D1091524

Empire and Society

New Approaches to Russian History

Edited by
Teruyuki Hara & Kimitaka Matsuzato

SLAVIC RESEARCH CENTER, HOKKAIDO UNIVERSITY
Sapporo, Japan

First published 1997
Copyright © Teruyuki Hara and Kimitaka Matsuzato 1997
Slavic Research Center, Hokkaido University
Kita-9, Nishi-7, Kita-ku, Sapporo 060, Japan
All Rights Reserved

edited by
Teruyuki Hara and Kimitaka Matsuzato

Empire and Society:
New Approaches to Russian History

List of Contributors: attached
Includes no index.
1. From Heresy to Harm
2. Notes on Working-Class Culture
3. The "Russian Idea" and the Ideology
4. The Habsburg and Russian Empires
5. Market Integration, Economic Intervention
6. The Development of the Russian State System
7. Land-Owning Nobles and Zemstvo Institutions
8. Stalin, Politburo, and Its Commissions
9. The Making of Foreign Policy
10. The Concept of "Space"

ISBN 4-938637-11-1 C3022

Printed in Japan

Contents

Foreword   i

Chapter 1
From Heresy to Harm:
  Self-Castrators in the Civic Discourse of Late Tsarist Russia
  by Laura ENGELSTEIN   1

Chapter 2
Notes on Working-Class Culture in Late Imperial Russia
  by Yoshifuru TSUCHIYA   23

Chapter 3
The "Russian Idea" and the Ideology of the February Revolution
  by Boris KOLONITSKII   41

Chapter 4
The Habsburg and Russian Empires: Some Comparisons and Contrasts
  by Orest SUBTELNY   73

Chapter 5
Market Integration, Economic Intervention of the State and
  the Decline of Empires: Austria-Hungary and Russia
  by György KÖVÉR   93

Chapter 6
The Development of the Russian State System
  in the Nineteenth and Early Twentieth Centuries
  by Pavel ZYRIANOV   107

Chapter 7
Land-Owning Nobles and Zemstvo Institutions:
  The Post-Reform Estate System in Political Perspective
  by Yutaka TAKENAKA   133

Chapter 8
Stalin, Politburo, and Its Commissions
  in the Soviet Decision-making Process in the 1930s
  by Takeshi TOMITA   151

Chapter 9
The Making of Foreign Policy under Stalin
  by Jonathan HASLAM   167

Chapter 10
The Concept of "Space" in Russian History
  — Regionalization from the Late Imperial Period to the Present —
  by Kimitaka MATSUZATO   181

Profiles of Contributors   217

Foreword

The political revolutions in the Slavic-Eurasian World, which took place from 1989-1991, changed the conditions for historical studies of those regions. The access to sources obviously improved. The sudden collapse of political regimes which seemed stable induced historians to doubt various axioms concerning the make-up of these regions. Of course, no external changes can advance academic activities, if they are not combined with the intra-academic achievements until the changes. In this sense, historical science would seem to be especially conservative. It is a challenge for historians to exploit new sources and promote new approaches.

This was the main theme of the International Symposium "Empire and Society: New Approaches to Russian History," held at the Slavic Research Center, Hokkaido University (Sapporo) on July, 13-15, 1994. This volume is based on the proceedings of that Symposium.

The first three chapters of this volume focus on subcultures and discourses. Laura Engelstein (Princeton University) spotlights self-castrators, a famous but rarely studied religious group. She analyses self-castrators not merely as a religious minority or a behavioral deviation, but as a "mirror" reflecting contemporary understanding of such fundamental concepts as sex, labor, crime, and so forth. Criticizing the traditional image of Russian workers as semi-peasants, Yoshifuru Tsuchiya (Nihon University) scrutinizes rituals, customs, and institutions which "urbanized" newcomers to factories. Boris Kolonitskii (the St. Petersburg Branch of the Institute of Russian History, RAS) reveals a complex intertwining of modern and traditional (or religious) concepts in contemporary interpretations of political events during and after the February Revolution. As a whole, these authors are extremely successful in anatomizing the collective consciousness in various phases of Russian history.

The next two chapters elucidate the formation and function of empires — a particularly up to date topic, since we witnessed the collapse of another gigantic empire only several years ago. Both Orest Subtelny (York University) and György Kövér (Budapest University of Economic Science) promote attractive comparative analyses between the Habsburg and Romanov empires. Their conclusions are similar too: both regard the former as being more viable than the latter. According to Subtelny, before World War I the Habsburg empire stood a good chance of transforming itself into a commonwealth, while the Russian government was strengthening its notorious Russification policy. Based on solid data elicited from surveys, Kövér refutes O. Jászi's thesis of the economic disintegration of the Habsburg empire before the war. Both conclusions might provoke a heated debate — a necessary process to advance an unfairly neglected issue: the *raison d'etre* of empires in the modern world.

Chapters six to nine analyze the relationship between the state and society, or the mechanisms of decision-making in Russia and the Soviet Union. Pavel Zyrianov (the Institute of Russian History, RAS) and Yutaka Takenaka (Osaka University) present arguments which have much in common with each other. First, both of them think that the Russian landed nobility could not be a social base for a constitutionalist, parliamentary development of the country. Second, for the non-violent development of a country it is very important to accumulate parliamentary experiences before its industrializing spurt: Japan got the timing right, whereas Russia did not. (It is not by chance that Zyrianov lists only two fatal defeats of Russian constitutionalists — 1825 and 1881, but not 1905, when Russian industrialization had already destabilized the society.) On the other hand, the authors place their accents on different points. Zyrianov emphasizes the anti-Weberian character of Russian bureaucracy, while Takenaka evaluates positively the development of a legal consciousness within Russian officialdom. Takenaka regards the estate system as a shock-absorber in the course of capitalist transformation, while Zyrianov denounces the tardy steps of Russia from an estate to a class society. Zyrianov elucidates structural faults in decision-making of the tsarist government, in particular, the role of the State Council.

The theme of the following two chapters (i.e., political decision-making during the Stalinist period) would seem to be particularly blessed by the opening of archive materials during the last several years. Takeshi Tomita (Seikei University) analyzes domestic policy, while Jonathan Haslam (Cambridge University) analyzes foreign policy. Criticizing primitive interpretations of "dictatorship," both authors emphasize the role of Stalin's entourage. Based on the abundant use of archive materials, Tomita clarifies institutional aspects of the political process.

The last chapter of this volume is dedicated to historical geography. Kimitaka Matsuzato (Hokkaido University) remarks that historical studies of Russia have been hampered by historians' negligent attitude toward geographic factors. As one of the first steps in overcoming this "geographic nihilism" he promotes a case study of the administrative-territorial division of Russia and the Soviet Union during this century.

As a whole, the editors are very glad to see that the contents of this volume do not betray its title: "new approaches to Russian history." On the other hand, to borrow O. Subtelny's words spoken during the Symposium, "newness does not guarantee the excellence of the study." It is the readers' prerogative to judge to what extent the "newness" of this volume will contribute to the development of historical studies of Russia.

June 12, 1997
The editors

Chapter 1

From Heresy to Harm:
Self-Castrators in the Civic
Discourse of Late Tsarist Russia

Laura ENGELSTEIN

In April 1772 it came to the attention of the ecclesiastical authorities in Orel province that a new heretical sect had emerged among the local villagers. They called themselves the Self-Castrators (*Skoptsy*), because surgical removal of all or part of the genital organs, of both women and men, was their distinguishing ritual feature. The group had broken away from an existing sect, the People of God, or Christ-Faith (*Khristovshchina*, or *Khlystovshchina*), which had earlier in the century separated from the priestless Old Believers. The tsarist regime looked unkindly on any deviation from institutional Orthodoxy; it found the *Skoptsy* most repugnant of all. This paper will describe the way in which this particular example of folk religiosity was interpreted by officials, interested observers, and professional men starting with the sect's discovery in 1772 and ending at the start of the twentieth century. It will focus on a number of exemplary texts, in order to show how reactions to the Skoptsy reveal the shifting terms of Russian public discourse.

Who they were

The Skoptsy shared the basic belief system and cult practices of the Christ-Faith. The latter was founded on the conviction that Christ had returned to earth in multiple incarnations to dwell among those who spurned the desecrations wrought by Patriarch Nikon in altering the liturgical practices of the Orthodox Church. The sect was organized in small congregations called "ships," each led by a preacher who called himself Christ and selected a female member as Mother of God. The followers forswore meat, alcohol, profanity, and sex. Outwardly conforming to Orthodox ways, they participated in secret ceremonies in which they felt themselves visited by the Holy Spirit. Constant repetition of the Jesus prayer in rhythmic cadences keyed to the movement of the breath (hesychasm) induced a sense of physical exaltation; ecstatic dances, in which men and women in separate groups whirled to the point of collapse, left them drenched in sweat and light-headed; sacred meals replaced the discredited sacraments; and inspired prophesy replaced the ministrations of priests. Most adherents were peasants or textile workers, some were merchants. Commercial networks centered on fairs held the community together. The sect was persecuted by government and ecclesiastical authorities, with varying degrees of intensity, throughout the eighteenth century, but to little effect.[1]

The Skoptsy crystallized as a separate sect in the 1760s, when a charismatic leader introduced two innovations into the Christ-Faith. Most important, he interpreted the injunction to sexual chastity in literal terms, as the act of physical castration. Second, he declared himself the unique reincarnation of Christ and his own congregation the central governing body. Though his origins are not clear, he appears to have been a runaway peasant, who called himself Kondratii Selivanov and wandered the land, in the fashion of the holy pilgrims, living on charity and avoiding the authorities. At some point he joined a Christ-Faith ship led by a woman of great prophetic conviction, named Akulina Ivanovna, who recognized him as the Son of God. All accounts describe Selivanov as a man of powerful appeal, who attracted a following of devoted converts ready to submit to the knife for the sake of purity and salvation. They called him Father-Redeemer (*Otets Iskupitel'*).[2]

When the existence of the group first came to light in 1772, the authorities arrested and interrogated about 60 peasants, including Akulina Ivanovna and two male prophets, but Selivanov himself escaped.[3] On the run for three years, he was eventually betrayed by members of the Christ-Faith hostile to his innovations. Selivanov tells the story of his capture, subjection to the knout, and experience of Siberian exile in a narrative entitled "The Passion of Kondratii Selivanov," which became the sect's principal sacred text.[4] On his way to exile, Selivanov claimed, he had encountered not only the Devil but also the Cossack rebel Emelian Pugachev. Pugachev had led his followers on a rampage of violence and destruction in the very years between the discovery of the Skoptsy in 1772 and Selivanov's subsequent arrest. In fact, this encounter could not have occurred, since Pugachev was executed in January 1775 and Selivanov marched off to exile only in June. Yet the fable had symbolic force. Both men had a popular following (though clearly, in Selivanov's case, relatively small); both exercised the charisma of Pretendership. As leader of the revolt, Pugachev had assumed the mantle of Tsar Peter III. It was in the name of the murdered emperor's legitimate authority that the rebel challenged Catherine's claim to rule. Upon his return from Siberia, Selivanov likewise began to call himself Tsar Peter III, as well as Jesus Christ. His fate, however, was not as grim as the one Pugachev encountered. Emperor Paul, undoing his mother's legacy, brought Selivanov back to St. Petersburg, where Alexander I then permitted him to reside undisturbed, surrounded by an entourage that included prominent figures well connected at court.[5] In 1820, however, Selivanov was confined to a monastery in Suzdal', where he died twelve years later, purportedly at the age of 112.[6]

The Skoptsy called the Redeemer's period of trial his Passion and his stay in St. Petersburg his Resurrection. They predicted a Second Coming, when at the end of time the Tsar-Redeemer would gather the faithful in Moscow for the Last Judgment and the onset of eternal happiness. Just as

Selivanov was not merely Christ but also Peter III, and the story of his life a rewriting of Christ's own story, so the Skoptsy combined sacred with secular history. In their accounts the Empress Elizabeth had given birth to Peter III, the Redeemer, who was castrated and then saved from death when a loyal guards officer allowed himself to be murdered in Peter's stead by the Empress Catherine's courtiers. Peter then wandered the earth, promoting the salvation of his followers. Alexander I, who had shown the Skoptsy relative toleration, was considered, honorifically, to be castrated as well.[7]

On what basis did the Skoptsy justify the transition from moral to physical chastity? Of what did the ritual consist? Some observers explained the transition to castration as a naive verbal slip: *iskupitel'* (redeemer) was but two vowels removed from *oskopitel'* (castrator).[8] The Skoptsy, for their part, cited chapter and verse in support of the practice. In Matthew 19: 12 Christ describes the three kinds of people for whom the injunction to marry does not apply: those who emerge eunuchs from their mother's womb; those made eunuchs by the hand of man; and those who make themselves eunuchs for the sake of the Kingdom of Heaven. In their extreme literal-mindedness, they read the third term as an injunction not to sexual renunciation but to the removal of sexual parts.[9] In this, the Skoptsy diverged from the host-sect, the People of God, but in another sense they perpetuated the distinguishing feature of the Old Belief in general. Boris Uspenskii argues that Old Believers defended the ancient rituals, spelling, and pronunciation as absolute expressions of the Divine and condemned Nikon's innovations for assuming that form was not synonymous with meaning. The new ritual emphasized the need to communicate through language and symbols; the old ritualists viewed the signs themselves as sacred. The latter thus rejected the use of metaphor as allowing for the play of interpretation. From the Old Believers' point of view, Uspenskii writes, "using words in their figurative meaning contributed to deviation from Christianity and, consequently, promoted a tendency toward heresy."[10] From the Church's standpoint, on the contrary, the Skoptsy's refusal to understand figurative speech was the source of their heresy.

In defense of castration the Skoptsy cited other biblical passages as well. In Epistle to the Hebrews 9: 22, Paul says, "without shedding of blood is no remission [forgiveness]." The Skoptsy believed Christ had bled twice: first at his circumcision, which they interpreted as castration, and second at the crucifixion. They also cited Matthew 18: 8-9, where Jesus says it is better to cut off the arm or pluck out the eye that offends you than to live in sin.[11] One testified in 1844 that he was following the lead of Jesus, who said (Luke 23: 29), "blessed are the barren, and the wombs that never bare, and the paps which never gave suck [*blazhenny neplodnye i utroby nerodivshie, i sostsy ne pitavshie*]."[12] The Skoptsy believed the Archangel Michael, who announced Mary's pregnancy, had been castrated, as had John the Baptist, who then castrated Christ.[13] Removing their own genitals, the Skoptsy suffered intense pain, bled in profusion, and deprived themselves of the instruments of sin. The threat of punishment did not deter them; they welcomed persecution and physical chastisement as elements of holy martyrdom.[14]

The Skoptsy were secretive about the details of the operations, but information about the practice emerges from trial testimonies and from a forensic medical study published in 1872. In the case of men, castration took two forms. The lesser operation, called the "minor seal" (*malaia pechat'*) — also, first seal, first whitening, or first purification — entailed removing the testicles. Either simultaneously, or, more commonly, in a separate operation, the penis itself could also be amputated; this was called the second, major, or "royal" seal (*tsarskaia pechat'*) — also, second purification or whitening. Originally the Skoptsy destroyed the testicles and part of the scrotum by applying a red-hot iron, a procedure known as "the fiery baptism." Later they used knives or razors and applied the incandescent iron only to staunch the flow of blood. Another technique was to twist the scrotum until the seminal vesicles were destroyed, blocking the flow of semen. As a result of twisting, the testicles sometimes dropped to the bottom of the scrotum, where they atrophied. In the case of women, the Skoptsy excised either the nipples or the entire breasts, or simply scarred the sides of the breasts. In addition they excised the labia majora, sometimes also the labia minora and the clitoris.[15] They were unable, of course, to reach the ovaries or womb.

The excisions were occasionally performed by adults upon themselves, but more often by elders or monitors (*nastavniki*) in a special ceremony. As the knife did its task, the words "Christ is risen!" were spoken.[16] In testifying before courts and commissions, ordinary sectarians chose two possible tactics. In the effort to prove they were not connected to the sect, membership in which was to be demonstrated by the fact of ritual castration, they claimed to have lost their genitals in the course of random accidents or assaults. In other cases, those interrogated eagerly assumed responsibility for having castrated others, thus shielding the few members who specialized in the role.[17] The Skoptsy seem to have chosen isolated places for the ritual: bath houses, grain-drying barns, basements, or the forest.[18] Nineteenth-century commentators disagreed about how often the operation proved fatal, but apparently few deaths came to the attention of the authorities.[19] Some subjects claimed to have felt no pain, while others bragged about its intensity. They seem not to have used narcotic substances or alcohol to dull their suffering.[20]

Some adults clearly elected to undergo the operation; some were convinced to do so (although the degree of coercion cannot be ascertained).[21] There are also many examples of children being put to the knife, sometimes by relatives who adopted the faith. Children also came into contact with the Skoptsy after being hired from their parents to work as apprentices and servants. Once among the sectarians, the children were raised in the spirit of the creed and allegedly kept from contact with their families. When questioned in court, almost all said they had sought castration of their own free will, as the road to salvation. Only one or two ever betrayed the identity of the person who had performed the operation.[22]

How they were understood

The Skoptsy disturbed contemporaries, just as they disturb us today. How nineteenth-century commentators expressed their discomfort reflected the changing cultural and political circumstances in which they lived. Over the course of one hundred years, no one ceased to deplore the sect's existence, but the reasons for condemning and trying to stop it shifted with the times. At first, the issue was false belief, then political subversion, and finally the inflicting of harm — to the self or the civic body. The sequence mirrored not only the political moods of succeeding reigns, but also the evolution of legal norms and principles in the direction of modern concepts of crime and repression.

Although Russian law guaranteed the status and dogma of institutional Orthodoxy and thus considered heresy not merely an error but a crime, Alexander I treated the Skoptsy with relative toleration. Interestingly enough, in precisely this period, when the state did not energetically fulfill its role as the guardian of true belief, the religious meaning of the Skoptsy was taken most seriously. The first published work on the sect was a brief pamphlet, issued in 1819, by a certain Martyn Piletskii (1780-1859).[23] Citing liberally from chapter and verse, Piletskii addresses the Skoptsy or potential converts in their own, religious terms. The tract was apparently intended to warn the common folk against the lure of the sect's all-too-literal reading of Scripture, though it is too complex to have attracted a popular readership. It might have affected the members of Selivanov's entourage, which included some influential people in these years, but could hardly have reached the largely unlettered peasants to whom Selivanov's teachings appealed.

By translating Christ's call for sexual chastity into the act of bodily mutilation, Piletskii argued, the sectarians failed to understand that sin originates in the soul not the body. Not only is moral causality reversed by castration, but destroying the instrument of sin actually impairs the believer's moral potential. Without the ability to enact his wicked desires, he considers himself superior to the ordinary person, thus succumbing to the sin of spiritual pride. In fact the psychological roots of desire survive the loss of the genital organs; indeed, frustration only intensifies lust. In the struggle against physical temptation, by contrast, the ordinary Christian achieves the humility essential to virtue. Deprived of the capacity to love, the castrate cannot direct this potentially dangerous impulse toward divine ends and therefore cannot achieve salvation.

Moral improvement through the infliction of physical pain was not only a mark of Christian martyrdom but also the guiding principle of corporal punishment. Mortification of the flesh by act of state or the paternal authority of landowners was thought to have a morally salubrious effect.[24] But inflicting pain upon oneself was a gesture of arrogance not self-abasement. It usurped not only the spiritual initiative of God but also the sovereign's political prerogative. The late eighteenth century was an age of physical violence, in which serfs were whipped by masters and felons beaten to bloody death with the knout, in the guise of corporal punishment; in which flesh was branded and nostrils slit. Pugachev's revolt, simultaneous with Selivanov's first public appearance, was a war in which rebels hacked and ripped the bodies of gentry inhabiting the manor houses they looted and burned; in which captured rebels were hung live from gibbets and malefactors chopped to bits and displayed, member for member, at the top of bloody pikes. In the self-administration of physical pain and bodily marking, the Skoptsy enacted a double turn: subjecting themselves to atrocious suffering and flagrant stigma, they spoke the language of holy martyrdom, while at the same time appropriating an idiom proper to the exercise of worldly power.

It was precisely their worldly implications that attracted the attention of the author of the century's most careful study of Skoptsy practice and belief. Not surprisingly this study was composed during the reign of Nicholas I. Devoted to the joint ideological monopoly of Orthodoxy and Autocracy, Nicholas appointed a top-secret commission to examine the sectarians' history and beliefs and evaluate the extent of their influence. In 1845 the commission issued four volumes of information on the various heretical sects, of which the third concerned the Skoptsy.[25] The work of Nikolai Nadezhdin (1804-56), it surveys existing knowledge of the sect, recounts its history from official records, the testimony of interrogated believers, and the sect's own songs and sacred texts, including Selivanov's account of his earthly and spiritual mission. It is not only a gold mine of information but also an eloquent articulation of the Nicholaevan political world view.[26]

Nadezhdin emphasized the sect's claim to political rather than moral authority, more interested in its challenge to secular principles than its spiritual pretensions. Focusing on the worldly implications of religious belief, he condemned any deviation from Orthodoxy as harmful to the integrity of the state. More specifically, Nadezhdin was alarmed by the subversive implications of Selivanov's second, political Pretendership.[27] Once Selivanov added the imperial persona to his divine claims, he called his congregation the "Royal Ship" (*Korabl'-Tsarskii*), to which, as Nadezhdin felicitously put it, the sect's other assemblies were tethered like "dinghies" (*legkie lodochki*) to the main craft.[28] The assertion of political as well as spiritual dominance, which Nadezhdin saw in Selivanov's title and in the sect's centralized structure of authority, was the group's distinguishing feature and the reason it ought to be repressed.[29]

But why should the deluded claims of a single self-mortifying peasant threaten the established order? Nadezhdin estimated that in 1845 the Skoptsy numbered 1,700, but he insisted that many more belonged to the sect than were physically castrated and certainly more than were ever apprehended. Though it is true that not all believers were physically marked, there is no evidence to confirm

Nadezhdin's claim that the proportion was two of every 400.[30] If this had been so, the sect would have numbered 300,000 at midcentury, but a German scholar writing in 1909 put the total (including the noncastrated) at no more than 100,000.[31]

Not only were they relatively rare, but the Skoptsy did not cause trouble in the usual sense. Concentrated mostly in the rural and urban lower classes (at least half were peasants), with some presence among junior military men, the sect also included some rich merchants.[32] In their home villages as well as in exile, the Skoptsy were known for sobriety, hard work, and economic success, both in agriculture and trade, and the community accumulated considerable wealth. Unlike Pugachev, Selivanov organized no mass movement, and he mobilized the cathartic power of violence as an instrument of group solidarity not a weapon of the weak against the strong. Yet, according to Nadezhdin, Selivanov and his followers represented a similar, no less ominous, threat. "In the dogma, dreams, and hopes of the Skoptsy," Nadezhdin believed, "political interests predominate over religious ones. . . No longer human, but still of Russian blood, the Skoptsy cannot imagine any other way to achieve the Kingdom of Heaven on earth than with the accession of Peter III to the Russian Imperial Throne. . . And this will occur not in peace and quiet, but with 'fearful and terrible thunder': led by the False-Tsar, the people will arrive by the legion, a mighty force, in military readiness!"[33]

Citing the mythological language of Selivanov's text as though it described the deliberations of an army command, Nadezhdin evoked a threat, which, not surprisingly, reflected the paranoid sensibility of Nicholas I's reign. United by the power of Selivanov's dominant personality, Nadezhdin warned, the sect formed a nationwide network of mutual support and subversive propaganda, a single "Brotherhood" or "Association" (*Bratstvo, Obshchestvo*), dedicated to the conversion of souls and the material sustenance of the flock. Operating in secret, beneath the cover of religious conformity, they recognized each other by secret signs, just as Freemasons did. "The Skoptsy brotherhood," wrote Nadezhdin, "is a solid, powerful union, sustained by active mutual support throughout the entire Empire in which its members are dispersed. From Petersburg to Siberia, from Siberia to the depths of Russia, everywhere they exchange letters, advice, instructions, and — money!" All the more dangerous for being unseen, the sect "permeates [the body politic] like an invisible poison that eats away at the common folk like a deeply embedded sore."[34]

In the middle of Alexander II's reign, the voice of science was added to the chorus of commentary on the Skoptsy. In 1872 Evgenii Pelikan (1824-84) published his study of the medical causes and consequences of castration. He described in detail the various techniques used to excise the genitals and tried to understand the physiological effects of their loss. In the case of men, only those castrated before sexual maturity showed signs of physical transformation: shrunken genitals, high voices, sparse body hair. The rest, he claimed, could be recognized by their listless demeanor and sallow complexion. The same traits were said to characterize the mutilated women as well, though disfigurement in their case had no effect on their reproductive system, as the physician was well aware.[35]

The contrast between the intellectual-political outlook of Nadezhdin, the Nicholaevan official, and of Pelikan, the medical professional, is nowhere better illustrated than by their respective opinions on how castration affected the experience of sexual desire. Nadezhdin in fact did not have a coherent position on this subject. At times he asserted that castration destroyed sexual desire, leaving the Skoptsy deprived of human feeling. But more often he emphasized the paradox that physical incapacity might not hinder, but even enhance, the thirst for physical satisfaction, until desire increased "to the point of savage, frenzied, even bestial rage [*neistovstvo*]."[36]

Where the bureaucrat saw the threat of passion raging out of control, demanding severe repression, the physician emphasized the social dangers inherent in the *loss* of desire, which deprived individuals of the opportunity for self-regulation. In so doing, he echoed, in a secular vein, the argument advanced by Piletskii, from a theological perspective. Where the latter extolled the moral value of sexual desire as a precondition of spiritual transcendence, the medical man defended sexual desire as a cornerstone of social existence: "Once he becomes sexually active, the normal man starts to find the opposite sex attractive: the first instinctive call of love also inspires him with the urge to noble action and great deeds and with devotion to the fatherland. The young man castrated before puberty knows none of this: he remains indifferent to his environment, lacking the smallest germ of noble aspiration, sense of duty, or civic obligation... The onset of puberty does not bring him family happiness; manly courage and lofty dreams are alien to him; rather, he acquires the vices of people with limited vision and crude morality: egoism, cunning, perfidy, and cupidity."[37] Secular virtue, in the physician's view, consisted not in the absence of desire or in submission to external controls, but in the ability to direct it toward socially constructive ends; indeed he considered desire a precondition of civic virtue.

Views on how the Skoptsy attracted and retained converts also shifted over the course of the years. Piletskii considered believers misguided but sincere and therefore took their theological claims seriously. Nadezhdin, by contrast, interpreted the process of conversion as one in which a core of desperate fanatics preyed on luckless victims, not so much either gullible or inspired, but rather objects of trickery and compulsion. Yet even Nadezhdin credited some of the sectarians' popular appeal to their mystical enthusiasm, folkloric rites, and naive spiritual idiom. He also conceded that the appearance of virtue among the Skoptsy aroused the peasants' admiration. In the end converts remained in the sect not on the strength of spiritual conviction, however, but driven by physiological need. The physical effect of the prayer meetings, with their repetitious movements and recitations, "exerted a powerful force on the body and soul," Nadezhdin believed, "like a magnetic enchantment, or, more simply, an intoxication that creates a dependency, which among crude natures, easily becomes an overpowering passion, like an incurable 'addiction to drink' [*zapoi*]."[38]

More mundane forms of compulsion also played a role, in his view. In addition to the understandable, though deceptive attractions of virtue, and the involuntary workings of physiology, Nadezhdin also cited material need as a strong inducement to join the sect and stay involved. He explained how the wealthy sectarian community provided shelter for vagrants and runaway criminals, whom they supplied with false papers and new names. To the poor peasant they offered relief from the military draft, escape from serfdom, economic support, and the hope of equality and fellowship. They adopted the children of their own needy relatives, took in orphans, and hired the offspring of impoverished villagers as apprentices.[39] Explaining the sect's appeal in material terms made the community seem sinister and mercenary, while converts were relieved of responsibility for their choice.[40]

Bringing the wisdom of science to bear on the question of what motivated the Skoptsy, Pelikan concluded that "mental blindness (or extremely one-sided mental development)" was the precondition for susceptibility to fanatical religious faith. But like Nadezhdin, who contrasted the calculated evil at work among the hard core with the naive vulnerability of their recruits, Pelikan also tried to have it both ways. On the one hand, as a forensic expert he insisted the Skoptsy were responsible for their actions and therefore competent to stand trial. Mentally limited, perhaps, but not insane, the Skoptsy revealed no organic abnormalities, did not behave strangely in everyday life, hallucinate, or rave. The sectarians' creed was systematically propagated and comprehensible to others, whereas the ideas of the insane were meaningful only to themselves. Skoptsy conversions, Pelikan maintained, might be the result of emotional contagion akin to mass hysteria, or simply the consequence of ignorance, but they were not signs of mental disease.[41]

Even the exalted mood that resulted from the ritual ceremonies was not a sign of mental imbalance but could be explained in physiological terms. As participants swirled and waved their arms, the body experienced an almost narcotic intoxication derived from pressure on the nerves and brain. The People of God and Skoptsy therefore used the expression: "to get drunk without drinking" (*chelovek plotskimi ustami ne p'et, a p'ian zhivet*).[42] Some physicians believed the flow of blood to the extremities produced a pleasurable light-headedness, "resembling a faint." The physical pressure weakened the rational faculties, stimulated the imagination, and loosened the inhibitions: "lubricious, selfish, and other, mostly base, inclinations come to the surface and struggle for satisfaction." The experts all emphasized the enhancement of erotic desire as a consequence of these physical exercises.[43] Thus, if believers joined the sect in their right, if simple, minds, they might emerge functionally deprived of reason.

If it is true that Skoptsy rituals induced states of exaltation and unreason in their participants, they also seem to have induced states of unreason in those who observed them. Not only Nadezhdin, but also Pelikan, the man of science, indulged extravagant fantasies on the subject of Skoptsy ritual practices, which bore a close resemblance to the myths that circulated about the Jews in Russia as well as Europe.[44] Pelikan reported accounts that accused the Skoptsy of eating the excised testicles or breasts of castrated members. He also repeated the claim that young girls were impregnated during sexual orgies and when they gave birth, their infant boys were pierced to the heart and drained of blood, which the Skoptsy used to take communion. They were also said to dry the dead infant's body, grinding the remains to a powder for use in baking communion bread. Though Pelikan rejected the charge that Skoptsy fed on severed breasts, he did not relinquish his belief that "the mortification of infants and communion with their blood is a religious-historical fact."[45]

Nadezhdin, for his part, emphasized the clannishness of the Skoptsy, who, like the Jews, constituted a "conspiracy [*zagovor* — note classic anti-Semitic vocabulary] against the rest of humanity."[46] Stressing the resemblance between Jews and Skoptsy, both supposedly possessed of great wealth, wrung from the labor of hapless employees, peasants, and subordinates, became a standard rhetorical turn.[47] While it is true that the sect had both wealthy, entrepreneurial, and poor, wage-earning members,[48] it is the language in which these social facts were described that calls our attention to the underlying structures of prejudice. It was a cliché of the antisectarian literature to describe the Skoptsy as ferociously money-loving. Having deprived themselves of human love and renounced all familial ties, they were said to pour their energies into the acquisition of wealth.[49] Like the Jews, they dealt in precious metal, lent money at interest, and in general were said to profit at the common people's expense. Many had become millionaires, partly, Nadezhdin asserted, as the result of commercial crimes. "Only the Yids," he remarked, "equal them in their wholehearted devotion to the Golden Calf."[50]

Issues in the law

In what terms were the Skoptsy condemned under the law? The sect was investigated in 1772 because it was heretical; the leaders were beaten and exiled but the followers allowed to resume their accustomed lives. Alexander I made the distinction between false belief and social harm. Only when the practice of castration threatened the welfare of others should it be the target of the law. The problem was, of course, that castration was itself the mark of false belief, and therefore it was difficult to distinguish between dogma and harmful acts.[51] The laws enacted in the reign of Nicholas I ignored this distinction. After 1842, the sects were divided into three categories, all criminal, but in degrees of increasing severity: heretical in terms of belief but not socially harmful; "especially harmful"; and "gruesome, fanatical, immoral, and vile."[52] Emphasizing the gravity of religious offenses demonstrated the regime's interest in protecting true religion as defined by the Orthodox Church, yet the state's involvement in disciplining false belief only helped erode the church's already weakened institutional authority.[53]

In the 1870s the Senate turned in the direction Alexander I had earlier taken, ruling that false belief itself should not be subject to penal sanction but that certain of its public manifestations were legitimate targets of the law. In relation to the Skoptsy, the Senators considered castration a criminal act insofar as it was motivated by religious fanaticism, although fanaticism in itself was no longer to be considered a crime.[54] This qualification signalled an attempt to avoid categorical prohibitions and focus instead on the character of individual acts. In another sense, however, the two moves seem to contradict each other: the first extended protection to private belief; the second made the element of belief the crime's defining feature.

The general trend, even in the conservative reign of Alexander III, was increasingly to focus on active manifestations of false dogma, while releasing the character of belief itself from the scrutiny of the courts. In 1883 the State Council reduced the three categories of heresy to two: benign and vicious, of which last the Skoptsy were the case in point.[55] This simplification did not, however, diminish the state's interest in repressing the practice of castration. But here the confusion set in. Now, separate statutes penalized the Skoptsy in particular for, on the one hand, spreading their faith (a specific action) and, on the other, merely for belonging to a sect with "vile and immoral" practices.[56] In the end, castration remained the mark of a crime defined as membership in a sect that promoted castration on the basis of false religious belief.[57] This tautological framing of the law did not satisfy legal experts, and some began to argue that controlling the spread of this distressing cult should not be the work of the courts.[58] Some observers took pity on the Skoptsy exiles, who showed remarkable ability to make the best of hard circumstances.

Despite their social virtues, they were nevertheless kept under extremely tight supervision and did not benefit from changes in the law, instituted in the 1880s and 1890s, that alleviated the situation of exiles and Old Believers.[59]

Even those who repented and wished to rejoin the Orthodox community lingered in a perpetual no man's land of the soul. One sympathetic observer turned the Skoptsy's surgical gesture of literalization into metaphor once again, when he described the sad fate of Skoptsy apostates: "Having left the people to whom they were joined by fanaticism and then by shared unhappiness, they cannot tie the knot that would unite them with the rest of the world. The artery is severed and circulation cannot be restored. The heart of the Skopets beats separately from the heart of the world."[60]

Despite their sufferings, spiritual and physical, the Skoptsy survived, even into the 1920s, when they were repressed by the Soviet authorities. The reason for the sect's appeal is not, however, easily explained. One cannot reduce the survival of the community over so long a period of time to the triumph of trickery and brute force. Nor is it obvious why members of an already stigmatized group (the Christ-Faith) wished to retreat even further to the social margin. Nor is the relation between economic success and bodily renunciation at all clear, since Old Believers, People of God, and Skoptsy seem to have shared the capacity for hard work and the talent for commercial success. It is clear that the naive literal-mindedness which characterized the Skoptsy's relation to Scripture neither constrained their economic behavior nor prevented them from devising ways to circumvent the law. Further research will have to determine, if possible, whether those who joined the sect were already set off from their host communities in some distinctive way before they assumed this additional burden. In the end it is genuinely difficult to understand why this particular signature of holy martyrdom should function as the door-keeper of community (especially when it did not apply to all concerned). Yet the extremity of the act must have exercised a powerful symbolic appeal to serve as the cornerstone of a coherent cultural formation that lasted for over one hundred years.

Notes

1 On the Christ-Faith, see John Eugene Clay, "Russian Peasant Religion and Its Repression: The Christ-Faith (*Khristovshchina*) and the Origins of the 'Flagellant' Myth, 1666-1837" (Ph.D. dissertation, University of Chicago, 1989).

2 K.V. Kutepov, *Sekty khlystov i skoptsov* (Kazan: Imperatorskii universitet, 1883), pp. 107-109, 116-117.

3 See N.G. Vysotskii, *Pervyi skopcheskii protsess: Materialy, otnosiashchiesia k nachal'noi istorii skopcheskoi sekty* (Moscow: Snegirevaia, 1915).

4 [N.I. Nadezhdin], *Issledovanie o skopcheskoi eresi* (n.p.: Ministerstvo vnutrennikh del, 1845), Appendix, pp.1-26, reprinted as "Strady Kondratiia Selivanova," in V.V. Rozanov, *Apokalipsicheskaia sekta: Khlysty i skoptsy* (St. Petersburg: Vaisberg i Gershunin, 1914), pp. 134-152.

5 See "Belye golubi," in A.S. Prugavin, *Raskol vverkhu: Ocherki religioznykh iskanii v privilegirovannoi srede* (St. Petersburg: Obshchestvennaia pol'za, 1909), pp. 87-95.

6 N.A. Gur'ev, *Sibirskie skoptsy, ikh ekonomicheskoe i pravovoe polozhenie* (Tomsk: K.A. Orlov, 1900), p. 8.

7 *Nadezhdin, Issledovanie*, pp. 101-108.

8 *Ibid.*, p. 199.

9 *Ibid.*, pp. 40-41.

10 Boris A. Uspensky, "The Schism and Cultural Conflict in Seventeenth Century," in Stephen K. Bataldenthe (ed.), *Seeking God: The Recovery of Relgious Identity in Orthodox Russia, Ukraine, and Georgia* (Dekalb, Ill.: Northern Illinois University Press, 1993), p. 121.

11 A. Orlov, "Missionerstvo, sekty i raskol: Khronika," *Missionerskoe obozrenie*, vol. 10-11 (1902), pp. 517-518. On misreading of Matthew, see also Martyn Stepanovich Piletskii-Urbanovich, *O skoptsakh* (St. Petersburg: Ios. Ioannesov, 1819), pp. 10-15.

12 Evgenii [V.] Pelikan, *Sudebno-meditsinskie issledovaniia skopchestva i istoricheskie svedeniia o nem* (St. Petersburg: V. I. Golovin, 1872), p. 92.

13 Nadezhdin, *Issledovanie*, pp. 293-294.

14 Pelikan, *Sudebno-meditsinskie issledovaniia*, p. 91.

15 *Ibid.*, pp. 3, 4-5, 43-44, 48, 60-61.

16 For an account, see *ibid.*, pp. 115-118.

17 *Ibid.*, pp. 99-100.

18 Nadezhdin, *Issledovanie,* pp. 209-212.

19 *Ibid.,* p. 212 (often fatal);   Pelikan, *Sudebno-meditsinskie issledovaniia,* p. 80 (rarely).

20 Pelikan, *Sudebno-meditsinskie issledovaniia,* p. 119.

21 On use of coercion: Nadezhdin, *Issledovanie,* pp. 216-217.

22 Pelikan, *Sudebno-meditsinskie issledovaniia,* pp. 38, 95-97.

23 Piletskii, *O skoptsakh.* The author was a member of the imperial court, who was asked to write the pamphlet by the emperor, but apparently Metropolitan Filaret considered it too sympathetic to the Skoptsy to allow it to be circulated: Kutepov, *Sekty,* p. 17.

24 D.N. Bludov, "Obshchaia ob"iasnitel'naia zapiska," in *Proekt ulozheniia o nakazaniiakh ugolovnykh i ispravitel'nykh, vnesennyi v 1844 godu v Gosudarstvennyi Sovet, s podrobnym oznacheniem osnovanii kazhdogo iz vnesennykh v sei proekt postanovlenii* (St. Petersburg: Tip. Vtorogo Otdeleniia Sobstvennoi Ego Imperatorskogo Velichestva Kantseliarii, 1871), lii.

25 The volumes were printed in only 50 copies, intended exclusively for official eyes (Kutepov, *Sekty,* p. 17). They were reprinted, however, in 1860-62 in London, under the editorship of Vasilii Kelsiev, a radical sympathizer, who considered religious sectarianism an expression of the people's desire to free themselves from the tyranny of church and state: see V.I. Kelsiev, (ed.), *Sbornik pravitel'stvennykh svedenii o raskol'nikakh,* 4 vols. (London, 1860-62), 1: introduction.

26 This volume remained the basic work on the Skoptsy, despite its polemical nature: see Kutepov, *Sekty,* pp. 30-31. Nadezhdin had been the editor of the journal that published Petr Chaadaev's "Philosophical Letter" in 1836; he later became a leading figure in the Imperial Geographical Society.

27 Nadezhdin, *Issledovanie,* p. 189.

28 *Ibid.,* p. 193 and 197 (two quotes, respectively).

29 For more on centralization and Selivanov's dominant role, see *ibid.,* pp. 270-271.

30 *Ibid.,* pp. 324-25; 334 (2: 400).

31 Karl Konrad Grass, *Die russischen Sekten,* vol. 2: *Die Weissen Tauben oder Skopzen* (1914; rpt. Leipzig: Zentral-Antiquariat der Deutschen Demokratishchen Republik, 1966), pp. 888, 891-892.

32 Nadezhdin, *Issledovanie,* pp. 327-328;   Pelikan, *Sudebno-meditsinskie issledovaniia,* appendix, pp. 7-8.

33 Nadezhdin, *Issledovanie,* pp. 366-367.

34 *Ibid.,* pp. 272, 284 (quote), pp. 286-287 (quote).

35 Pelikan, *Sudebno-meditsinskie issledovaniia,* pp. 69, 71-79.

36 Nadezhdin, *Issledovanie,* p. 352. This opinion repeated, almost word for word, in Efim Solov'ev, *Svedeniia o russkikh skoptsakh* (Kostroma: Gubernskaia tipografiia, 1870), i.

37 Pelikan, *Sudebno-meditsinskie issledovaniia*, p. 87.
38 Nadezhdin, *Issledovanie*, 336. Such reasoning became a clich-ea; see Solov'ev, *Svedeniia*, pp. 78-80.
39 Nadezhdin, *Issledovanie*, pp. 337-341; on offering loans and excusing debts on condition of castration, see Pelikan, *Sudebno-meditsinskie issledovaniia*, pp. 95. For persistence of accusations of bribery, enslavement of children, see A.A. Levenstim, "Fanatizm i prestuplenie," part 2, *Zhurnal ministerstva iustitsii*, No. 8 (1898), p. 6.
40 Same emphasis on poverty as motive for joining and wealth as source of community's strength: Solov'ev, *Svedeniia*, ii-iii, p. 17.
41 Pelikan, *Sudebno-meditsinskie issledovaniia*, pp. 103-106.
42 *Ibid.*, p. 129.
43 *Ibid.*, pp. 133-134, 136.
44 See Laura Engelstein, *The Keys to Happiness: Sex and the Search for Modernity in Fin-de-Siègcle Russia* (Ithaca: Cornell University Press, 1992), chapter 8.
45 Pelikan, *Sudebno-meditsinskie issledovaniia*, pp. 148-149, 162, 164.
46 Nadezhdin, *Issledovanie*, p. 349.
47 Orlov, "Missionerstvo," p. 516 (kagalnoe obshchestvo, kagalnye bogatstva); Nadezhdin, *Issledovanie*, 347-348 (on conflict between rich and poor among the Skoptsy).
48 See, for example, Gur'ev, *Sibirskie skoptsy*, p. 24; also V. I-n [V. I. Iokhel'son], "Olekminskie skoptsy: Istoriko-bytovoi ocherk," part 2, *Zhivaia starina* (1894), pp. 315-316.
49 Nadezhdin, *Issledovanie*, pp. 347-348.
50 *Ibid.*, pp. 351-352, 362-363 (quote, 361-362).
51 I.P. Iakobiia, "Ob ugolovnoi nakazuemosti prinadlezhnosti k izuvernym sektam," *Zhurnal ministerstva iustitsii*, No. 5 (1912), pp. 104-106.
52 "Khronika: 203 st. ulozheniia o nakazaniiakh po tolkovaniiu Pravitel'stvuiushchego senata," *Zhurnal ministerstva iustitsii*, No. 1 (1896), p. 238 ("izuvernye, soedinennye s proiavleniiami fanatizma ili s protivonravstvennymi, gnusnymi deistviiami"); Levenstim, "Fanatizm," part 2, p. 31; Iakobiia, "Ob ugolovnoi nakazuemosti," pp. 105, 107-108; Ardalion [Vasilevich] Popov, *Sud i nakazaniia za prestupleniia protiv very i nravstvennosti po russkomu pravu* (Kazan: Tipografiia imperatorskogo universiteta, 1904), p. 473.
53 Popov, *Sud i nakazaniia*, pp. 509-511.
54 V.N. Shiriaev, *Religioznye prestupleniia* (Iaroslavl: Tipografiia gubernskogo pravleniia, 1909), p. 378; Iakobiia, "Ob ugolovnoi nakazuemosti," p. 112.
55 Shiriaev, *Religioznye prestupleniia*, p. 348.
56 "Khronika," pp. 238-240. For the statutes on the religious sectarians, see Articles pp. 196-204, in N.S. Tagantsev (ed.),

Ulozhenie o nakazaniiakh ugolovnykh i ispravitel'nykh 1885 goda (St. Petersburg: Gosudarstvennaia tipografiia, 1901), pp. 225-237. On contradiction between these two articles, see Iakobiia, "Ob ugolovnoi nakazuemosti," pp. 112-114.

57 Complaining that the law against castration actually penalized belief: I-n, "Olekminskie skoptsy," p. 317.

58 Iakobiia, "Ob ugolovnoi nakazuemosti," p. 131.

59 See I-n, "Olekminskie skoptsy," pp. 317-320.

60 *Ibid.*, p. 319.

Chapter 2

Notes on Working-Class Culture
in Late Imperial Russia

Yoshifuru TSUCHIYA

Introduction

Over the past three decades, the "culturist" approach has
come to prevail in Western historical research on popular
movements and working classes in Europe. This approach
rejects the reduction of culture to social and economic
conditions and makes much of cultural roles in historic
transformations. For example, E.P. Thompson suggests that
the working class was not automatically formed by changes in
the economic structure and productive relations, but that it
took form only when it achieved class consciousness through
the experiences of struggle and protest. He considers that the
working class emerged due to interactions between economic
and cultural factors. Some younger researchers (such as G.
Rude) not only emphasize the autonomy of culture, but also
even claim that popular culture created the popular
movement.[1]

Needless to say, the formation of working classes cannot be
attributed to culture alone; such an approach, however,
appears to be somewhat useful in the study of Russian
workers. Scholars in the former Soviet Union almost
exclusively analyzed social and economic conditions in order to
illustrate the formation processes of classes, and Western
historiography has long paid much attention to the connection
of workers with villages and stressed their peasant-like
character. However, this emphasis in Western historical

research began to change early in the 1980s, and some recent studies seem to be more or less characterized by the forementioned style of approach.[2] This study is a modest attempt to analyze the world of Russian workers for the purpose of acknowledging their cultural autonomy and its changes.

1. Traditional Customs and their Social Functions

A typical Russian worker was born and raised in a rural area, and came to a city to work in a factory in his/her early teens. A detailed scrutiny of such workers' early lives in the countryside is beyond the scope of this study, but we may suppose that the customs, values, morals, behavior, and social bonds would remain intact even after his/her arrival in a new urban environment. According to Anne Bobroff, who studied the social bonding patterns of female workers in the central industrial region of Russia, there were differences in expected roles between boys and girls in childhood, and difference of gender had some influence on their future activities as workers.[3] It is well known that *zemliachestvo* was an important bond which helped workers to enter urban life.[4] Whether brought from the countryside or not, some traditional customs and rituals in workers' daily lives reinforced their social bonds, *sociabilité*, and their identities of belonging to certain communities.

The concept of *sociabilité* represents the interrelations of people who are connected by some particular social bond. Generally, people live in "multiple *sociabilité*" (from family to political party) and *sociabilité* ordinarily creates a certain community of interest. The community has specific unwritten rules and a self-controlling ability exercised by norms based upon these rules. When people are aware of the common norms among themselves, *sociabilité* becomes the basis of community.[5] Such *sociabilité* as *zemliachestvo*, neighborhood, and some bonds in a workshop or factory which appear as workshop or factory "patriotism" have been hinted at in

Russian workers' history.[6] This writer once pointed out that there were two important foci in the urban working class milieu: factory and neighborhood (or residential quarter).[7]

Among traditional customs and rituals, drinking and "collective fistfights" were very important in reinforcing the identities of workers. Educated Russians and consciously advanced workers regarded temperance as a mark of cultural development, but in the male brotherhood of workers the use of vodka was an essential sign of membership.[8] As many workers' memoirs reveal, a new worker was required to treat his fellow workers to a bottle of vodka in a nearby tavern. This custom (called *prival'noe*) prevailed among metal and textile workers. Comradely relations between the newcomer and his seniors were established only after *prival'noe* occurred. Following that, all possible cooperation and support was given to the newcomer, and he could depend on those. It was impossible to obtain such support without offering *prival'noe*,[9] as Shapovalov described:

> "If a new worker refused to offer *prival'noe*, even if he were to starve or die, other workers made him unable to remain in the factory by various harassments; on the gear of his machine a nut was put, his machine got broken, and he would be fired. Or they enjoyed the following activity: they secretly attached tails made of a piece of cloth or dirty dustcloth to the worker [who neglected *prival'noe* — Y.T.] and enjoyed watching him walking about in the workshop without noticing his own tails. Sometimes they set these tails on fire. When the worker was surprised and took the tails off, burning his hands, everyone threw ridicule upon him."[10]

This custom, which was part of the traditional drinking culture,[11] was firmly maintained, so that even if a new worker had spent all of his assets during his unemployment and had no money, he still had to practice *prival'noe*. If he had no money and could not borrow from anybody, he resorted to *peregonka*, — that is, he bought goods in the factory shop on credit, sold them to local shops at a discount of 40-50 %, and got money to treat others with.[12] *Prival'noe* was not simply consumption of alcohol, but a distinctive ritual.

The abuse of alcohol had a bad influence on the lives of workers. Thus the habit of daily drinking at taverns, which David Christian defined as the "modern drinking culture," was the target of a sobriety movement led by reformist liberals, conscious workers, and socialists who wished to improve the quality of workers' lives. However, even daily drinking unrelated to rituals might strengthen the social and collective bonds among male workers.

In addition to *prival'noe,* collective fistfights are often also cited in workers' memoirs as important amusements. This traditional pastime, which originated in the sixteenth or seventeenth century,[13] was mainly practiced during the winter, and remained common even in the early twentieth century.

The scenario of a collective fistfight was: two sides — for example one factory vs. another or one district vs. another — formed "a wall against a wall (*stenka na stenku*)" to struggle for control of a disputed no-man's-land.[14] S. Kanatchikov (a worker at the Gustav List plant) wrote, "In the wintertime, when the Moscow River was frozen, we would go to the wall of the dike and had fistfights with workers from the Butikov factory. In the evening we would return home with our black eyes and our broken bloody noses."[15] And V. Sergeevich, who worked at the Neva shipyard in Aleksandro-Nevskaia district of St. Petersburg, described the "wall" of Smolenskoe village against that of Mikhail Arkhangel' village.[16]

There were some rules among the fighters, — not to strike those who had fallen, not to hit an opponent in the eye, and to fight only with bare hands. During intense fighting, however, these rules were often violated; rocks and knives were used as weapons, and some men were killed or seriously wounded.[17] The fight usually began with a young "wall" of teenage boys, followed by their seniors. The number of participants sometimes reached 500.[18] A strong fighter was a hero respected by other workers.

As Daniel Brower pointed out, the level of violence in these fights appeared barbaric and epitomized the crude and backward aspects of popular life to any Russian for whom culture meant learning and rational discourse. However, what outsiders judged as uncivilized had a different meaning to workers. Although they were bloody and brutal, collective fistfights created bonds of comradeship which helped urban immigrants to form a community to which they could turn in times of need. This community gave them a sense of belonging to a place of their own in the city.[19] Brower's claim is certainly relevant, although this writer cannot agree with his association of such fistfights with labor violence in Russia. Violence within a community, as an object of analysis, should be distinguished from that which was directed toward the world outside of the community.[20]

Thus, customs and rituals such as *prival'noe* and collective fistfights, hand-in-hand with other factors of the urban milieu like communal residence, reinforced workers' bonds in a certain *sociabilité* and helped to form the workers' community. Such informal *sociabilité* and community were all the more important because most Russian workers had no formal organization before the first Russian revolution. (A very few examples of formal organizations through which workers reinforced their identities were: Khar'kov Mutual Aid Society, mutual aid organizations of printers in St. Petersburg, and the communal dormitory organized by bakers in St. Petersburg.) The forementioned customs and rituals were despised by educated society, but among workers they fulfilled certain social functions.

2. Workers' New Aspiration for Self-Enlightenment

Workers' lives did not remain entirely traditional. For example, by the end of the nineteenth century, workers' meals had already become "urbanized," characterized by the consumption of meat and tea independantly of particular religious opportunities.[21] As to workers' manner of dress, there indeed were peasant-style workers who wore rustic *rubashka* with a belt, and high boots into which the cuffs of their trousers were tucked. They also had their hair cut in the shape of an inverted bowl.[22] Such styles rapidly became urbanized as workers became accustomed to their new environment.[23] According to Shapovalov, even among textile workers (known for their peasant-like way of life) the younger ones had already changed their hairstyles into urban styles, and they wore jackets on holidays.[24] Z.T. Trifonov, a worker at the Wagon works, dressed himself in the "German" style in order to gain admittance to the Summer Garden, after twice being refused admittance by policemen because of his disheveled clothes.[25]

Among the new inclinations which were promoted in the industrial and urban milieu, the aspiration to enlightenment or self-education was highly important. While, as is well known, the workers' literacy rate was relatively high,[26] it is said that their literacy had been acquired before they came to the city.[27] This means that even in the countryside, boys especially might receive an elementary education, as some workers' memoirs reveal.[28]

Michael Share has pointed out that when young, future members of the Central Workers' Circle of Petersburg regarded education as "the major vehicle for a release from their destination"; many had attended *zemstvo* or village schools, though all considered this education to be inadequate.[29] Trifonov was taught to read by his uncle, who was asked to teach the boy by Trifonov's illiterate mother who eagerly wanted to make him literate. At the same time, his elder sister was not allowed to learn despite her hope to do so, because "a girl need not go into the army." Trifonov's learning proved to be entirely inadequate when he entered a village school.[30]

Thus boys had possibilities to learn even in the countryside and many future workers learned reading, writing, arithmetic, and religion. Girls had fewer opportunities to learn because at a rather early age they had to perform such work as being nursemaids (*niania*) in order to augment family incomes.[31] However, the earnest desire to learn might be encouraged in the city, where there were numerous institutions and opportunities for workers to study, such as evening-Sunday schools, various museums, libraries, popular reading meetings (*narodnoe chtenie*), and the like.

Some public and private initiatives to broaden elementary education began in the 1860s and early 1870s. They included the Sunday school movement, establishment of factory classes, the spontaneous movement for expansion of formal elementary education, and the new law promulgated in 1872 by the Ministry of Education for urban elementary education.[32] Of course, these trends did not immediately transform the cultural outlook of urban workers, but in the 1870s there had already emerged the workers' intelligentsia. These were a small number of skilled worker who were distinguished from the rest of the urban working class by their level of literacy, social traits, economic and political positions, and their "urge to discover the outside world." They were generally apolitical, and merely sought the cultural and economic improvement of their current conditions.[33]

In the 1870s, the inclination toward self-education was still limited to a very small percentage of workers — that is, the workers' elite. However, due to the growing number of full-time urban workers and the forementioned trends toward expansion of elementary education, more and more workers had availed themselves of educational opportunities by the end of the nineteenth century. Especially after the first Russian revolution, workers' aspirations for education and knowledge had become evident.

In 1900 the number of Sunday schools, which had been established by various groups and private interests, totaled 286 in 75 cities, with 50,000 students. In 1905, some 112,000 worker-students were learning in evening classes and special courses for workers.[34] In the Ligovskie evening classes in St. Petersburg, 686 students were present in 1906/1907 and 1,030 in 1907/1908. In the Prechistenskie courses in Moscow, 1,137 students were learning in 1906, and 1,500 in 1908; in subsequent years there were between 1,500 and 2,000 students. In the case of Prechistenskie, when each school year began, 3,000 or more hoped to enter the courses, but some had to be disappointed because of limited capacity.[35] A similar phenomenon was seen in the general situation of urban elementary education. According to Brower, economic opportunity provided a powerful incentive for expanded elementary education. There was a strong demand for free public (or parish) schooling. One simple indicator of this demand was the number of unsatisfied school applications in large cities. In Moscow in 1877 there were 600 more admission applications than openings; in 1890, despite a sevenfold increase in municipal expenditures on education, there were 2,600 excess admission applications. At the end of the 1890s, Khar'kov's schools, which had doubled in number since 1893, still had to refuse admission to 500 children.[36]

As is well known, the curriculum of evening classes and Sunday schools often contained political and social themes. V. Sergeevich wrote, "Lessons in the Sunday school (Smolenskaia school in the Neva district of St. Petersburg — Y.T.) were infused with political tendentiousness. Even in purely scientific subjects, much was spoken about politics. For example, the chemistry teacher often changed the topic from Lavoisier to the French Revolution... Thus, the school was a sort of local political club and a uniting focus."[37]

For those workers who sought enlightenment and knowledge, however, it did not matter whether lessons at educational institutions were socialistic or not. Thus various initiatives taken by the government or liberal reformists could attract a considerable number of workers. For example, the popular reading meetings organized by the Sobriety Society in St. Petersburg were held on 1,032 occasions and attracted attracting a total of 182,200 participants (including many workers) in the years 1892-94. Similar meetings were held 3,711 times from 1906 to 1912, attracting a grand total of 429,500 participants.[38] Z.T. Trifonov offered unqualified praise to N.A. Vargunin, a factory owner, and the Neva Society of Popular Entertainments he established.[39] According to a survey conducted among worker-students in 1910-1912, those who (rejecting a utilitarian purpose regarded multi-faceted general improvement as their main reason for studying comprised more than half of the respondents. At the same time, a fairly large number of workers demanded that evening classes should provide opportunities to continue learning in order to prepare for examinations for graduation from a secondary school, to acquire a teaching credential, or to become an agronomist.[40]

After the first Revolution, new workers' organizations devoted to enlightenment and cultural growth appeared. These were called "workers' clubs." According to I.D. Levin, such clubs in St. Petersburg had three different origins: the initiatives of evening class workers, the personal initiatives of activists, and the initiatives of workers at one or more factories. Though these organizations were unstable and not always long-lived, they sponsored in various activities such as organizing evening classes, lectures, literary-musical parties, reading or drama circles, and the like.[41]

In any case, it is beyond doubt that a substantial number of workers participated in these educational organizations in large cities. It is true that many workers could not complete the regular course of evening or Sunday schools for various reasons, or were unable to pay the membership fees for workers' clubs. However, experiences in such organizations could not but influence the cultural conditions of workers.

3. Changing Attitude toward Religion among Workers

Life in urban and industrial environments and contacts with various educational entities seemed to contribute to the secularization of workers. For many workers who had just come to the city, religion was very important, although they often disliked priests. A. Buiko, a Putilov worker, noticed that religion or the "religious narcotic" had long captivated him.[42]

Semen Kanatchikov first feared the pattern makers ("students" of the Gopper factory near his Gustav works) because they did not believe in God and might be able to shake his faith as well, which could have resulted in eternal hellish torments in the next world. On the other hand, he admired them because they were so free, so independent, and so well-informed about everything.[43]

Religious sectarianism also flourished among urban workers in the late nineteenth and early twentieth centuries. On this point, Sergeevich has noted:

> The workers' movement in the late nineteenth and the early twentieth centuries caused lively activity in various religious sects. At first sight, any connection between the workers' movement and religious sectarianism may seem strange, but it nevertheless existed. Restrained by the nets of ignorance and darkness, Russian workers could not and were afraid to break away from God and religion... On the other hand, it was also impossible to come to terms with religion as presented by priests. Churches and priests played a disturbing role in the workers' emancipation struggle... Sectarianism was the golden mean which was suitable, above all, for less advanced, less conscious masses. Here God was not denied and religion was admitted, but priests, Churches, and their regulations were not admitted.[44]

While a teenage worker at the Pal' cotton mill in St.Petersburg, A. Artamonov fell under the influence of a group of worker-*pashkovtsy*, that is, workers of some sect at the factory. He began to tell his shocked mother about his new beliefs: "that icons were thought up by people, that they were not necessary, that the Church should be in the soul of every individual, and that priests were deceivers, hawkers, and pharisees."[45]

Thus religious sectarianism among workers appeared to be the product of a combination of their anti-clerical feelings and faith in God. At the same time, religious sectarianism played a certain role in weakening workers' religious faith. Again, according to Sergeevich, "when I visited the meeting of *pashkovtsy* (for the first time — Y.T.), I decided to debate them if necessary, because I regarded myself as being well versed in the Bible. . . At the meeting of *pashkovtsy*, I didn't hear anything abominable; on the contrary, many things seemed true. After that, I often attended their meetings, thought over what they said, and observed the reality. In my own notion of religion, a deep fissure gradually formed, and my belief in God slowly disappeared."[46]

As regards the waning of religious faith among workers, it is plausible that scientific education in evening and Sunday schools or workers' circles, as well as revolutionary propaganda, played important roles. Courses in physics, geology, geography, astronomy, and other subjects were taught in those schools.[47] Trifonov referred to one particular lesson:

In the second year of the Smolenskie evening-Sunday classes, A.A. Baikov, a young teacher, once brought a big human skeleton, a live frog, and a microscope. Comparing the structure of the frog's heart with that of the human, as well as circulation of blood, he said that humans might have evolved from such a frog, and in all cases, the nearest ancestors of humans were monkeys. Such a comparison inflicted a blow upon my religious faith. I became unsettled, and was about to leave the classroom in resentment, but a classmate kept me in the class. . . The teacher disassembled the skeleton into parts and explained the significance of the inner mechanism of each bone. . . His clear, persuasive explanation gradually began to penetrate my consciousness. . . When the class was over, I felt ashamed of thinking about leaving imprudently just to protect my own faith that God had created Adam.[48]

Shapovalov associated his own loss of religious faith with his study of science: "comparing the conclusions of science to the stories of the Bible, I arrived at the definitive conclusion that there was no God, that God had not created man, but rather priests had thought up the concept of God to deceive the people." A. Boldyreva stated that scientific answers to various questions aroused a worker's curiosity and "impelled him to seek answers to the questions that troubled him, not in priests' sermon, but in books."[49]

Indeed, such a distinct departure from religious faith might have been limited to a small number of workers, but mass secularization of workers was indeed taking place. The propagandist S.G. Strumilin found few "church enthusiasts" among workers — religion was less important to them, he felt, than for village peasants. N. Krupskaia similarly noted that urban workers had less need for religion than did peasants; workers were more educated and more aware of the "practical application of knowledge."[50] When he talked with students of the Prechistenskie classes in June, 1910, Lev Tolstoy found that they had no religious view of their lives. The "religious seeking" of young workers was essentially a quest for new, non-religious, and ethical ideals which corresponded to their social and political aspirations. According to a young Tolstoian worker, S.T. Semenov, "what interests them are newspapers articles, current works of young writers, the factions in the State Duma, and national problems."[51] This trend seemed to be more clearly shown in reading preferences as well.

Though many workers first began to read with religious books, their urban milieu was farremoved from that of the peasantry, and moral teachings in religious literature seemed implausible. Workers preferred secular to religious literature. As one indication, 22 percent of the holdings of the Pushkin Reading Room in St. Petersburg were religious in nature, but in 1888 only 2 percent of the books checked out came from this category.[52] The traveling library of the Vladikavkaz Railroad received only 55 requests for religious-moral literature out of 15,319 total requests. The wane of religious faith among workers was noted everywhere in the reports of bishops after the first Revolution. They were inclined to think that this process could not be reversed because the idea of 1905 was too much alive in the workers' consciousness. As if to confirm this, the percentage of religious literature in all publications decreased from 29 percent in 1901 to just 9 percent in 1913.[53]

Of course, such attitudes toward religion and the popularity of secular literature did not always lead directly to an acceptance of socialism, although the departure from religious faith was often a step toward an "advanced and self-conscious" worker.[54] In one Petersburg workers' club, *Prosveshchenie*, requests for books in 1907-08 were as follows: social literature — 41 percent, and *belles lettres* — 42 percent; in 1908-09, 26 percent for the former and 55 percent for the latter; and in 1909-10, 17 percent for the former and 66 percent for the latter. During the time of what is termed "a reaction," there may be seen such a tendency of declining interest in social literature, i.e. social problems. That tendency was common in popular lectures as well.[55] And the mass circulation of detective stories (*"Pinkertonovshchina"*) was such that a working-class newspaper associated such a phenomenon with the failure of the revolution and the breakdown of workers' organizations and democratic publications.[56]

Generally speaking, working-class culture was comprised of old traditional popular culture and newer customs, values, morals, and attitudes formed in urban and industrial environments, and was created from their mutual interactions. Some traditional aspects were regarded as "dark," and the backwardness of the populace became the target of reformist and socialist enlightening activities. Even such "dark" aspects performed important social functions among workers, so they seemed difficult to eradicate. On the other hand, the new milieu in which workers came to live provided them with various opportunities (all the while their political, social, and economic conditions indicated their position in society), arousing their aspirations for new cultural attainments. On this point, both liberal reformists and socialists were successful to some extent, if not completely.

In order for Russian working-class culture to be fully illuminated, numerous questions remain to be analyzed: gender roles in workers' families, the socialist influence on working-class culture, the relationship of working-class culture with bourgeois culture or peasant culture, shop floor culture, and so forth. When these problems are scrutinized, it would probably be shown that in the early twentieth century, workers possessed specific cultural characteristics different from those of the urban middle classes and village peasants.

Notes

1 This epitome is based upon Michio Shibata, "Joshō," *Minshu-Bunka, Series Sekai-shi he no Toi,* No. 6 (Tokyo, 1990), pp. 1-14.
2 For example, see David L. Ransel (ed.), *The Family in Imperial Russia* (Univ. of Illinois Press, 1978); Victoria E. Bonnell (ed.), *The Russian Worker: Life and Labor under the Tsarist Regime* (Univ. of California Press, 1983); Daniel R. Brower, *The Russian City between Tradition and Modernity 1850-1900* (Univ. of California Press, 1990); and Mark D. Steinberg, *Moral Communities: The Culture of Class Relations in the Russian Printing Industry, 1867-1907* (Univ. of California Press, 1992).
3 Anne L. Bobroff, "Working Women, Bonding Patterns, and the Politics of Daily Life: Russia at the End of the Old Regime," Ph.D. Dissertation (Univ. of Michigan, 1982).
4 On the role of *zemliachestvo,* see Robert E. Johnson, *Peasant and Proletarian: The Working Class of Moscow in the Late Nineteenth Century* (Rutgers Univ. Press, 1979). It should be noted that *zemliachestvo* did not always indicate the peculiar bonds of peasants.
5 Michio Shibata, *Pari-no Furansu Kakumei* [The French Revolution in Paris] (Tokyo, 1988), pp. 71-76. See also; Hiroyuki Ninomiya, "Joshō," *Shakai-teki Ketsugo, Series Sekai-shi he no Toi,* No. 4 (Tokyo, 1989), pp. 1-14.
6 On neighborhood, see Laura Engelstein, *Moscow 1905: Working-Class Organization and Political Conflict* (Stanford Univ. Press, 1982); on workshop and factory patriotism, see Steve A. Smith, "Craft Consciousness, Class Consciousness: Petrograd 1917," *History Workshop,* 11 (1981).
7 Yoshifuru Tsuchiya, "Rōdōsha-no Sekai: Peteruburugu ni okeru sono kōsatsu," [The Workers' World: The Theory Applied to St.Petersburg], *Roshia-shi Kenkyu,* No. 40 (1984).
8 Brower, *The Russian City,* pp. 145-146.
9 For example, V. Sergeevich, *Zavod-Kuznitsa revoliutsii: Rabochii o starom i novom zhit'e-byt'e* (M.,1929), pp. 21-23; and P. Timofeev, *Chem zhivet zavodskoi rabochii* (SPb., 1906), pp. 33-34.
10 A.S. Shapovalov, *Na puti k marksizmu* (L., 1926), p. 30.

11 David Christian, *Living Water: Vodka and Russian Society on the Eve of Emancipation* (Oxford Univ. Press, 1990), p. 75. According to Christian, traditional drinking cultures tended to be collective in their approach to drinking, while modern drinking cultures were (and are) more individualistic. In the traditional world, drinking was a social and ceremonial activity, shaped more by convention than by individual whim. Daily drinking in a tavern can be classified as "modern" rather than "traditional." The "modern" aspect of workers' drinking culture not only damaged their health, but also impacted their family finances. It was thus a very common scene that on payday, wives waited for their worker-husbands at the gate of the factory so that they might prevent their husbands from spending all their wages in taverns. See Bobroff, "Working Women, Bonding Patterns and the Politics of Daily Life," pp. 130-138. A.M. Buiko, *Put' rabochego: Vospominaniia Putilovtsa* (L., 1964), p. 15; and Sergeevich, *Zavod-kuznitsa revoliutsii,* pp. 44-45.

12 On *"peregonka,"* see Buiko, *Put' rabochego,* p. 15; and Sergeevich, *Zavod-kuznitsa revoliutsii,* pp. 21-22.

13 Brower, "Labor Violence in Russia in the Late Nineteenth Century," *Slavic Review,* 41 (3) (1982), p. 425.

14 Brower, *The Russian City,* p. 147.

15 Reginald E. Zelnik (trans. & ed.), *A Radical Worker in Tsarist Russia: The Autobiography of Semen Ivanovich Kanatchikov* (Stanford Univ. Press, 1986), p. 13.

16 Sergeevich, *Zavod-kuznitsa revoliutsii,* pp. 43-44.

17 Buiko, *Put' rabochego,* pp. 20-21.

18 Brower, "Labor Violence," p. 425 and Shapovalov, *Na puti k marksizmu,* p. 24.

19 Brower, *The Russian City,* p. 148.

20 See also the critical comments by Johnson and Koenker — Robert E. Johnson, "Primitive Rebels? Reflections on Collective Violence in Imperial Russia," and Diane Koenker, "Collective Action and Collective Violence in the Russian Labor Movement," *Slavic Review,* 41,(3) (1982), pp. 432-435, 443-448.

21 *Rabochii klass Rossii ot zarozhdeniia do nachala XX v.* (M., 1983), p. 249; Yoshimasa Tsuji, *Roshia Kakumei to Rōshi Kankeino Tenkai* [The Russian Revolution and the Development of Labor Relations] (Tokyo, 1981), pp. 73-75; and M. Matossian, "The Peasant Way of Life," in Wayne S. Vucinich (ed.), *The Peasant in Nineteenth-Century Russia* (Stanford Univ. Press, 1968), pp. 12-14.

22 Zelnik, *A Radical Worker,* p. 8; on the urban hair styles, see pp. 20-21, and *Vospominaniia I. V. Babushkina 1893-1900* (L., 1925), pp. 36-40.

23 V.Iu. Krupianskaia, "Evoliutsiia semeino-bytovogo uklada rabochikh," in *Rossiiskii proletariat: Oblik, bor'ba, gegemoniia* (M., 1970), p. 281.

24 Shapovalov, *Na puti k marksizmu*, p. 86.

25 Z.T. Trifonov, "Vospominaniia," in *Avangard: Vospominaniia i dokumenty piterskikh rabochikh 1890-kh godov* (L., 1990), pp. 304-306.

26 For example, see S.N. Semanov, *Peterburgskie rabochie nakanune pervoi russkoi revoliutsii* (M.-L., 1966), p. 52.

27 Jeffrey Brooks, "Readers and Reading at the End of the Tsarist Era," in: William Mills Todd (ed.), *Literature and Society in Imperial Russia, 1800-1914* (Stanford Univ. Press, 1978), pp. 143-144.

28 Zelnik, *A Radical Worker*, pp. 3-4; Trifonov, "Vospominaniia," pp. 295ff; and Buiko, *Put' rabochego*, pp. 11ff.

29 Michael B. Share, "The Central Workers' Circle of St. Petersburg, 1889-1894: A Case Study of the 'Workers' Intelligentsia'," Ph.D. Dissertation (Univ. of Wisconsin [Madison], 1984), pp. 136-137.

30 Trifonov, "Vospominaniia," pp. 295-296.

31 Bobroff, "Working Women, Bonding Patterns, and the Politics of Daily Life," pp. 178-180.

32 See, for example, Brower, *The Russian City*, pp. 154-155; L.M. Ivanov, "Ideologicheskoe vozdeistvie na proletariat tsarizma i burzhuazii," in *Rossiiskii proletariat: Oblik, bor'ba, gegemoniia*, pp. 318-319, passim; Share, "The Central Workers' Circle of St. Petersburg," pp. 43-46; and Zelnik, " 'To the Unaccustomed Eye': Religion and Irreligion in the Experience of St. Petersburg Workers in the 1870s," *Russian History*, 16, nos. 2-4, 1989, p. 308.

33 Share, "The Central Workers' Circle of St. Petersburg," pp. 36, 40-41, 97.

34 Ivanov, "Ideologicheskoe vozdeistvie," p. 321. The number of students in four evening and Sunday schools along the Shlisserburg highway was as follows:

school year	males	females	total
1883 / 84	240	0	240
1884 / 85	309	165	474
1885 / 86	459	335	794
1886 / 87	508	316	824
1887 / 88	500	274	774
1888 / 89	498	298	796
1889 / 90	490	277	767
1890 / 91	708	256	964
1891 / 92	811	190	1,001
1892 / 93	691	163	854
1897 / 98	988	290	1,278

E.Ia. Vainerman, "Obrazovatel'noi i kul'turnyi uroven' peterburgskikh rabochikh v 90-kh godakh XIX veka," *Uchenie zapiski Leningrad, gos. ped. in-ta im. A.I. Gertsena*, t. 78 (1948), p. 180.

35 I.S. Rozental', "Dukhovnye zaprosy rabochikh Rossii posle revoliutsii 1905-1907 gg.," *Istoricheskie Zapiski*, 107 (1982), p. 78.

36 Brower, *The Russian City*, pp. 157-158.

37 Sergeevich, *Zavod-kuznitsa revoliutsii*, p. 62.

38 Ivanov, "Ideologicheskoe vozdeistvie," p. 331.

39 Trifonov, "Vospominaniia," pp. 304, 314-318. About Vargunin, see also Share, "The Central Workers' Circle of St. Petersburg," pp. 44-45 and Ivanov, "Ideologicheskoe vozdeistvie," p. 328.

40 Rozental', "Dukhovnye zaprosy rabochikh Rossii," p. 80.

41 I.D. Levin, *Rabochie kluby v dorevoliutsionnom Peterburge: Iz istorii rabochego dvizheniia 1907-1914 gg.* (M., 1926).

42 Buiko, *Put' rabochego*, p. 19.

43 Zelnik, *A Radical Worker*, pp. 27-28.

44 Sergeevich, *Zavod-kuznitsa revoliutsii*, pp. 51-52.

45 Cited in Deborah L. Pearl, "Tsar and Religion in Russian Revolutionary Propaganda," *Russian History*, Vol. 20, nos. 1-4, 1993, pp. 97-98.

46 Sergeevich, *Zavod-kuznitsa revoliutsii*, pp. 53-54.

47 On the programs in evening-Sunday schools, see Share, "The Central Workers' Circle of St. Petersburg," pp. 46-47; on the educational program of the workers' circle, also see, pp. 202-203.

48 Trifonov, "Vospominaniia," p. 307.

49 Pearl, "Tsar and Religion," pp. 105-106.

50 Ibid., p. 103.

51 Rozental', "Dukhovnye zaprosy rabochikh Rossii," p. 87.

52 Brooks, "Readers and Reading," p. 140.

53 Rozental', "Dukhovnye zaprosy rabochikh Rossii," pp. 86-87.

54 Pearl, "Tsar and Religion," p. 96.

55 I.D. Levin, *Rabochie kluby*, p. 116.

56 Rozental', "Dukhovnye zaprosy rabochikh Rossii," pp. 81-82.

Chapter 3

The "Russian Idea" and the Ideology of the February Revolution

Boris KOLONITSKII

Recently in Russia considerable (possibly too much) attention has been devoted to studying the so-called "Russian idea." Participants in this discussion, however, argue about different things: many do not define what they mean by the "Russian idea" in any way, and for the majority of people these arguments appear simply to be about "Russian," "Russians," or "Russia." The attempts that have been made to provide such a definition have usually been unsatisfactory.[1]

Granted, it is quite difficult to speak about some single "Russian idea": its adherents were and often are opponents and at times even political adversaries. Still, amongst all the different interpretations of the term "Russian idea" and the various concepts joined together by this notion, the following characteristics, in my opinion, stand out:

1. The paths of development of Russian civilization (of Russian culture and society) are fundamentally different from those of Western civilization (different authors evaluate the significance of this distinction differently).

2. Russian culture contains certain elements that not only distinguish it from all the rest of the world, but also contain the preconditions for the salutary transformation of the latter — the idea of the Russian people being "divinely chosen" and "divinely sustained," of faith in their "world-wide historic" mission.

3. Political attitudes are not separated into an independent sphere. Politics is seen through a prism of moral and moral-

religious views. The "Russian ideas" are absolutely whole, undifferentiated. Therefore, the political ideal of the "Russian idea" is also syncretic (*"sobornost'*," "theocratic empire," "universal theocracy," etc.).

A distinctive variation of the "Russian idea" was inherent in the official ideology of Imperial Russia, especially during the reigns of Alexander III and Nicholas II.

Discussions about the national roots of the February Revolution are today extremely ideologized. The question "Why?" is very often replaced by the question "Who is to blame?" — which is completely in keeping with Russian tradition. To a certain degree, however, this also reminds one of the controversy in Western historical literature in the 1940-50s over the interpretation of German Nazism. While certain Anglo-American authors saw the entire history of Germany as nothing more than the prehistory of Nazism, many German authors of both a conservative and liberal orientation tried to emphasize the foreign origin of the doctrines that influenced the formation of Hitlerism.

Likewise, the February Revolution is also at times interpreted as an exclusively Russian phenomenon, an evaluation usually accompanied by negative connotations. Historian Richard Pipes describes the uprising in Petrograd in the following way:

> The air was thick with that peculiar Russian air of generalized, unfocused violence — the urge to beat and destroy — for which the Russian language has coined the words *pogrom* and *razgrom*....
>
> ...It was not really a military mutiny of the kind that broke out during the war in other armies, including the French and German, but a typical Russian *bunt*, with powerful anarchist overtones.[2]

It is unclear exactly how the mass disorders that accompanied political revolutions in other countries are different from the "truly Russian" pogroms.

On the other hand, the foreign nature and enmity of revolution to the Russian political tradition was and often is emphasized. People of various ideological orientations supported and continue to support describing February as a foreign and non-Russian conspiracy against Russia. Here is a typical example taken from a publicist writing during the Civil War: "Now, however, it is clear to everyone that our entire Revolution is not of Russian origin, that it was both begun and continued by those in Russia who possessed neither Church nor Fatherland, those who from childhood were taught to spurn everything native, to treat everything that carries the stamp of Russian originality with contempt."[3]

N.A. Berdiaev expressed his own special view on the roots of the Russian Revolution in 1918 (he later changed his views on this question): "The Russian Revolution was anti-national in character; it transformed Russia into a lifeless corpse. Nevertheless, the national peculiarities of the Russian people are reflected in its anti-national character, and the style of our unhappy and destructive Revolution is the Russian style."[4]

More often, however, the February Revolution, which overthrew the autocracy and repudiated the ruling ideology, is interpreted simply as an unsuccessful attempt at modernizing the political and social system of the country along the lines of Westernization (a democratic, bourgeois-democratic revolution) that radically departed from the political tradition of pre-revolutionary society. A. Ianov suggests that the "Russian idea" suffered a "deafening defeat" in 1917 (although he defines the "Russian idea" simply as the theoretical core of the "new Russian right").[5] At times the disparity between the February Revolution's ideology and the "Russian idea" is thought to be the main reason for its lack of success.

Such an approach is extremely simplistic. The complex phenomenon of the 1917 Revolution arose from the interaction of several revolutionary trends that at first reinforced and then stifled one another.[6] The February Revolution was without doubt in certain respects both democratic and bourgeois. But at the same time it was also anti-imperial, anti-war, and, to a certain degree, anti-militarist. If the ideas of a "state based on law" inspired the agents of the Provisional

Government, then anti-Western, anti-modernist attitudes were an integral part of the peasant revolution. The various components of the "Russian idea," it seems to me, were inherent in a number of important revolutionary trends.

1. Religious Revolution

Many contemporaries joyously welcomed the February Revolution and interpreted it not only as a political revolution, but as a total moral revolution as well: "...the political victory may be understood by many as just a political victory, but it was a general victory for the Russian spirit over passivity and morbidity, which prevents one from living, breathing, and creating." The fall of the autocracy was explained by its "sinfulness": "The Russian people forgot the very reason why it is necessary to live in a union and not alone. And the Russian people forgot this truth for a simple reason — they were divided into rich and poor, into the aristocratic and those without rights. All the tsar's power rested upon this terrible sin." Many contemporaries sincerely thought that after the Revolution lying and stealing, foul language and games of chance, jails and fences would disappear. They happily fixated on both actual and merely wished for changes. S.L. Frank wrote, "People became more attentive and courteous to one another; an acute, almost intoxicating feeling of general national solidarity awoke among the people."[7] In this regard February was an extreme form of a "revolution of high expectations."

Of course, a similar consciousness also marked other revolutions. The Russian synthesis of moral-political expectations, however, had its own peculiarities. The Russian Orthodox Church and the autocracy were connected both institutionally and ideologically. Many believers were accustomed to treating the state religiously; the "tsar" was not only the head of state: an official cult of the monarchy was interwoven with a religious cult. Some religiously oriented contemporaries believed that this was the most important reason for the Revolution. E.N. Trubetskoi wrote:

> Why was the tsarist autocracy in Russia destroyed? Because autocracy *became an idol* for the Russian autocrat. He placed his authority above the Church, and in this there was both self-adulation and a grave offense to sacred objects.... Damage to the origin of spiritual life — this was the fundamental reason for [the autocracy's] downfall.[8]

Many believers saw the various religious experiments by a portion of the political elite, including even some representatives of the tsar's family (the infatuation with Rasputin and other intrigues), as blasphemy. Just as the social crisis on the eve of the Revolution was manifest in ecclesiastical life, so too the political revolution could not but lead to a revolution in the religious sphere as well.[9]

The Revolution soon influenced church services. Metropolitan Evlogii recalled:

> From the very first day after the Revolution the question was put to me as the head of the Volhynia eparchy: whom to remember and how at church services? At first, before the abdication of Grand Duke Mikhail Aleksandrovich, this was quite simple. Later it became more complicated. In the end it was decided to remember the "Good-faith Provisional Government".... The deacons sometimes got confused and said "May the Good-faith Provisional Government last for many years"...[10]

A contemporary and member of the Irkutsk Public Committee remembered the March days of the Revolution in the following way:

> Together with serious affairs we wasted a lot of time on trifles.... Along came a synodic archpriest with the question of whom "to proclaim" at the end of the ektene.
> - It was suggested to the Right Reverend Bishop that the clergy conclude their proclamation: "for Russian power and the piety of her rulers"....

- So let it be proclaimed![11]

What this demonstrates is just how quickly priests turned to the new temporal power; only Soviet power could find a way out of this situation, could both treat this question as "trivial" and at the same time find a quick solution to the problem.

Subsequently, the Petrograd Ecclesiastic Consistory and the Synod adopted special resolutions on the unification of ceremonial "proclamations."[12]

Many contemporaries' first reaction to the new regime was to organize a thanksgiving service. "The first swallow of the Revolution," the first news of the Revolution, for Metropolitan Evlogii was a telegram from a priest: "The workers have requested that a service be said in honor of the Revolution." Red banners with the slogan "Long Live the Democratic Republic" were carried in front of icons during ceremonial processions.[13]

A number of priests adorned themselves with red bows. The Revolution also intruded upon the internal furnishings of churches. Z.N. Gippius' sister, T.N. Gippius, who enthusiastically participated in the activities of the Petrograd Religious-Philosophical Society, wrote:

> Currently in the Kazan Cathedral at the foot of the crucifix where there is a little funereal table for the repose of the soul, someone placed at the feet of Christ a red silk scarf and flowers.... This *too* is a red banner. And it is very clever. I had just written about the cross, and this scarf caused me to shiver with that internal agitation that one experiences in rare moments, and I *specially* kissed the feet of Christ like never before.[14]

Church administration became disorganized. In many eparchies there was at times a tendency to call laymen and lower church officials "social-deacons" and "social-psalm-readers," respectively. A wave of enthusiasm for "overthrowing bishops" and electing new ones flowed over Russia (sometimes laymen were advanced as candidates for these positions). The Synod was overwhelmed by petitions demanding that the episcopate be elected. The policies of the "revolutionary" Ober-Procurator of the Holy Synod, V.N. L'vov, who "acted like a dictator," replacing the Metropolitan of Moscow and completely reconstituting the Synod, had a contradictory influence on the development of this situation. A number of high-level church officials and priests were dismissed by local soviets. The revolutionary masses demanded a "purge of the clergy" and the sending of church officials to the front for being a "superfluous element."

The movement for autocephaly (Georgia, Ukraine) was the central element of the crisis for the Church administration. This movement merged with national independence movements and was strongly politicized; the supporters of autocephaly had no intention of waiting for canonical decisions. Thus, the programs of a number of Ukrainian parties contained a demand for the independence of the Ukrainian Church. The Central Rada adopted a similar resolution, which it saw as a blow to the Russian counter revolution. Not surprisingly, army organizations began to examine ecclesiastical questions; thus, the Third All-Ukraine Army Congress resolved on 1 (14) November, "To recognize the need for the autocephaly of the Ukrainian Church. Services should be conducted in Ukrainian." Sometimes the movement for autocephaly was also revolutionary in its "form": a contemporary recalled with horror the "short-haired and shaved" Ukrainian army priests with their rifles and greatcoats who played an active role in the all-Ukraine Church Assembly.[15]

The Church administration's crisis was interwoven with the country's power crisis; the problem of dual power, for example, can be seen in believers sending every imaginable petition on religious questions to both the soviets and committees. The monks of the Alexander Nevskii Monastery made the following appeal to the Petrograd Soviet: "Believing in your committee as a just body of truth, we appeal to you for the removal from the Alexander Nevskii Monastery of the monster tyrant governor-general of the monastery,

Archimandrite Filaret." Laymen sometimes complained about priests to the soviets and demanded that they be removed.[16]

A number of priests were elected to soviets and military committees, and sometimes they adopted fairly radical positions. Thus, P.N. Wrangel recalls having clashed with a priest who represented a group of Cossacks at a joint meeting. A.I. Vvedenskii, the future creator of the so-called "Living Church," was a member of the Petrograd Soviet. Many priests were elected to rural volost committees.[17]

The congresses and meetings of the soviets and committees sometimes discussed initiatives relating to the Church. In April, for example, at a session of a congress of the Western front a priest named Elashentsev demanded that valuables be removed from churches so that they could be used for "the strengthening of freedom and the completion of the war." The assembly greeted this appeal with an ovation and resolved to print the text of his speech and have it sent to the clergy.[18]

That such extreme revolutionary sentiments were widespread within the Church can be seen from the Pomestnyi Sobor's creating a special "Commission on Bolshevism in the Church." At one of the Commission's sessions it was acknowledged that "Bolshevism has captured a large number of clergymen" (at that time "Bolshevism" was a term used for any radical movement).[19]

A portion of the intelligentsia had long ago suggested that the struggle against the autocracy should be carried out in the sphere of religion. A number of the leaders of the February Revolution held such views. At one of the meetings of the Petrograd intelligentsia on 29 October 1915, A.F. Kerenskii declared: "Politics is empiricism and autocracy is a religion... one must fight this religion with the same weapons, i.e., with religion, with religious consciousness." D.S. Merezhkovskii, another participant in this discussion, also expressed similar views.[20] Soon, a number of different trends appeared that attempted to unify the revolutionary movement and a renewal of Orthodoxy: "Gogolian Christianity," "Christian Revolutionaryism," "Religious Revolution," etc.[21]

Attempts to combine religion and revolution or religion and socialism intensified after February (examples include the activity by part of the Petrograd Religious-Philosophical Society to organize meetings and printing houses, and the attempts to create a Society of revolutionary-religious propaganda). In these circles the overthrow of the autocracy was regarded with religious enthusiasm. T.N. Gippius wrote: "The atmosphere has been purified. The universal resurrection of the dead.... Thank God that sobornost' triumphs over *partiinost'*."[22]

A number of contemporaries, on the other hand, felt their religious convictions justified overthrowing the tsar, but saw the Revolution as the beginning of a blasphemous campaign against religion and the Church. Such feelings persist today; in 1992 Priest Aleksei Ostaev called the February Revolution "godless" and condemned the Pomestnyi Sobor of 1917-18 for accepting it. In his opinion:

> The orthodox "with one voice and one heart" profess only and exclusively that which we were taught by the One and Holy Synodic and Apostolic Church, that is the Orthodox Church. In terms of the state structure this is an autocratic monarchy in harmony with Orthodoxy. Within the Church the Tsar is ascribed the special rank of bishop of world affairs.... Christianity and democracy are incompatible concepts; the very combination of the words is blasphemous.[23]

It is indisputable that in 1917 many priests as well as laymen thought that February was "godless," and the religious experiments discussed above contributed to this. Thus, despite the dangers many priests continued "to remember" the tsar and to carry out monarchist propaganda. For their efforts a number were even arrested.[24]

For many believers the news of the tsar's abdication came as a serious religious shock. F.F. Iusupov recalled, "The church was full of crying peasants: 'What will become of us?'

they repeated, 'they have taken the tsar away from us'."
Metropolitan Evlogii paints a similar picture: "The manifesto
announcing the Sovereign's abdication was read in the
cathedral; the archdeacon read it and cried. Amongst the
praying many sobbed."[25]

One can be sure that both the supporters and the opponents
of the Revolution often interpreted this grandiose upheaval
not only as a political, but also as a religious experience.[26]

From the very beginning, however, the Revolution was also
directed against the participation of the Church in political
life; the February Revolution was also an anti-clerical revolution. A number of contemporaries embraced this current of the
Revolution in an extremely oversimplified way. Z.N. Gippius
wrote in her diary: "Some sincerely think that 'they overthrew
the tsar' means 'they overthrew the Church,' 'the institution is
abolished.' They are used to joining them together utterly and
inseparably. And logically... amongst the more illiterate this
was even clearer: 'I myself have seen it written: down with
the monarchy. Meaning, beat up all the monks'."[27] (The
illiterates' confusion to which Gippius refers arises from the
Russian words for monarch [monarkh] and monk [monakh]
being near homonyms, trans.)

The fact that the victims of the February Revolution were
interred without priests and without services had special
significance. Burying them without a burial service aroused
indignation from some believers. The Cossacks from the
Petrograd Garrison refused to participate in the ceremony for
this reason.

A number of socio-political experiments were also directed
against the Church: for example, already on 25 March the
Nicholskii Union of Anarchist Communists decided to send
delegates to the Shmakovskii Men's Monastery with the
suggestion that they join the union, change their monastic
regime, and that those not wishing to live the life of Soviet
communism move away "to a more remote location." Rural
assemblies often adopted decisions on removing priests from
their parishes; further, many such resolutions contained a

demand that church valuables be removed to repay emancipation redemption loans.[28]

Many of those who held anti-clerical outlooks, however, continued to remain under the influence of a deep religious tradition, even though they often did not know it. This tradition exerted influence on the politicization of society: the mass consciousness, which in form was political, was organized as a religious consciousness. The symbols, institutions, and leaders of the Revolution became objects of quasi-religious worship.[29]

Contemporaries compared the Revolution to a "revival," a "rebirth," a "resurrection" of Russia and her people:

> Christ has arisen ! Thundering, chains have fallen,
> The heavens rejoice — rapturous night...
> Regards to you and greetings, miracle Russia
> — the steppes,
> Greetings to you my wintery, native land!

> Before you — space. Before you — Glory,
> Hosanna ! The radiant cry announces from heaven.
> Everything, everything is before you, Slavic Power,
> Russia, Eternal God, has indeed risen![30]

A soldier in the Russian expeditionary corps in France wrote:

> As pealing bells from trench to trench
> Emotion wafts: The people have arisen.
> They have begun to live. With anguish Europe looks
> At deeds daring, at wonders' rapid march.[31]

At the same time his compatriot, fighting in an expeditionary corps in Macedonia, suggested:

> The suffering face of Russia, I believe
> Will brighten once again and blossom splendidly.
> To her the long desired Messiah will come
> And to a new and better life will lead...[32]

Other paschal poems sounded similar motifs:

> ...For you the Messiah has come
> In this bloody, awesome, and dreadful year,

Profoundly pained Russia,
Saintly martyred people...[33]

It goes without saying that the poems of amateur poets are a highly specific kind of historical source. Nevertheless, both in many resolutions (sentences, orders) and in personal correspondence one can trace the same motif: faith in the rebirth (resurrection) of suffering (unhappy) Russia and her people. As one soldier wrote home: "I wish you happiness on this great holiday — The Resurrection of the Great People of all Russia."[34]

The theme of resurrection and rebirth — the rebirth of a nation and of man — is present, no doubt, in the self-consciousness of any revolution. In the Russian Revolution of 1917, however, one can trace a special connection between this theme and religious consciousness.

The Revolution led to the mass politicization of society, and this process was both harmful and self-contradictory. In compensating for their lack of corresponding political knowledge and experience, contemporaries sometimes used — consciously or unconsciously — customary and familiar ethical and religious concepts to evaluate events. And such a grandiose revolution as this was compared to (and at times also experienced) as an Easter holiday. G.N. Gippius wrote in a letter on 26 March that "The first revolutionary night was like an Easter night in its sensation of miracles near, close by, all around you." Many of those who participated in the actual events compared the Revolution to Easter in their diaries and memoirs.[35] Even the rituals of Easter were often used by contemporaries to express their attitudes toward what was happening. One teacher recalled a meeting with a colleague: "This was the first time that I had seen many of my comrades since the break in classes; along with shaking their hands and greeting them I said to each: 'Christ has arisen!' and then many of us kissed three times."[36] Both conscious and unconscious orientations toward the Easter holiday were manifest in people unfamiliar with each other (often soldiers) kissing on the city streets.

Such an approach — evaluating the Revolution as an important religious event — was even sanctified by the authority of religious thinkers. D.S. Merezhkovskii wrote that "perhaps since the time of the first Christian martyrs there has been no phenomenon in history that was more Christian, more Christ-like, than the Russian Revolution." The religious publicist V.P. Sventsitskii remarked during those days:

> The Russian Revolution brought defeat to the "devil." And for this reason it is so clearly like a *miracle*.... We knew that "revolutionary organizations" existed. But let every man tell the truth — including the most extreme revolutionaries — did he ever imagine that in three days the Russian people would rise from the dead? Of course no one ever dreamed of this. But behold, they have indeed arisen![37]

It is curious that a number of clerical figures also treated the Revolution in this way: "Father Ivan (from a pastoral school), despite his position, greeted me with 'Christ has arisen! Christ has arisen!' and in response to my admonitions that he be more reserved he objected, 'You don't understand anything...' Then I understood that he had torn the tsar's portrait off the walls of the school and hidden it somewhere."[38]

But if the Revolution was often compared with Easter, Easter was also sometimes compared with a revolution. The celebrating of the Easter holiday became politicized: "I gave the Easter morning service in the cathedral, packed with soldiers. The atmosphere in the temple was revolutionary, awe-inspiring.... To the salutation 'Christ has arisen!' amongst the rumble of 'He has indeed arisen' a voice shouted 'Russia has arisen!!'" [39] The campaign for sending Easter and May first presents to the front was conducted under the slogan: "Send red revolutionary eggs."

The salutations sent to the organs of power (the Provisional Government, soviets of various levels) on the Easter holiday had a political character. A group of soldiers wrote to the Provisional Government:

Christ has arisen! Most esteemed defenders of freedom, the 7th Company of the BDRP of the 35th Infantry Division wish you a solemn holiday of Christ's Easter resurrection and hope that you will meet and celebrate this holiday with the same emotion and delight with which we and the entire country met the freedom for which you fought.[40]

The Tauride Palace was called the "Temple of Freedom," the "Temple of Revolution;" the Ministers of the Provisional Government were called "Priests of Freedom": "We swear to believe in you, to guard the brilliant sun of freedom, and to protect you, its foremost priests," declared the delegates of the 40th corps.[41] N. Berdiaev objected to this attitude toward the Revolution: "To swear to earthly gods in the name of the Revolution is to enslave the spirit and commit idolatry."[42]

The religious tradition also exerted an influence on the symbology of the Revolution: many flags copied the form of ecclesiastical banners; red banners sometimes portrayed angels with trumpets that seemed to be warning the oppressors of the harsh judgement to come — the Revolution.[43]

Sacralizing is always inherent in politics. In 1917, however, the process of mass politicization merged for a time with both the anti-clerical movement and with religious revolution; political problems were interwoven with religious ones. The mass consciousness was political only in form; in its essence politics became an ideological surrogate for religion. This process of sacralizing politics was described at that time by N.A. Berdiaev: "A new kind of idolatry has begun; many new idols and earthly gods have appeared — 'revolution,' 'socialism,' 'democracy,' 'internationalism,' 'proletariat'."[44] The cult of revolution went on to influence the formation of Bolshevik political culture during the Soviet period.[45]

Faith in the Miracle of the political, economic, and moral Resurrection of the country and the nation became an important element in the mass political (political-moral-religious) consciousness. When this Miracle failed to occur, its absence was "explained" by the intrigues of general political enemies who were demonized in simplified forms (the "internal German," "enemy of the people," "bourgeois").

People often compare the 1917 Russian Revolution to revolutions of other eras, but we would do just as well to compare it to religious conflicts and battles over faith.

2. The "Russian" Revolution

The February Revolution provided an impetus for movements in non-Russian regions of the Empire — movements for reform in those areas, for autonomy, and in a number of cases even for leaving the Russian Empire. But at the same time many contemporaries saw February as a revolution for *Russian* liberation:

> We soldiers, fearless and brave
> Against the tsarist lackeys went!
> For the great Russian cause!
> For a land's great joy![46]

The Revolution was sometimes interpreted as a particularly Russian phenomenon without analog in world history, as proof of Russia's special mission. In his article "The Russian People's Revolution," E.N. Trubetskoi wrote: "This Revolution is the only one or almost the only one of its kind. There have been bourgeois revolutions and proletarian revolutions. But up to now there have been no national revolutions in the broad sense of the word like the Russian revolution."[47]

S.L. Frank believed that the Revolution manifested an "instinct for national self-preservation." His treatment of the Revolution contained mystical tones: "... the people's soul, full of great suffering and insulted in this suffering by unscrupulous tsarist power, overthrew this power in a single burst." P.B. Struve, according to his friends, spoke of the "patriotic necessity" of a coup.[48] This is how the authors of the "Vekhi" circle evaluated the February Revolution.

Many contemporaries tenderly saw in the Revolution's being "great and bloodless" a confirmation of the special unique character of Russians. One often heard: "Just imagine!... in Russia there was a great revolution and not a drop of blood was spilled! This is an unprecedented phenomenon in the history of revolutions. The Russians are a holy people..."[49] In the "Declaration" of the Petrograd intelligentsia the Revolution was interpreted as "the most miraculous of all known revolutions in the history of the world."[50] It is instructive that the Revolution was immediately called the "Great" February Revolution.

A number of politicians expressed similar views. Prince G.E. L'vov, the head of the first Provisional Government, declared on 9 March: "Honor and glory to all Russian people. The sun of freedom shined on Russia and immediately illuminated the profound depths of the lake of the Russian people's genius." Characterizing L'vov's attitude during the Revolution, his biographer wrote: "The 'Mother Country' was on the brink of destruction.... And could he possibly doubt at this hour the 'profound wisdom' of the Russian people, the divine principles living in her soul, her benevolence, her love for peace, and her humility?" A similar idealization of Russia and her people also influenced the process of adopting political decisions.[51] The ideology of Slavophilism exerted great influence on the formation of L'vov's world view. The idea of "revolutionary messianism" found reflection in a number of his speeches:

> The Great Russian Revolution is truly miraculous in its majestic, calm procession. It is miraculous in its non-fairy-tale upheaval, its lack of colossal change, its lack of force and haste in its onslaught and assault on power, and in the very essence of its leading ideas. The freedom of the Russian Revolution is permeated by elements of a world, universal character. An idea, which grew out of small seeds of freedom and equality thrown on black-earth soil a half century ago, captured not only the interests of the Russian people, but the interests of all peoples of the entire world. The soul of the Russian people turned out to be a universal democratic soul by its very nature. It is prepared not only to merge with the democracy of the whole world, but to stand

at the head of it and lead it along the path of developing humanity on the great principles of liberty, equality, and fraternity.[52]

Many people believed that the greatest accomplishment of the Revolution was the creation of a truly national government. The future ideologue of the *smenovekhovstvo* N.V. Ustrialov wrote: "From now on in Russia there will be no border between power and country. From now on the Russian government and the Russian people are one, and this unity is the Russian nation." N.A. Berdiaev, in assessing the Provisional Government and its head, remarked: "In this government... there is something characteristically Russian, the Russian dislike for governing."[53]

The Revolution was seen as a signal to fulfill the historic mission of Russia. M.Ia Fenomenov, who described himself as a socialist, declared: "Our Russian patriotism is very different than crude German chauvinism.... The liberation of people is the historic task of the great Russian people."[54]

The Revolution was often seen as a patriotic revolution encompassing all peoples, a "revolution in the name of victory" summoned to avert a national catastrophe, to suppress "conspiracies" and "treachery," and to replace the anti-people power. After February N.A. Berdiaev wrote: "The Russian Revolution was patriotic in terms of its foundations and its character." "The Russian Revolution was a highly national, a highly patriotic, a highly inclusive revolution, in which all classes and groups who opposed the anti-patriotic system of power participated...." "It was not the social class struggle that led us to a political revolution, but rather the intransigent clash between the old power and all the classes of society, all the Russian people, all nations."[55]

Many rank-and-file participants in the events of the Revolution described the situation after the Revolution as a distinctive kind of opposition, a confrontation between the "Russian people" and the "enemies of the people," the "traitors to the people's cause."[56]

The theme of victory over the "internal enemy" was sometimes interwoven with the theme of "resurrection":

Much blood, torment, suffering, and tears
Russia's patient people endured through years —
Until her cup of patience overflowed!
Russia has arisen, her internal enemy broken,
From its nightmarish dream the country has awoken,
And glory to her resurrection bestowed.[57]

The victory over the "internal enemy" was interpreted as the most important factor in the victory over the "external enemy": "Once they had dealt with the internal enemy, the liberated people turned their sights toward a more crafty and clever enemy — Wilhelm and his faithful robbers, who had always helped the autocracy keep the Russian body and soul in bondage."[58]

Even a number of representatives of the royal house shared this view. According to F. Iusupov, Grand Duke Nicholas Nikolaevich declared upon being named to the post of supreme commander in chief: "Finally, we can now triumph over the enemies of Russia."[59]

That anti-Germanic sentiments permeated an important part of post-revolutionary attitudes cannot be disputed: the Revolution was sometimes interpreted as a patriotic anti-German revolution, and pre-revolutionary anti-monarchist agitation was marked by features of Germanophobia and rumors about a change of religion. Anti-German sentiments were also manifest during the February Revolution: appeals were made against the Empress-German, and many officers, bureaucrats, and simple civilians who had German surnames were arrested and even killed. The well-known publicist D.V. Filosofov wrote in his diary on 1 March:

At ten o'clock yesterday Nuvel' telephoned. Soldiers came and dragged him and his brother into the street under arrest because they had "German surnames." Out on the street they explained that their name was French. Then [the soldiers] said to him: "Ok, scram." A member of the

State Council, Ikskul' (the former Secretary of State?), who was living with them was arrested because of his surname and dragged on foot to the Duma; there, they sorted it out.

Even foreign newspapers wrote about this. The English *Times* reported that "a strong anti-German mood predominates in the population." Foreign newspapers (English and German) reported on the persecution of people with German surnames.[60]

An anti-German mood also predominated amongst the supporters of renewing the Church: "The regime of the German police state established in Russia during the so-called 'imperial' period of its history could not help but exert its deadening, chilling influence on ecclesiastical life."[61]

A committee of the 9th Finish Rifle Company declared: "Greeting the great historical fact of the fall of the monarchy, and along with it the pernicious domination of the Germans..."[62] One also encounters similar attitudes in personal correspondence. One soldier wrote home, "Greetings on the occasion of the new Russian and non-German government." A review of soldiers letters prepared by the military censor pointed out: "The opinion is often repeated that the overthrow of the old regime was the salvation of Russia from the Germans, who would inevitably have acquired Russia under the former Minister-Traitors."[63]

Anti-monarchist and anti-German attitudes were interwoven in the cheap, mass-produced "anti-Rasputin" literature, in analogous theatrical productions, and in folklore:

... You led a campaign
    With Wilhelm one and all,
And the simple people cursed
    You scoundrels.
Eh, you princes, my princes
    You butlers!
True Holsteins
    You Germans![64]

The wide-spread belief in a conspiracy between the Tsar and Germany left a profound imprint on the mass historic consciousness: even decades later many tourists who visited the former imperial palaces tried to figure out exactly where the telephones were located that the Tsar and Tsarina used to "give away secrets" to the Germans.

The question of the presence of xenophobia in the ideology of the Russian liberation movement is one that needs special study. In 1917, however, such attitudes had an even more immediate source: chauvinistic and militaristic agitation during World War I influenced many interpretations of February. In the "patriotic" literature of the war period victory over the "internal German" was seen as a precondition for victory over the "external German." This is precisely the terminology that we encounter in many of the resolutions after February.

The logical construction "Germans are our enemies, our enemies are German" influenced the political struggle after the February Revolution. Political opponents were accused of Germanophilism and treason. Initially, such accusations were aimed at left socialists and later even at moderate ones. Many soldiers, however, accused the Supreme Commander of treason: they were convinced that L.G. Kornilov, who had escaped captivity, had actually been allowed to escape.

Before February many authorities had pointed out that unrestrained anti-German propaganda represented a danger for state security. After the revolution anti-Germany propaganda was supported in all kinds of ways by the army command. A "Letter to the Motherland," printed and distributed by a sailor, said: "Germans living in Russia and the old government committed a great treason.... But one should not forget that even now in our country there is a German for whom Russian freedom is nauseating."[65]

It was precisely this interpretation of the Revolution (as a patriotic revolution in the name of victory, as an anti-German revolution) that was advanced by the propaganda of the allies in Russia.

It should be pointed out that Russian soldiers, and in a number of cases Russian workers, were sometimes the initiators and conduits of the radicalization of revolutionary movements in the non-Russian outlying areas at the same time that local social activists were assuming more moderate positions.[66] This, it would seem, also left an impression on perceptions of the Revolution as a Russian revolution.

3. Anti-bourgeois Revolution

Neither the "religious revolution" nor the "patriotic revolution" was a fundamental current of the Revolution. Socialist parties of various persuasions played a most active role in this process; they were the ones who exerted the greatest influence on the formation of the language of the Revolution and on the origin of its symbols. In this respect the "bourgeois" February Revolution was from the beginning also an anti-bourgeois revolution. One might think that the internationalist ideology of socialists would oppose the "Russian idea." The red flag literally became the state flag, and even the liberal press viewed attempts to demonstrate under the national banner as "monarchist demonstrations." N.A. Berdiaev reproached socialists for their lack of patriotism:

> International social democracy is completely German in spirit. It is, in fact, one of the German influences that is preventing the Russian people from comprehending that there is a great world-wide historic struggle taking place between the Slavic and the Germanic peoples, between two hostile forces of history, that the Slavic race will either emerge from this struggle victorious, will repel the pretensions of Germanism and fulfill its mission in history, or it will be degraded and pushed aside.

Nevertheless, we do encounter traces of the "Russian idea" in studying the socialist subculture of 1917. Even N.A. Berdiaev himself pointed out in 1917 the connection between socialism and the Russian political tradition: "Russian revolutionary socialism is a completely reactionary phenomenon; it is merely the legacy of the processes that have been breaking down old Russia."[67]

Even many moderate socialists considered Russia to be the center of international revolution. I.G. Tsereteli declared in one of his speeches, "... with the joint efforts of all the living forces of the country we will carry our Revolution through to the end and, perhaps, spread it to the rest of the world."[68]

The revolutionary masses, assimilating the propaganda of the socialists, began to see themselves as the "vanguard" of the international workers' movement — this is precisely how the soldiers of the reserve battalions in the Russian Guard called themselves. "The most democratic in all the world," is how many resolutions described their country. "Oppressed peoples of all countries," they constantly summoned, "should follow the example" of Russia, or the Russian people: "German people, follow our example in the struggle with your government."[69]

Revolutionary messianism was manifest in the creation of symbols for the new Russia: on many of the banners and emblems of that time one encounters representations of the earth, where the planet was sometimes adorned with the figure of a Russian worker carrying a red flag. Representations of the globe also appeared in the drafts of a new state coat of arms for Russia.[70] This also had an influence on the formation of coats of arms during the Soviet period.

In characterizing these kinds of attitudes many publicists began to speak of "inside-out Slavophilism." The well-known sociologist P. Sorokin wrote:

> When you see how the ignorant proletariat — up to 80% of whose members are illiterate and whose remaining part is just barely able to read and write Russian — being under the hypnosis of revolutionary phraseology, seriously begins to think that he is indeed the "vanguard," the most enlightened and best detachment of the International — when you see all this, it involuntarily reminds one of the Slavophiles and Dostoevskii's "Russian schoolboy."[71]

It is also possible to discuss the mutual influence of the religious and the anti-bourgeois currents of the Revolution. This shows up, in particular, in the creation of various models of Christian socialism and in analogous combinations of parties and religious organizations. Thus, the Union of New Christian-Socialists, while characterizing the overthrown order as "completely anti-Christian," considered it their task to establish the kingdom of God on earth. Various attempts were made to create Christian-socialist and "Church-socialist" parties. A number of contemporaries even criticized V.N. L'vov for "dressing" the Orthodox Church "in the clothes of Christian socialism."[72]

On the other hand, the movement for religious renovation also developed under the influence of the "fashion for socialism." A union of democratic clergy and laymen expressed their support for the struggle with capitalism, and a pre-assembly meeting of the Russian Orthodox Church came out in favor of abolishing capitalism.[73]

The socialist and anti-bourgeois mass consciousness was also connected to religious tradition. In a paper entitled "The Revolution and the Russian National Self-Consciousness," read before the Solov'ev Moscow Religious-Philosophical Society on 18 October 1917, A.M. Ladyzhenskii wrote:

> As yet nothing is at all certain. Are the masses animated only by personal egoism, does our Revolution lack ideals, are the refusals of regiments to go on the attack provoked only by a desire to escape danger. No, in the masses, along with purely self-interested motives, at the present moment there is a deep faith that they are creating an extraordinarily just system, that within a few years and maybe even a few months the kingdom of God on earth will emerge. There are people who relate to Bolshevism with a purely religious faith. [It is not by chance that soldiers force priests to add before the final words of their prayers to the Lord for world peace the phrase "without annexations or indemnities."][74]

In his work "The Religious Foundations of Bolshevism," N.A. Berdiaev expresses a similar idea: "Bolshevism is socialism reduced to religious tension."[75]

Various models of Russian "national socialism" appeared under the "fashion for socialism." The Union of Evolutionary Socialism presented a liberal version with its motto which stated "Through a people's Great Russia — to socialism." At the same time the trashy right, chauvinistic Malen'kaia gazeta (to which even V.P. Sventsitskii contributed) called itself "the paper of non-party socialists."[76]

It should be pointed out that both xenophobic ideas and extreme forms of anti-bourgeois ideology shaped a similar mentality at the center of which one finds the idea of a powerful conspiracy of "dark forces": in one case a conspiracy of the "internal enemy," in the other, a conspiracy of the bourgeoisie. P.B. Struve wrote about this phenomenon even before the Revolution:

> The essence of both white and red Black Hundredism (*Chernosotenstvo*) consists of an educated (cultured) minority of the people being contrasted to the people as an evil force, a force that was, is, and should be culturally alien to it. Just as Marxism is the study of the class struggle in societies, Black Hundredism of both colors is its own kind of study of cultural struggle.[77]

Of course, anti-bourgeois, "anti-*burzhui*" attitudes were sometimes shaped not only by class conflicts, but also by socio-cultural ones: people with anti-Western, anti-urbanist attitudes used the term "bourgeois" as a derogatory label for any opponent.[78]

But even the propaganda of left socialists at times contained elements of xenophobia. Thus, anti-bourgeois and anti-imperialist agitation was directed to a large degree against French and, especially, British capitalists, who oppressed the Russian people, used them for their own purposes, etc. Such propaganda overlapped with German military agitation printed in Russian in which anglophobic motifs predominated.

It appears that the elements of the "Russian idea" that I singled out at the beginning were characteristic of various political tendencies in 1917. They are found in a wide variety of sources. These components were present in both program and propaganda materials and in the mass consciousness. Parts of them were used subsequently by official Soviet ideology at various stages of its development.

But how broadly disseminated were the diverse versions of the "Russian idea?" During which stages of the Revolution did they enjoy popularity? To what degree were they "programmatic" components of ideology, and to what degree were they merely tactical devices? These problems demand special investigation.

In so doing it would be worth examining the question of the correlation between ideology and traditional political culture and between the mass consciousness and the political mentality. For example, in a number of cases a democratic ideology was superimposed on an authoritarian mentality; fashionable political slogans interacted with deep religious and communal traditions. One might conjecture that the political tradition often deformed and adapted the external ideological systems that were hostile to it. In this respect it is instructive that within a few weeks of the radical anti-monarchist revolution there arose in Russia — without the influence of any kind of external coercive power — a cult of the omnipotent leader-savior, the cult of A.F. Kerenskii. This cult then influenced Bolshevik and Soviet political culture.

Translated from Russian by Gregory D. Crowe

Notes

1 "In our view, the real 'Russian idea' is the entire aggregate of Russian history, culture, and philosophy, and just a little bit more. This 'little bit' is a certain irrational subjective-objective 'I,' which gives a qualitative definitiveness to our self-perception through our national character," V.A. Bobakho, S.I. Levikova, and L.T. Retiunskikh, "'Russkaia ideia' v igre (O nekotorykh mekhanizmakh

formirovaniia natsional'nogo samosoznaniia)," *Vestnik Moskovskogo universiteta*, Series 12: *Sotsial'no-politicheskie issledovaniia*, No. 6 (1993), p. 44.

2   Richard Pipes, *The Russian Revolution* (New York: Knopf, 1990), pp. 275, 281.

3   Cited in V.P. Ivanov, *Tserkov' i revoliutsiia* (Tomsk, 1919), p. 3.

4   N. Berdiaev, "Dukhi russkoi revoliutsii," S.A. Askol'dov et al. (ed.), *Iz glubiny: sbornik statei o russkoi revoliutsii* (Moscow: Novosti, 1991), p. 55.

5   A. Ianov, "Russkaia ideia i 2000-i god," *Neva*, No. 9 (1990), pp. 143, 154.

6   On the significance of this approach see: P.V. Volobuev, "Istoricheskie korni Oktiabr'skoi revoliutsii," *Anatomiia revoliutsii: massy, partii, vlast'* (St. Petersburg, 1994), pp. 38-39. Following Kharuki Vada, the author suggests that we look at the Russian Revolution as "a complex of revolutions during an era of world wars."

7   N.Ia. Abramovich, Podpol'e russkogo intelligentstva (Moscow, 1917), p. 4; N.N. Pchelin, Staryi i novyi poriadok (Moscow, 1917), p. 7; S.L. Frank, "O blagorodstve i nizosti v politike," *Russkaia svoboda*, No. 3 (1917), p. 28.

8   E. Trubetskoi, "O khristianskom otnoshenii k sovremennym sobytiiam," *Russkaia svoboda*, No. 5 (1917), pp. 3-4.

9   Concerning a number of aspects of this crisis see: G. Freeze, "Tserkov', religiia i politicheskaia kul'tura na zakate starogo rezhima," V.S. Diakin et al. (ed.), *Reformy ili revoliutsiia? Rossiia, 1861-1917: materialy mezhdunarodnogo kollokviuma istorikov* (St.Petersburg:. Nauka, 1992), pp. 31-43. Religious, political, and social contradictions were also interconnected during the 1905 Russian Revolution. On this see: P.N. Zyrianov, *Pravoslavnaia tserkov' v bor'be s revoliutsiei 1905-07 gg.* (Moscow: Nauka, 1984).

10 Evlogii, Metropolitan of Western Europe, *Put' moei zhizni: vospominaniia mitropolita Evlogiia* (Paris: YMCA, 1947), p. 285.

11 V.S. Voitinskii, *1917-i: god pobed i porazhenii* (Benson, VT: Chalidze Publications, 1990), p. 21.

12 G.L. Sobolev, *Revoliutsionnoe soznanie rabochikh i soldat Petrograda v 1917 godu (Period dvoevlastiia)* (Leningrad, 1972), pp. 188-189; E.S. Osipova, Abstract to "Politika pravoslavnoi tserkvi v period podgotovki Oktiabr'skoi revoliutsii (mart-oktiabr' 1917 g.)" (Dissertation for the degree of Kandidat of Historical Sciences, Moscow, 1968), p. 10.

13 Evlogii, *Put' moei zhizni*, p. 284. Manuscripts' Division, Rossiiskaia natsional'naia biblioteka (hereafter, OR RNB), f. 481, op. 1, d. 174, l. 20(ob). On the thanksgiving services see also: Sobolev, *Revoliutsionnoe soznanie*, p. 41.

14 OR RNB, f. 481, op. 1, d. 174, l. 15: letter from T.N. Gippius to D.V. Filosofov dated 17 March 1917.

15 N. Zernov, *Russkoe religioznoe vozrozhdenie XX veka* (Paris, 1974), p. 208; N.P. Vevziuk, Abstract to "Ukrainskaia avtokefal'naia pravoslavnaia tserkov' v gody grazhdanskoi voiny" (Dissertation for the degree of Kandidat of Historical Sciences, Odessa, 1989), pp. 13-14; *1917 god na Kievshchine*, p. 354;.Evlogii, *Put' moei zhizni*, p. 308.

16 Tsentral'nyi gosudarstvennyi arkhiv Sankt-Peterburga (formerly TsGAOR Leningrada), f. 7384, op. 9, d. 148, l. 1; Sobolev, *Revoliutsionnoe soznanie*, pp. 193-194.

17 P.N. Vrangel', *Vospominaniia generala barona P.N. Vrangelia* (Frankfurt: Izd. Posev, 1969), pp. 44-45; *Vechernee vremia* (Petrograd), 5 August 1917; E.S. Osipova, "Politika pravoslavnoi tserkvi," pp. 16-17.

18 *Kievlianin*, 16 April 1917.

19 Rossiiskii gosudarstvennyi istoricheskii arkhiv (hereafter RGIA; formerly TsGIA SSSR), f. 833, op. 1, d. 33, l. 29.

20 OR RNB, f. 601, op. 1, d. 1606, l. 112, 115.

21 O.V. Ostanina, Abstract to "Obnovlenchestvo i reformatorstvo v Russkoi pravoslavnoi tserkvi v nachale XX veka" (Dissertation for the degree of Kandidat of Philosophical Sciences, Leningrad, 1991); Jutta, Scherrer, *Die Petersburger Religiös-Philosophischen Vereinigungen: die Entwicklung des religiösen Selbstverständnisses ihrer Intelligencija-Mitglieder (1901-1917)* (Wiesbaden: Harrassowitz, 1973), pp. 159-184.

22 OR RNB, f. 601, op. 1, d. 1635.

23 A. Ostaev, "Demokratiia sataninskaia...," *Moskovskie novosti*, 15 November 1992. See also Ivanov, *Tserkov' i revoliutsiia*.

24 Sobolev, *Revoliutsionnoe soznanie*, pp. 40-41.

25 F.F. Iusupov, *Pered izgnaniem, 1887-1919* (Moscow: AO Moskovskii tsentr iskusstv, 1993), p. 187; Evlogii, *Put' moei zhizni*, p. 285. In the reports of the military censor it is pointed out: "Almost all the peasants' letters expressed the desire to see the tsar at the head of Russia. It is obvious that monarchy is the only form of rule capable of being understood by peasants." Here is another example: "We want a democratic republic and a tsar-father in three years," OR RNB, f. 152, op. 3, d. 98, l. 34. One soldier's letter, cited in a review by the military censor, stated: "It would be great if they would give us a republic with a sensible tsar," Rossiiskii gosudarstvennyi voenno-istoricheskii arkhiv (hereafter RGVIA; formerly TsGVIA SSSR), f. 2003, op. 1, d. 1494, l. 14. It would seem that many peasants saw the terms "kingdom" [*tsarstvo*] and "state" [*gosudarstvo*] as synonyms, just as many people today believe that the words "state" and "country" are synonyms.

26 On this score S.L. Frank wrote:

Of all the achievements of Western European culture Russia from time immemorial embraced only one: strong state power, which originally grew in her not from a process of secularization and not in a struggle with theocracy, but rather from the very depths of orthodox faith: the "Tsar-Father," the anointed sovereign of God, was in the people's consciousness the only bearer and the supreme instance of the empirical-social realization of religions truth, the only link that united religious faith with historic construction.... From the moment when the monarchy, that unique support in the people's consciousness for the entire state-judicial and cultural structure of life, collapsed – and it crashed down on the people's religious faith in the "Tsar-Father" with the force of a wreck – all the principles of state and social life in Russia must have collapsed, because they lacked an independent foundation, they were not implanted in spiritual soil.

S.L. Frank, "Religiozno-istoricheskii smysl russkoi revoliutsii," M.A. Maslin (ed.), *Russkaia ideia* (Moscow: Respublika, 1992), pp. 336-337.

27 Z.N. Gippius, "Peterburgskie dnevniki, 1914-1919," in her *Zhivye litsa: stikhi, dnevniki* (Tbilisi: Merani, 1991), p. 302.

28 *Russkoe slovo*, 28 March 1917; Osipova, "Politika pravoslavnoi tserkvi," pp. 16-17, 19.

29 The writer L. Andreev's diary gives examples of the cult of revolution, formerly an integral part of the subculture of the radical intelligentsia. He even writes about the "religion of revolution," and the "holiness of revolution." See "Iz dnevnika Leonida Andreeva," Istochnik 9, No. 2 (1994), p. 42.

30 Iu.L. [Iurii Lisovskii], "Khristos voskres!," *Voennaia gazeta: dlia russkikh voisk vo Frantsii*, No. 21 (1917).

31 E. Verestin, "Russkaia revoliutsiia," *Na chuzhbine: sbornik proizvedenii russkikh voinov* (Paris, n.d.), p. 149.

32 N. Taryshev, "Ia veriu," *Na chuzhbine*, p. 161.

33 B. Kamenskii, "Khristos Voskrese!," *Izvestiia Soveta deputatov armii, flota i rabochikh Abo-Olandskoi ukreplennoi pozitsii*, 2 April 1917.

34 Tsentral'nyi gosudarstvennyi arkhiv Rossiiskoi federatsii (hereafter TsGARF), f. 6978, op. 1, d. 244, l. 27.

35 Letter of T.N. Gippius to D.V. Filosofov dated 26 March 1917, OR RNB, f. 481, op. 1, d. 174, l. 18; K.M. Oberuchev, *V dni revoliutsii: vospominaniia uchastnika velikoi russkoi revoliutsii 1917-go goda* (New York: Izd. "Narodopravstva," 1919), p. 49; P.A. Sorokin, *Chelovek, tsivilizatsiia, obshchestvo* (Moscow: Izd. politicheskoi literatury, 1992), p. 228; G.A. Kniazev, "Iz zapisnoi knizhki russkogo intelligenta vo vremia voiny i revoliutsii 1915-1922 g.," *Russkoe*

proshloe, No. 2 (1991), p. 114; O. Mirtov, "Khristos Voskrese," *Russkaia volia,* 10 March 1917; S. Pushkin, "Paskhal'nyi zvon," *Soldat-grazhdanin* (Moscow), 1 April 1917; *Lukomor'e,* Nos. 9-10 (1917) (This entire issue is devoted to this theme). On the atmosphere of "general brotherhood" and of a "public holiday" during the February Revolution see: V.M. Zenzinov, "Fevral'skie dni," D.S. Anin (ed.), *Revoliutsiia 1917 goda, glazami ee rukovoditelei* (Rome: Edizioni Aurora, 1971), pp. 151-157.

36 Cited in O.N. Znamenskii, *Intelligentsiia nakanune Velikogo Oktiabria: fevral'-oktiabr' 1917 g.* (Leningrad: Nauka, 1988), p. 117. V.S. Ianovskii writes on the influence of Easter traditions on perceptions of important political events: "On Sunday, 22 June 1941 after the liturgy, our dear compatriots in Marseilles as well as Nice kissed, greeting each other with an Easter spirit," V.S. Ianovskii, *Polia Eliseiskie: kniga pamiati* (St. Petersburg, 1993), p. 32.

37 D.S. Merezhkovskii, "Angel revoliutsii," *Russkoe slovo,* 1 April 1917; V. Sventsitskii, "Krest i pulemet," *Malen'kaia gazeta,* 7 March 1917.

38 Evlogii, *Put' moei zhizni,* p. 285.

39 *Ibid.,* p. 285.

40 TsGARF, f. 1778, op. 1, d. 80, l. 15.

41 *Malen'kaia gazeta,* p. 8 March 1917; TsGARF, f. 1778, op. 1, d. 80, l. 50.

42 N. Berdiaev, "Kontrrevoliutsiia," *Russkaia svoboda,* Nos. 10-11 (1917), p. 6.

43 P.K. Kornakov, "Znamena Fevral'skoi revoliutsii," G.V. Vilinbakhov (ed.), *Geral'dika, materialy i issledovaniia: sbornik nauchnykh trudov* (Leningrad: Gos. Ermitazh, 1983), p. 22.

44 N.A. Berdiaev, "Pravda i lozh' v obshchestvennoi zhizni," *Narodopravstvo,* No. 4 (1917), p. 7.

45 B. Kolonitski, "Revolutionary Names," *Revolutionary Russia* 6, No. 2 (1993), pp. 222-223.

46 Chuzh-Chuzhenin, *Pesennik revoliutsionnogo soldata,* first collection (1917), p. 8.

47 E. Trubetskoi, "Narodno-russkaia revoliutsiia," *Rech',* 4 March 1917.

48 S.L. Frank, "Demokratiia na rasput'e," *Russkaia svoboda,* No. 1 (1917), p. 13; idem, *Mertvye molchat* (Moscow, 1917), p. 9; idem, *Biografiia P.B. Struve* (New York: Izd. im. Chekova, 1956), p. 108.

49 Evlogii, *Put' moei zhizni,* p. 290.

50 Cited in Znamenskii, *Intelligentsiia,* pp. 114-115.

51 T.I. Polner, *Zhiznennyi put' kniazia Georgiia Evgen'evicha L'vova: lichnost', vzgliady, usloviia deiatel'nosti* (Paris, 1932), pp. 231-232, 244.

52 Cited in I.G. Tsereteli, "Vospominaniia o Fevral'skoi revoliutsii," *Ot pervogo litsa,* compiled by I.A. Anfertev (Moscow: Patriot, 1992), p. 96.

53 N. Ustrialov, Revoliutsiia i voina (Moscow, 1917), p. 21; N. Berdiaev, "Vlast' i otvetstvennost'," *Russkaia svoboda*, No. 6 (1917), p. 4.

54 M.Ia. Fenomenov, *Russkii patriotizm i bratstvo narodov* (Moscow, 1917), pp. 5, 24.

55 N. Berdiaev, "Psikhologiia perezhivaemogo momenta," *Russkaia svoboda*, No. 1 (1917), p. 6; idem, *Narod i klassy v russkoi revoliutsii* (Moscow, 1917), p. 12; idem, *Vozmozhna li sotsial'naia revoliutsiia* (Moscow, 1917), p. 2.

56 Tsentral'nyi gosudarstvennyi arkhiv voenno-morskogo flota (hereafter TsGA VMF), f. R-95, op. 1, d. 103, l.114.

57 D. Semenov, "Pala staraia vlast!..," *Soldat-grazhdanin* (Moscow), 24 March 1917.

58 B. Rozov, "K russkim soldatam," *Voennaia gazeta: dlia russkikh voisk vo Frantsii*, No. 27 (1917), p. 5.

59 Iusupov, *Pered izgnaniem*, p. 188.

60 D.V. Filosofov, "Dnevnik," *Zvezda*, No. 2 (1982), p. 190. V.F. Nuvel' was a member of the association "World of Art;" Ikskul' von Gildenbrandt was a Baron and Secretary of State (1904-09); RGIA, f. 1470, op. 2, d. 89, l. 63.

61 N. Fioletov, *Tserkov' v obnovlennoi Rossii* (Moscow, 1917), p. 1.

62 TsGARF, f. 1778, op. 1, d. 80, l. 55.

63 RGVIA, f. 2003, op. 1, d. 1496, l. 18, l. 39(ob).

64 Chuzh-Chuzhenin, *Pesennik revoliutsionnogo soldata*, p. 16. See also the *chastushka* written in Petrograd province: I buy for my Sashukha dear / Gold rings to put upon her ears / For the Russians she has sold / And cheaply I am told, Menshevik Ivan, *Narodnye revoliutsionnye chastushki* (Petrograd, 1917), p. 9. "Sashukha" refers to Empress Aleksandra Fedorovna.

65 TsGA VMF, f. R-95, op. 1, d. 64, l. 1.

66 On this see: Andreas Kapeller, *Russland als Vielvölkerreich: Entstehung, Geschichte, Zerfall* (Munich: Beck, 1992), p. 288.

67 N. Berdiaev, "Patriotizm i politika," *Narodopravstvo*, No. 10 (1917), p. 3.

68 Tsereteli, "Vospominaniia o Fevral'skoi revoliutsii," p. 109.

69 Sobolev, *Revoliutsionnoe soznanie*, p. 180; TsGA VMF, f. R-95, op. 1, d. 14, l. 83.

70 Kornakov, "Znamena Fevral'skoi revoliutsii," pp. 12-26; idem, "Opyt privlecheniia veksilologicheskikh pamiatnikov dlia resheniia geral'dicheskikh problem," *Novye numizmaticheskie issledovaniia*, No. 4, Trudy Gosudarstvennogo Istoricheskogo muzeia, 1986, vyp. 61:134-48; idem, "Simvolika i ritualy revoliutsii 1917 g.," *Anatomiia revoliutsii, 1917 god v Rossii: massy, partii, vlast'* (St. Petersburg, 1994), pp. 356-365.

71 P. Sorokin, "Slavianofil'stvo na iznanku," *Volia naroda*, 12

September 1917; see also *Rech'*, 18 April 1917; and *Delo naroda,* 20 April 1917.

72 *Soiuz novykh khristian-sotsialistov* (Kiev, 1917), 6-7; A. Levitin and V. Shavrov, *Ocherki po istorii russkoi tserkovnoi smuty* (K«nacht: Institut glaube in der 2 Welt, 1978), 1:32; Kh.M. Astrakhan, *Bol'sheviki i ikh politicheskie protivniki v 1917 godu* (Leningrad: Lenizdat, 1973), p. 356; A letter from T.N. Gippius and Z.N. Gippius to D.S. Merezhkovskii and D.V. Filosofov dated 30 June 1917, OR RNB, f. 481, op. 1, d. 217, l. 18(ob). See also: *Katekhizis khristianina ili sotsialista* (Ekaterinslav, 1917), 15 pp.; A.A. Mudrov, *Khristos-sotsialist, ili khristianstvo i sotsializm* (Ekaterinslav, 1917), 15 pp.; *Evangelie khristianskogo sotsializma* (Tver', 1917), 8 pp.

73 Matthew Spinka, *The Church and the Russian Revolution* (New York: The MacMillan Co., 1928), p. 69; Zernov, *Russkoe religioznoe vozrozhdenie,* p. 209.

74 Manuscripts' Division, Institut russkoi literatury (Pushkinskii dom), f. 185, op. 1, d. 1576, l. 4. The section enclosed in square brackets was crossed out in the manuscript version in the archives.

75 N. Berdiaev, "Religioznye osnovy bol'shevizma," Russkaia svoboda, Nos. 15-17 (1917), p. 3.

76 B.A. Gurevich, *Cherez narodnuiu Velikuiu Rossiiu k sotsializmu* (Petrograd, 1917); R.Sh. Ganelin et al. eds., *Natsional'naia pravaia prezhde i teper': Istoriko-sotsiologicheskie ocherki,* Part I: *Rossiia i russkoe zarubezh'e* (St. Petersburg: Institut sotsiologii RAN, 1992), pp. 111-124. See also *Partiia russkikh natsional'nykh sotsialistov: Osnovy partii* (Moscow, 1917), 1 p.

77 P.B. Struve, *Patriotica — politika, kul'tura, religiia, sotsializm: sbornik statei za piat' let 1905-1910 gg.* (St. Petersburg: Izd. D.E. Zhukovskago, 1911), p. 16. Cf. "The completely concrete-historical fury and destructiveness of the Russian Revolution was born not only from an economic-class alienation, but also from a profound spiritual-cultural gap between the Russian national masses and the educated estates of Russian society, who tried to implant the European culture in Russia and who themselves became partially saturated with it," S.L. Frank, "Religiozno-istoricheskii smysl," p. 337.

78 B.I. Kolonitskii, "Antiburzhuaznaia propaganda i 'antiburzhuiskoe' soznanie," *Otechestvennaia istoriia,* No. 1 (1994), p. 17-27.

Chapter 4

The Habsburg and Russian Empires: Some Comparisons and Contrasts

Orest SUBTELNY

1. Empires: Some Introductory Generalizations

For much of recorded history, most people have lived in empires. Until the twentieth century, empire was the most prevalent and effective way of uniting a variety of peoples and extensive territories under single rule. It was — until the very recent emergence of regional blocs and global organizations — the only way of establishing and maintaining political order in the face of cultural, ethnic, social hereogeneity. This unity was usually imposed by force. We can, therefore, view empire as the rule or control, direct or indirect, political or economic, of one state, nation or people over similar groups.[1]

A reflection of the unifying and stabilizing role that empires usually played is the fact that they were invariably associated with the concept of peace, law and order: we have, for example, Pax Romana, Pax Mongolica, Pax Ottomanica, Pax Russica (and, most recently, Pax Sovietica and Pax Americana). By the same token, life outside of empire or without empire often viewed, by those within empire, as anarchistic and barbaric, a primitive struggle of one against all. The merits of empire were captured in the oft-repeated Middle Eastern aphorism: one day of anarchy is worse than forty years of tyranny. Thus, whatever their disadvantages, empires, especially at their high point, offered stability and security. And this was prized by all peoples at all times.

The life span of empires usually had two distinct if frequently overlapping phases: an initial, relatively brief phase, characterized by military conquest and a subsequent, extended phase, where the main focus was on stability, law and order (system maintenance). In general, creating empires was easier than maintaining them. Military conquests, no matter how impressive, were efforts of short or sporadic duration. While they provided impetus to empire-building, they never guaranteed the durability of an empire. It was the second, maintenance phase that demanded long term, consistent, and multi-dimensional success. An empire's longevity was testimony to the consistent skill of its rulers in the difficult task of keeping a variety of peoples together.

For the survival of empires, it was necessary that an implicit quid-pro-quo relationship between ruler and subjects be established and maintained. In this relationship, what imperial rulers expected from their subjects was clear and explicit: they demanded obedience and taxes. But subjects also had their expectations of the rulers, even though these were rarely explicitly expressed: in return for obedience and taxes, they expected their rulers to provide them with security, law and order. Empires in which this trade-off functioned effectively and consistently could expect a lengthy existence. Those which failed to maintain this quid-pro-quo arrangement invariably had a short life span.

In order to rule effectively, that is, to maintain the above-mentioned trade-off, imperial rulers invariably applied integrative policies. Integration was the only way an empire could fulfill its function of uniting various peoples and vast territories. An emperor could not keep his side of bargain with subjects if he did not, sooner or later, to greater or lesser extent, attempt to draw political and economic components of the empire closer together; to impose standard laws, currency, obligations; to introduce a common language, culture and ideology. Integration, therefore, consisted of centralization and standardization.

Centralization was the attempt to control and to direct key aspects of politics, economics, and culture in the various, widely scattered parts of the empire from one center, more specifically, from the imperial capital and the imperial court. It was, invariably, a difficult task, involving conflicts between the imperial center, which sought to monopolize power, and the regional or local elites that did everything possible to keep some of it in their hands. To make their task of governing the heterogeneous societies easier, imperial governments, and especially their bureaucracies also attempted to obliterate local, regional cultural differences, that is, to standardize. Thus, these policies pitted imperial systems against deeply-ingrained and fiercely defended aspects of the subject societies. To overcome these particularistic tendencies over long periods of time required a high level of political skill.

In terms of structure, most empires rested on two key institutional pillars: the army and the bureaucracy. The function of the first was to extend borders of the empire when the opportunity arose or to assure internal order when necessary. Bureaucracy's main function was to secure funds for the support of the army. These two institutional pillars of empire were linked by a third, over-arching institution, that of the emperor and his court. Its function was to coordinate and direct the army and bureaucracy and to serve as the incarnation of empire. Such, in bare outline, were the basic features and functions of most empires.

From a global perspective, we may now move to a European one. The Europeans produced two distinct types of empires. One, which fit the universal pattern established by the empires of antiquity, might be called the classic type.[2] It served as the basis for the preceding discussion. And the territorial conglomerates accumulated by the Habsburgs and Romanovs in central and eastern Europe fall into this category. The other type included the more recent, commercial-capitalist overseas or colonial empires built by the British, French, Spanish and other west European powers.

Among the empires of the first or classical category, geopolitical motives seem to have played the primary role in motivating expansion; among those in the second or colonial category, it is generally accepted that economic considerations provided the key driving force for expansion. This is not to say, however, that the impetus for expansion was simple and clear-cut. In every case of expansion, in every type of empire, a variety of motivating factors were always involved. Nonetheless, the classical/geopolitical and the colonial/commercial dichotomy is useful for purposes of analysis because it aids us in focusing on general tendencies in one type of empire or another. As we will see later, it also helps to situate the Habsburg and Romanov realms in the context of other empires.

At this point, several comments of a historiographical nature are in order.[3] Although empires are as old as history, imperialism is a modern concept. The man commonly credited with introducing it is the Englishman, J. Hobson. In 1902, he wrote a book entitled *Imperialism,* which was a critical analysis of how and why the British became involved in the Boer War. In it Hobson concluded that this episode of British expansionism, as well as many others, was primarily motivated by the need of British capital to find higher returns on capital in the face of shrinking returns at home.

While Hobson's work initiated the study of imperialism, it also skewed it. It identified empire and imperialism, first and foremost, with a) colonial empires like those of Britain and other European industrialized countries b) with the forces of capitalism and c) with modern imperialism of the late 19 and 20th centuries, that is, with the age of capitalism. This approach was enthusiastically adopted and elaborated by Lenin, Hilferding, Luxemburg, Bukharin and, later, by legions of leftist scholars who established, ironically, established a near monopoly on the study of imperialism. Consequently, most work on the topic were often ideologically biased tracts which attempted to demonstrate, in more or less scholarly terms, the methods, phases and varieties of capitalist exploitation of the Third World. Rarely did these Marxist scholars focus their attention of imperial structure, organization, functioning and maintenance, that is, on the empires as such. Not unexpectedly, they concentrated on imperial failings while ignoring the imperial achievements. In short, the predominant Marxist-based approach to the study of imperialism was more about capitalism than about empires.

Works treating imperialism from a non-economic perspective appeared later and, until recently, were in the minority. A groundbreaking study in this regard was J. Schumpeter's, *Imperialism and Social Change* (1919). Seeking to explain how the great powers of Europe could have embarked on such a self-destructive conflict like World War I, he concluded that answer lay in the realm of the irrational. To prove his point, Schumpeter analyzed the emergence of the ancient empires of Egypt, Assyria, Persia and Rome. And he argued that their expansion was propelled by atavistic tendencies, specifically by the survival of deeply ingrained but no longer essential warrior traditions in the military elites of these societies. In each case, he claimed, imperialistic societies developed war-machines which at a certain point were no longer necessary for self-preservation. In order to justify their existence and in response to deeply ingrained psycho-social tendencies, these military elites then embarked on war. Thus, it was a case of conquest for the sake of conquest. Schumpeter implied that similar motivations were at work in modern imperialism as well. Moreover, he emphasized that capitalism not a driving force in imperialism; on the contrary, it actively discouraged imperialism.

In recent decades, a variety of other non-economic explanations for imperialism have appeared.[4] Most traditionalist is the view that imperialism could best be understood in terms of international (political) competition, that it is competition between states that has been simply extended to a global level. Others prefer to treat imperialism in terms of modernization. They argue that not only did modernization create great political, economic and military disparity among the people of the world, but it also brought them into greater proximity to each other. The result was an almost natural tendency of the more developed, responding to a power vacuum, to impose dominion over the less developed. German scholars have been especially attracted to social imperialism, that is, the creation of empires as a means to ease social tensions at home. Meanwhile, the Englishman, D. Fieldhouse introduced a useful corrective to the studies of imperialism by pointing out that imperial expansion originates not only in the imperial center but also on the periphery of empire.[5] For example, expansion frequently occurred due to the machinations and initiative of local imperial administrators working with local collaborators. Often acting without the acquiescence of the imperial center, they pushed into new territories when opportunities appeared and for reasons of self-aggrandizement. In other cases, a turbulent frontier, specifically, the need to impose order and maintain security upon it, led empires to expand further than they originally intended. Despite the considerable differences among them, these approaches concur in that profit was not the primary motive for empire-building. And that, essentially, the primary goals of empire have been to exert power and control.

2. The Habsburg and Romanov Empires: Some Common Features

As noted above, the Habsburg and Romanov empires form a distinct category among the European empires.[6] They are the only European empires that are of the classical type. We will, therefore, focus on the features that they shared and that distinguished them from the others European empires.

(1) Imperial heritage — both Austrian and Russian territorial conglomerates were originally peripheries of other

empires. In the case of Austria, it was the eastern frontier (Österreich) of the Carolinian and Holy Roman empires. Muscovy formed the western periphery of the Mongol empire. In addition, during the Kievan period and after, Moscow was exposed to the influence of the Byzantine empire. When the empires of which they were a part collapsed, both Habsburg and Muscovite rulers embarked on their own empire-building careers. Unlike England, France or Spain, they did not experience a period as relatively homogeneous, nationally-based kingdoms. The point is that both Austria and Muscovy emerged within empires and then sought to re-create similar conglomerates on their own. They knew no other political form of political organization except empire.

The heritage of empire was evident in the *Weltanschauung* of the two dynasties. They tried to trace their genealogies back to Rome, they laid claims to lands by arguing that they once belonged to empires to which they claimed to be the legitimate successors, they envisaged themselves as universal monarchies, and they steered clear of narrow, ethnic identification. Finally, they saw their mission in classical terms: to attain predominance over numerous peoples and vast territories and, in the process, to bring order and security to these lands.

(2) Continental location — both empires consisted of contiguous land masses, They did not extend their rule overseas like the English, French or Spanish. Because they tended to subjugate their immediate neighbors, cultural differences, or more accurately difference in levels of development were, generally, not as great among Habsburgs or Romanovs and their subjects as they were in the case of the colonial metropolises and their colonies. Indeed, some Moscow's subjects, for example, the Livonians, Ukrainians or Poles, were more highly developed than their rulers. And in the Habsburg case, it is difficult to say which were the more developed lands, Bohemia and Italy or the Austrian heartland.

Because some of the conquered peoples, or at least their
elites, possessed highly-developed administrative, military,
commercial or cultural skills, they were coopted by Habsburg
and Romanovs. Consequently, the ethnic intermixture in the
imperial centers was extensive. Vienna teemed with Italians,
Hungarians, and Poles. The readiness of Moscow to accept
Tatars in its service is well known. Later came Baltic
Germans, Ukrainians, and Poles. Under such conditions, the
idea of basing their empires on a single nationality had little
appeal to the Habsburgs and to the Romanovs. Like the classic
empires, they were cosmopolitan in their world view. This
stands in sharp contrast to the west European colonial
empires, each of which was based on the predominance of a
single nationality and in which it was impossible for colonial
subjects to attain positions of power at the imperial center.

(3) The turbulent frontier — For both Austria and Russia
securing their frontiers was a constant and pressing problem.
Indeed, the attempt to secure their frontiers was one of the
major reasons for their expansion. For centuries, the
Habsburgs had to confront the Ottoman threat. And as they
slowly pushed the Ottomans back, the Habsburgs acquired the
"liberated" lands of Hungary, Transylvania and Croatia. Only
because Vienna gained these east European lands by right of
conquest was it able to impose absolute rule upon them.

From the very outset, Moscow had to struggle for its very
survival with the nomads of the steppe. And initially its the
greatest expenses were the maintenance of defense systems
against incursions by the Tatars. It was the need to capture of
Tatar base of operation in the Crimea that finally brought
Russia to the shores of the Black Sea and involved it in an
extended conflict with the Ottoman empire. A similar threat
to the frontier led to Russian expansion into parts of Siberia,
Central Asia and the Caucasus where the Kirghiz and
Kalmuks nomads and Caucasian tribesmen posed a constant
threat. Thus, for both Austria and Russia, imperial expansion

was, to a large extent, a function of establishing secure borders.

The importance of frontier warfare for both empires is reflected in the fact that both empires there evolved social groups specializing in border defense. In Russia the well-known Cossacks fulfilled this function.[7] Meanwhile in the Habsburg lands, especially in the Adriatic region, this role was performed by the Grenzers. But defending the borders was not only the function of these irregular troops. Both Muscovite and Habsburg regular forces were used in border defense. In fact, the process of organizing border defense played a formative role in the creation of the Romanov and especially the Habsburg regular armies.

The turbulent frontier was a crucial and common experience for both the Habsburg and Russian empires. While their imperial heritage might have pushed both Habsburgs and Romanovs to think in terms of universal rule, instability on their frontier pulled them into expansion. It was, therefore, a case of push-pull effects at work in the building of empire. Finally, it was traditional empire building in the sense that involved the classic trade-off: in return for their obedience, the new subjects of the Habsburgs and Romanovs received security.

(4) Defenders of Christianity — By pushing back the Tatars and Ottomans, both empires also prevented Islam from establishing a foothold in eastern Europe and the Balkans. In fact, in both both cases the defense of Christianity was a major theme in their growth. The Habsburgs especially emphasized their role as the *antemurale* of Christianity and did their best to strengthen Catholicism in newly acquired lands. Moscow also stressed its role as defender of Orthodoxy. For example, it repeatedly used the argument that Orthodox Ukrainians should accept Moscow's sovereignty because the tsar was their best defense against the Catholic Poles and Muslim infidels. Consequently, churchmen in Ukraine soon became the most enthusiastic proponents of Russian overlordship in their land.

For centuries, Russia's attempts to expand its influence in the Balkans was associated with its claims that it was defending Orthodoxy in that region.

Religion and empire-building have often been closely related. But there was a crucial difference in the Austrian and Russian approach to religion when compared to that of the west European colonial empires. The latter functioned as propagators of Christianity, supporting missionaries who attempted to convert the colonial peoples. The two east European empire, however, were defenders of Christianity. Missionary activity was not an important feature of their expansion. And Russia, for the most part, showed considerable tolerance in the treatment of its Muslim subjects. Finally, both empires became bulwarks of Christianity in large parts of southeastern and eastern Europe. Indeed, Russian extended Christianity to the shores of the Pacific.

(5) Struggle with democracy and nationalism — While the two empires served as patrons of religious Europeanization of the eastern part of the continent, they had an ambivalent attitude about introducing political Europeanization into their domains. In this connection, it should be emphasized that none of the major ideas, values, institutions commonly associated with European political culture were developed in the east, in the realms of the Habsburgs and Romanovs. Their historical role, especially after the French Revolution, was to stifle or to impede the spread of western political concepts and ideologies eastward. But, of course, rejection of the West was not total. Techniques and technologies that were useful to two empires, in an instrumental sense, were eagerly accepted and implemented. Even absolutism as a concept was adopted (since it fitted in so well with ancient concepts of imperial rule).[8] For the most part, however, western conceptual innovations, especially those that were political-ideological in nature, were treated with suspicion if not outright enmity by the imperial governments. In this sense, both empires were similar to rest of the non-Western world in their confrontation

with Westernization: they were willing to accept western techniques but not western concepts. (esp. political) Thus, on the one hand, they helped to westernize the eastern part of the continent. But on the other hand, they contributed greatly to the creation of the crucial differences between its eastern and western parts.

Crucial in this regard was their struggle against the two western ideologies: democracy and nationalism. Throughout the 19th century and until their collapse, the two empires attempts to contain the social and political impact of these ideologies was the central feature of their history. Indeed, they were the first empires to confront — and to succumb — to movements awakened by these political-ideological forces. This is yet another way in which the two empires were similar to each other and different from other European states: for them democracy and nationalism were mortal threats while for the west European nation-states (if not their colonial empires) they were a sources of strength.

It took a revolution in 1848 to force Vienna to accept constitutionalism and universal civil rights. In Russia this occurred in, in part, in 1905. And as the power of the imperial centers weakened, the component parts of the empire, fueled by nationalism, began to pull apart. Decentralization, a process that contradicts the very nature of empire — was well underway in the Habsburg realms before World War I. In Russia there was only talk of a possible federalization of the empire. But the rapidity with which the Russian empire disintegrated in 1917 indicates that the forces of nationalism and decentralization would have swept through that empire as well. It was the fate of the Habsburg and Romanov empires to be the first to prove that, in the face of democratization and nationalism, empires were no longer viable. The world would have to find another way of bring about the peaceful coexistence of its variegated peoples.

(6) Initiators of modernization — in the eastern part of Europe there is a deeply-ingrained tradition of initiating and

introducing change and modernization from above. While there is a variety of reasons for this tendency, certainly both empires, by the very nature of their centralized decision-making process, did much to maintain it. The most recent proponent of rapid modernization in the region — the USSR — also introduced it from above. Interestingly enough, the Soviet Union's border coincided closely with those of both the Romanov and Habsburg empires.

3. The Habsburg and Romanov Empire: Some Differences

(1) The political/ideological context — For a large part of their collective career, the Habsburgs were imperial rulers more in theory than in practice. For almost five centuries they presided over the Holy Roman Empire which, as Voltaire quipped, was neither Holy, nor Roman, nor an empire. It was, rather, a loose federation of largely Germanic principalities which paid lip-service to the ideal of a Christian empire, regularly elected the Habsburgs to preside over it, but insisted on doing what suited their interests. The basic political values and institutions which prevailed in the Holy Roman Empire were those of feudalism. And it was in confrontation with these principles that the Habsburgs attempted to establish a centralized controlled universal state. Even though the Habsburgs frequently came into conflict with these feudal ways, they were intimately familiar with them and willing to coexist with them. Thus the context from which the Habsburgs emerged was Germanic /Catholic/ feudal.

Only in the 18th century, when the 1000-year old Holy Roman Empire was on last legs, did the Habsburgs focus attention on east Europe and proceed to develop there the classic forms of an centralized, integrated, uniform imperial state. But even then, their aspirations were repeatedly challenged, most notably by the Hungarians. Thus, Habsburg imperial rule, despite its illustrious pedigree, was never completely accepted by its subjects and frequently found itself on the defensive.

The Russian empire emerged from a Slavic /Orthodox/ Byzantine/Mongol environment.[9] It was, obviously, much further removed from European institutions and values than the domains of the Habsburgs. But although its imperial heritage was not as illustrious as that of Austria (Moscow's ruler tried to claim that their genealogy reached back to Rome but Vienna scoffed at this), its imperial rule was much more extensive and real. Moscow did not have to deal with the limitations which political feudalism imposed on the Habsburgs. The patrimonial principles which it espoused — and which its subjects generally accepted — fitted in well with an emperors traditional claims to absolute power. Moreover, from the outset the Orthodox Church supported Moscow's imperial claims. Its creation of the so-called Third Rome theory is only one example. For contrast, one need only recall the long and decisive conflict between the popes of Rome and the Holy Roman emperors which unsettled central Europe. True, later the Catholic church did support the Habsburgs, and visa-versa. But this was only after an emperor's claim to supreme authority was shattered in Europe in general, and in particular in the lands where the Habsburgs emerged. In short, the theoretical basis for Habsburgs claims to predominance were weaker than those of the Russian rulers.

(2) The physical and social environment — There were vast differences as to the types of areas into which the two empires expanded. The Habsburgs operated in a relatively developed setting. Many of their lands were in the heart of Europe and even those in eastern Europe were not a "different world." Their subjects were almost all Christians. When compared to the Russian empire, Habsburg territories were not vast because the Habsburgs were always surrounded by powerful neighbors.

Russia, in contrast, had almost unlimited room for expansion, especially in the East and southeast where a power vacuum existed. Covering 1/6 of the world's land mass, it encompassed a tremendous variety of peoples and cultures. It encompassed peoples who had barely emerged from Stone Age cultures and the highly sophisticated Baltic Germans or Polish aristocrats. What is striking about the Russian empire is that it included many peoples who were culturally more advanced than the Russians while in the Habsburg lands, German-speaking people were considered to be the most culturally advanced. In geopolitical terms, Russia had a much more advantageous position than the Habsburg empire. When it met resistance to expansion in the west, it could always focus its attention on aggrandizements in the East and visa-versa. Unlike the Habsburg domains, the Russian empire was both a European and an Asian power (and, briefly, an American one as well).

(3) Methods of expansion — As is well known, the Habsburg acquired many of their lands not by conquest but by judicious marriages ("Let others go to war, you, fortunate Austria, marry") or political arrangements. Only in Hungary and the Balkans was war a means of gaining territory. Because the Habsburgs often could not apply the law of conquest but had to respect the rights and privileges of the lands they acquired by negotiation, they often encountered major obstacles in their attempts to exert complete control. In the Russian case, conquest was the primary means of expansion. And in cases where Russia negotiated the acquisition of new lands such as in Ukraine, Livonia, Georgia sooner or later it felt that it could ignore the commitments it made to respect local "rights and privileges." Therefore, the tsars had fewer problems in claiming unlimited authority.

(4) Rationales for expansion — The Habsburgs generally used four types of arguments to justify their claims for territory and authority, especially in eastern Europe. One was based on legality, that is, they claimed that lands belonged to them as part of a matrimonial agreement. The second type of

argument was a moral one and it emphasized their role as defenders of Christianity against the Ottoman onslaught (Hungary) or of Catholicism against Protestantism (Bohemia). Political pragmatism characterized the third type of argument, namely that lands freed from Turks were Vienna's by right of conquest (Hungary). And the fourth type of argument rested on Habsburg promises to provide more effective and just government than that which previously existed in a given land (Poland).

Initially, the tsars also utilized the inheritance argument, although it rested on flimsier, less legally-binding grounds than that of the Habsburgs. Moscow claimed that by "gathering the Rus lands" it was reclaiming its patrimony. However, the rulers of Lithuania could and did challenge this right to the Kievan inheritance. By the same token, in the East, Moscow's rulers, referred to themselves in terms of Chingisid titulature − white tsars − and claimed their right to "gather" the Chingisid inheritance. But here too they could be challenged by the various khans of nomadic hordes who were the direct descendents of Chinghis Khan.[10]

Much more characteristic of Russian claims to hegemony were arguments of a messianic nature. Even inheritance claims had strong element of mission, of moral duty to restore what had existed before. However, the intermingling of hegemonic tendencies and moral obligation was most striking in the so-called "Third Rome theory" which emerged in 1400s and argued that Muscovy, as the bastion of Orthodox holiness, was the true and final successor to the Roman and Byzantine empires. The defense of Orthodoxy was also used to legitimize Mocow's expansion into Ukraine and Balkans in the 17th and 18th centuries. In the 19th century, the mixture of hegemony and messianism took on racial overtones when Russia emerged as defender of Slavs and proclaimed its mission to unite them all under its leadership. It has often been argued that Moscow's attempt to defend the interests of the proletariat around the globe was, at least in part, a reflection of this combination of messianic and hegemonic tendencies.

Indeed, Russia's insistence on acting as the exclusive peacekeeper in the CIS today might be seen as a reflection of these well-established traditions. To summarize: Habsburg arguments for hegemony were more rationalistic while Russia's tended to be more messianistic.

(5) System maintenance — Given the legal, traditional and practical limits on their authority, the Habsburgs were often forced to compromise with their subjects. The most famous case is the agreement reached with the Hungarians in 1867 which created Austria-Hungary. Less well-known but equally characteristic was the agreement which gave the Poles control of Galicia in return for their support of Vienna. And just before World War I, another compromise between Vienna and the Czechs was in the making. This willingness (or necessity) to compromise meant that Habsburg rule was generally regarded as not being overly oppressive. For example, in the emotion-laded field of cultural policy, Germanization, a typical imperial policy, was pursued for the practical purpose of easing communication between the empire's various peoples and the imperial government. The Habsburgs had little hope or desire to turn their subjects into Germans (or Austrians).

Although there existed a clear-cut gradation among the approximately dozen nationalities of the Habsburg empire in terms of influence, privileges and prestige, no one nation predominated, especially after 1867. In fact, the Habsburg demonstrated considerable ability in accommodating the demands of their ever-restive peoples. In the process, they were gradually transforming their empire into a federation. But even though, in functional terms, their empire was becoming a fiction, the Habsburg sought of retain their predominance by providing a context in which the various east European nations could coexist. For this reason even such critics of the empire as the Czech leader, Palacky, acknowledged that if the Habsburg empire collapsed it would be necessary to restore it.

The rulers of Russia, in contrast, were extremely loath to compromise on their autocratic prerogatives. Autocracy was deeply ingrained in Russia, political feudalism never developed there. Therefore, not the art of compromise, but the tactics of the carrot-and-the-stick were usually utilized to keep the empire together. When new lands were acquired, the local elites were usually lulled into subservience by generous socio-economic privileges (but not political ones). But if they resisted, retribution was severe and uncompromising. Because the tsars saw themselves as the sole centers of power, they could not envisage their empire as anything but a unitary state. Consequently, they were adamant in not allowing locally-, territorially-, regionally-based seats of power to exist or develop. The tsar, not one's patria, had to be source of loyalty. Therefore the tsarist imperial government insisted on, and often succeeded, in weakening the ties of local elites with their homelands, something that the Habsburgs could never do.

Unlike the Habsburgs and their policies of Germanization, when the Russian imperial government introduced Russification in the latter part of the 19th century, it actually believed that non-Russian could be turned into Russians. The fact that Russians constituted about 50% of the Russia empire while German-speakers were only 24% of the Habsburg empire account in part for these differing perceptions. In fact the identification of the empire with Russia (*Rossiia*), a kind of supra-ethnic, Russian-speaking identity, reflected the imperial rulers suspicion of ethnically-based differentiation, their insistence on unitarianism which was incorporated in the slogan — one and indivisible Russia. The belief that the tsar, as the personification of *Rossiia*, that is, the empire, could be the only source of political loyalty also explains why the Russian imperial government was so fierce in its persecution of all political dissenters. It severity in dealing with revolutionaries is well known. But perhaps even more uncompromising was its treatment of certain nationalities, especially the Ukrainians and Belorussians (until 1905 their language was banned from schools and they were forbidden to publish in it). For example, the government considered the Ukrainians to be a variant of Russians and would not allow further discussion of the issue. Characteristically, in 1863, P. Valuev, minister of the interior declared that "the Ukrainian language never existed, does not exist, and will never exist in the future." In short, when confronted with nationalism, the Habsburgs tried to come to terms with it. But the Russian imperial government attempted to suppress it.

(6) Response to challenges of modernity — There is an inherent contraction between empire and modernity, especially in political and ideological terms. Democracy, civil rights, national sovereignty are obviously incompatible with unlimited rule of emperors. Therefore, that imperial rule would be sorely tested in the modern period was unavoidable. The essential question was how imperial rulers would respond to these challenges.

It appears that the Habsburg empire was more successful in adapting to modernity. It was closer to the West, the source of modernization. Modern ideas and techniques seeped in more gradually and evenly. And there was a longer period of adjustment. Already in the 1780s, Joseph II introduced educational reforms, in 1848 there was a constitution, from 1867 onward there was a growing tendency toward the decentralization of the empire. Nonetheless, it was generally acknowledged that many aspects of modernization — the railroads, industrial developments, education, medical care, defense — could best be attained with aid of empire. Even many members of the Austro-Hungarian socialist and nationalist intelligentsia, desired the continued existence of the empire. They believed that, in the context of Austria-Hungary, they could — the short term — attain many of their goals. Their relatively benign attitude toward the empire was based on the premise that the empire would continue to change, to respond to social and national pressures.

Nationalism, of course, was the central problem. However, the crucial point about nationalism in Austria-Hungary was that it was not primarily directed against Vienna. More often than not, the nations of the empire were in conflict with each other. And Vienna's role as an arbiter in these struggles was generally accepted, especially by weaker peoples like the Ukrainians or Slovaks, in their confrontations with the more influential Poles or Hungarians. Before World War I, the Habsburg empire stood a good chance adjusting to modernity by transforming itself, much like the British did later, from an empire to a commonwealth. It would, of course, no longer be an empire but its demise could have gradual and graceful.

Modernization in the Russian empire was more rapid, extreme and contradictory. An example of the rapidity of the process is the fact that in about one decade, the 1890s, Russia achieved a level of industrialization that was comparable to that which took Europe almost a century to attain. The extremes were even more striking: the most unbending autocracy confronted the most radical revolutionary movement in Europe; excellent universities existed side-by-side with extensive illiteracy; huge, modern factories functioned amidst of a sea of primitive villages; a brilliant, activist intelligentsia was surrounded by vast, apathetic masses. Modernizaton also created a much more contradictory situation in Russia than it did in Austria-Hungary. While society modernized, the political system remained militantly traditionalist. The more nationalism grew among it various people, the more the establishment insisted on "one, indivisible Russia." As Russia exploited such newly acquired regions as Central Asia, its most developed regions were exploited by European capitalists. Under such conditions, a significant portion of the intelligentsia believed that their only option was to bring down the system by force.

If nationalist conflicts were the greatest threat to the Habsburgs, social upheaval posed the greatest danger to the Romanovs. An interesting question is why socialism, not nationalism, became the focal point of opposition in Russia. A simple answer is that the Russian intelligentsia was in the majority and it defined opposition in social terms. But why did so many non-Russians choose to fight tsarism as members of Russian organizations rather than their own? Here we have a major achievement of the Russian intelligentsia. It convinced itself and many non-Russian intellectuals as well that the non-pluralistic, unitarian approach to opposing the autocracy, one based on socialist (not nationalist) agitation, was the one and only way to confront autocracy. Thus, the Russian revolutionaries, like their imperial opponents, demonstrated little willingness to compromise with diversity. They, too, insisted on all-encompassing, centrally-directed solutions to heterogeneity, be it nationally-based or otherwise. It is not surprising, therefore, that they eventually created a new, Soviet empire. Thus, unlike the Habsburg empire, the Russian empire appeared to be capable of reincarnation.

Notes

1 This definition is taken from W. Langer, *The Diplomacy of Imperialism.*

2 For the concept of empire in medieval, as especially of the continuity of the Roman imperial idea in the West, see R. Folz, *The Concept of Empire in Western Europe* (1969)

3 For a discussion of historiographical and theoretical aspects of the study of imperialism see W. Mommsen, Theories of Imperialism.

4 These are surveyed and systematized in M. Doyle, *Empires* (1986).

5 See D. Fieldhouse, *The Colonial Empires* (1965).

6 By the Habsburg empire we mean the lands dominated by the Vienna-based branch of the family, especially after 1648.

7 The literature on the Cossacks is vast. For a relatively recent overview see L. Gordon, *Cossack Rebellions* (1983). However, most insightful is still G. Stockl, *Das Entstehens des Kozakentums* (1963). Literature on the Grenzers is summarized in G. Rothenburg, *The Austrian Military Frontier.*

8 For a discussion of absolutism in eastern Europe see O. Subtelny, *Domination of Eastern Europe* (1986)

9 A recent and excellent study of the Russian empire is A. Kappeler, *Russ-land als Vielvölkerreich* (1992). This groundbreaking work is the first modern study of Russia as a multinational empire.

10 Ibid, pp. 29-50.

Chapter 5

Market Integration, Economic Intervention of the State and the Decline of Empires:

Austria-Hungary and Russia

György KÖVÉR

Oscar Jászi's famous book on the dissolution of the Habsburg Monarchy formulated the following thesis: "By 1913, the Austro-Hungarian Monarchy was already a defeated Empire from the economic point of view, and as such it went into the World War in 1914."[1] The origin of this statement came from speculations on the "tragedy of the free trade-policy" of the Habsburg Monarchy, in a chapter where the free-trade was discussed as one of the centripetal forces in the Monarchy. The book was written in the late twenties and Jászi was one of the followers of the idea of the "Danubian Confederation," i.e. a multinational political and economic integration."

Forty years later, in a "historical contribution to the current integration-problems" Krisztina Maria Fink considered that "das retardierende Moment eigentlich vom 1867er Vertrag in den Ablauf der Dinge gebracht wurde."[2] From the base of the institutional "Grossraumswirtschaft" her main argument compared the Monarchy directly to the European Economic Community: "... [sie] in der dritten, zweistaatlich-konstituellen Phase keine Übertragung auf eine von beiden Teilen anerkannte supranationale Organisation fanden, deren Entscheidungen auch ohne Zustimmung der Mitgliedsstaaten für dieselben verpflichtend gewesen wären."[3] From this point of view the peak of the process of the economic integration in the Habsburg Monarchy was undoubtedly the period of Neoabsolutism (1849-1860). (We can take for a great fortune, that Fink choose as a forerunner of the EEC not the last years of the Russian Empire.)

Whether we put the starting point of the preponderance of centrifugal economic forces in the Monarchy at 1867 (Fink) or at the beginning of the 20th century (Jászi) in a global institutionalist view the political dissolution ought to be preceded and prepared by the economic disintegration.

The Hungarian version of the law of 1867 sharply differentiated the *common affairs* (foreign and military affairs and the related financial matters) from *the affairs of common interest*. The former resulted from the law called Pragmatica Sanctio (1723), but the latter came from affairs newly founded during the neoabsolutist period. If we look more thoroughly at these affairs of common interest, we can find in this "basket" of the Compromise exclusively economic matters: the apportionment of the Habsburg state debt, the railway lines built across the border between the two halves of the Empire, the consumption taxes imposed according to the same principle in both parts of the Monarchy, the contractual form of the customs union and the common monetary system.

Different regulations applied to the several historically rooted types of affairs. Finances related to the common affairs (after all tariff revenue had been applied to) fell to the two halves of the Monarchy in a ratio (the so called 'quota') following principally the distribution of the number of citizens and their taxpaying capacity. Actually the quota was set by political negotiations (1868 - 70 : 30; 1899 - 65.6 : 34.4; 1907 - 63.6 : 36.4). To the payment by installments — from the official Hungarian point of view the Habsburg debt was undertaken without Hungarian approval — Hungary contributed only "from fairness, and political considerations." By the unification of debt denominations in 1868 the two partner-states settled for Hungary yearly a fixed amount of payments. While after 1873 the rate of interest diminished for a long period, this way of installments became unfavorable for Hungary (although the idea came originally from the Hungarian minister of finance). Concerning the so called affairs of common interest the Compromise was subject to renewal at stated intervals (as a rule every ten years).

The periodical renewal of the agreements has been judged differently by contemporaries and by historians. From one point of view the discussions in the press, in the parliaments and at the governing level shook and destabilized the Monarchy every ten years.[4] According to the opposite view, without the periodical renegotiations the rigid system of Dualism would have collapsed earlier than it did. In this opinion, the periodical renegotiations formed the dynamic element of the Dual Monarchy.[5]

Moreover after 1867 in the areas not covered by the affairs of common interest, there were articulated *autonomous Austrian and Hungarian economic policies* (disregarding at the moment the other ethnic and provincial corporative economic interests). Neoabsolutism introduced the interest guarantee system to construct an imperial railway network centered on Vienna. The Hungarian government adopted it after 1867 to build Budapest centered radial main lines in Hungary. The direct tax-system of the Empire formed in 1850-1851 did not belong to the affairs of common interest after 1867. It became different step by step in the two parts of the Monarchy. The Hungarian acts for the industrial promotion (1881, 1890, 1899, 1907) contained tax exemption, interest-free credits, and later the subsidies clearly intended to substitute for Hungary's lack of her own protective tariffs.

The range of effect of these converging and diverging tendencies in the area of the institutional system and the instruments of economic policy was determined by the framework of the *market*. Until the war the institutions and the economic policy operated solely through means conforming to the market system. The development of the market in the Austro-Hungarian Monarchy is one of the preferred topics of the latest clinometric researches. Examining the wholesale prices of the Empire David F. Good reinforced the earlier formulation, that the commodity-market integration peaked in the 1850-1860s.[6] The institutional and political background behind the price convergence which is usually mentioned is the formation of the customs union and the building of the main railway lines of the Empire.

An other important finding of Good's work is the money-market integration of interest rates within the Monarchy during the first half of the 1880s. The institutional framework included a uniform interest rate policy at the branches of the Austro-Hungarian Bank and the newly prescribed legal maximum interest rate. Through the inconvertible "parallel currency-system" (with fluctuating rate of exchange between the "paper currency" and the silver Gulden) the Monarchy before 1892 (and in Russia till 1895) fit in a contradictional way into "the fragmented international capital market."[7]

As for Russia the institutional approach of the Empire would indicate the permanent growth of centripetal forces. There was no sign of any "Compromise" in this respect, the trend has been the opposite to the Austrian "bicentralisation." "Self-government" given for conquered territories at the first period after that they "joined" to the Russian Empire was lost. "Sooner or later, for one reason or another, the privileges granted to conquered peoples were retracted, contracts were unilaterally abrogated, and subjects, together with their territories, were incorporated into the regular administration of the Empire."[8] It is true, the latest step in this respect was made namely in the field of economic matters. The Finnish constitution for example was suspended in 1899, followed by the centralization of taxes only in 1910, during the so called "campaign against Finland."[9]

Behind the bureaucratization and centralization the market integration emerged in Russia as well. Measuring with different methods the bias of agrarian prices the pioneers of Soviet "new economic history" also pointed out that "to the 1880s comes to the end the formation of the unified all-Russian agrarian market."[10] From our comparative point of view the exact timing of the fulfillment of the process is not so relevant as the statement, that the market integration in Russia developed slower and later than in the "bicentralized" Monarchy.

Intending to emphasize centrifugal forces as the greatest economic problems of the Austro-Hungarian Monarchy before the War, authors usually deal more with the international balance of payments and trade of the customs union as a whole than with the commodity and capital turnover between the two halves of the Dual Monarchy. Jászi's main economic argument mentioned at the introduction of this paper also was based on the statistical observation that after 1907 the balance of trade of the Monarchy became passive, followed by an increasing indebtedness. Actually the growth of imports into both parts of the Monarchy from outside the customs territory was much quicker that that of exports during the last prewar cycle (1908-1913 trough to trough). But the situation was the same during the previous period of time (1901-1908) as well. The principal reason for the passive balance of trade of the whole Monarchy was the turn to deficits in the Cisleithanian commodity balance (Graph I).

Since 1901 we can follow the customs inland traffic between the two halves of Austria-Hungary not only from Hungarian, but also from Austrian statistical sources. In this "Zwischenverkehr," after some years of Hungarian active balance in the first years of the century (the data are different in the Austrian and Hungarian statistics, presumably because of diverging pricing methods), from 1905-1906 a large Hungarian deficit accumulated. The growth rate of turnover decreased somewhat in the period 1908-1913 in comparison to 1901-1908, but it does not show any dramatic breakdown or irreversible change. Behind the increased customs barriers of 1906, the two countries of the newly formed "customs alliance" maintained the same traditional commodity trade to which they had become accustomed in the well proved division of labour within the Habsburg Empire since the late 18th century. The real foreign trade outside the Austro-Hungarian customs territory is indivisible from the inland traffic between the parts of the Monarchy. "The Monarchy's striking import surplus – the result of massive Austrian imports of raw cotton and wool, plus yarn and thread – never attained the absolute size of Austria's export surplus of textile goods in her trade with Hungary." The accelerating exports outside of the customs area consisted first of all of new products, which find their way abroad.[11]

Concerning the capital account, the negative balance of commodity trade almost as a matter of course coincided with an increase in security export before the War. We know from summary estimates that the outflow of bonds and shares from the Monarchy was obviously higher, while data collections disregarded direct emissions and considered short term monetary movements to be unmeasurable.[12] In the Austro-Hungarian Monarchy, with its inconvertible crown-currency belonging to the outer periphery of the international gold standard, according to a contemporary analysis during "external drains" when "the Bank of England redeems its notes in gold, the Austro-Hungarian Bank in gold bills, viz., gold in foreign hands... To have the requisite stock of Devisen and able to meet any demand, the bank sends gold abroad and procures bills in exchange."[13]

The enormous growth of the passive balance of trade and the rapid increase of discounting bills at home sharpened the situation on the foreign exchange market (Graph II). The balance sheets of the Austro-Hungarian Bank show the radical parallel diminution of the metallic reserve and the stock of gold bills during the years 1910-1912. The bank had to raise its rate of interest which peaked in 1913. In the year 1913 – according to the normal path of the business cycle – the stock of gold and gold bills started to increase. It was the direct result of diminishing discount at home and that of the decrease of import surplus. The gold buying activity of the bank, was totally missing in years 1912-1913.[14]

Examining Russia from a strictly economic point of view and disregarding the level of indebtedness the position of this empire looks less problematic. The Russian balance of trade remained continuously active up to the war, which means

Russia was able to counterbalance the flow of foreign loans by his forced agricultural exports.[15]

This way the question related to the economic "defeat" raised by Jászi seems insolvable in itself and at a comparative level too. Neither the institutions and the economic policy, nor the structure and cyclical movements of the market predetermined the economic dissolution of Austria-Hungary before the war. The Austro-Hungarian Monarchy dissolved not for economic reasons, but it was dissolved. Could have such a few influence the centripetal, integrative forces of the market?

We could not accept the argument of the relatively "close correlation" between economics and military forces of powers − represented by Paul Kennedy. "While it would be quite wrong, then, to claim that the outcome of the First World War was predetermined, the evidence ... suggests that the overall course of that conflict ... correlates closely with the economic and industrial production and effectively mobilized forces available to each alliance during the different phases of the struggle."[16] Our comparison of Austria-Hungary and Russia suggests other consequences.

*   *   *

Alexander Gerschenkron's famous thesis on the role of "relative backwardness" in Europe contrasts the German and Russian type industrialization. It is "common place" now in economic history, that in Germany the bank, and in Russia the state substituted the factors required for the so called "great spurt." It is not so well known, that in Gerschenkron's concept the Austro-Hungarian Monarchy was divided into two halves from the point of backwardness and substitution: Austria (Cisleithania) belonged to the German-type, Hungary (Transleithania) to the Russian-type development.

When we talk of the economic activity of the state in Austria-Hungary and Russia during the World War I, some comparative questions and points are evident. The first point comes immediately from Gerschenkron's above mentioned thesis: the difference in the tradition and practice of the state interventionism in the two empires. There are, of course, some common features of backwardness in the central and eastern part of Europe. Some of them (the low level of internal capital accumulation, the traditional structure of society) was emphasised very strongly in the last decades in the historiography. "It is not the peculiar and specific role of the state, but the import of capital, promoted and motivated by the state activity, which may be regarded as a feature distinguished Eastern Europe from the rest of the Continent in the modern transformation of the economy."[17]

But on the eve of World War I, the contrast in the state activity seems to us much stronger, as similarities. Not only between Austria and Russia, but between Austria-Hungary together (as an economic entity) and Russia as well. The indices of the financial system of the two empires sharply differ: the amount of assets of financial institutions in comparison to the GNP was higher in Austria-Hungary, namely 220%, while in Russia only 158%. From the other side, the foreign indebtedness of Austria-Hungary reached 50%, that of Russia 65% of the GNP. The different level of the monetarisation required different redistributive activity by the governments.

The income side of the state budget shows very well the differences too. In Austria-Hungary the state revenues based mainly on tax system, which differed in direct, but were identical in indirect taxes in the two halves of the empire. In Russia before the War the main items of government income came from tax on vodka-distillation and the state railways (26 and 24% respectively). The weight of the defence expenditures marks also important differences: "The proportion of armaments expenditure to national income on the eve of the war amounted in Germany to 3.5%, in Britain to 3.6% and in Austria-Hungary to about 4%. Russia engaged in even higher armaments expenditure: some 6% of national income."[18] Low level of monetarisation, restricted possibility of modern taxation, high level of military expenditures and foreign indebtedness — this is the background of Russian war finance before the war.

Prohibition of vodka-distillation at the very beginning of the war and permanent chaos in the railway traffic very early reduced the government revenues in Russia.[19] There was an other possibility to raise the income, to increase the direct taxation of the firms and the population, which was carried out extensively. In introducing new taxes (for example the income tax) the tsarist government was not very active. Only in 1916 did they start to impose them. Issuing war obligations — because of the weak development of financial institutions and the low rate of saving — was not a great success. From the beginning of the war to the February Revolution they issued 6 domestic bonds: in nominal value some 8 billion rubles. Due to the creditor activity of the Allies, Russia also received substantial foreign loans during the war. In constant price we can say that these measures were only enough to hold the of pre war expenditure level.[20]

Austria-Hungary — belonging to the Central Powers — had not had the same opportunity to use the foreign stock market for war finance purposes. The Austrian and the Hungarian Governments exploited domestic sources to a greater extent. The 8 War Loans in both side of the Monarchy (35 billion K in Cisleithenia; 18 billion K nominal in Hungary) increased the importance of the domestic state debt.[21] This process, however, diminished the possibilities to increase the state-revenue through new taxes. In this respect the difference between the two halves of the Monarchy was not without importance: Austria employed since 1896 a modern personal income-tax system, which was introduced very late, only in 1916 in Hungary (incidentally in the same year as in Russia). All these measures lead — in a different way from Russia — in constant prices, to the same result: roughly to the pre-war expenditure level of the dual Monarchy. In this respect we can formulate a very modest conclusion of the above discussed problems about the war finance. The tradition and earlier practice of the state intervention in two relatively backward empires determines usually only fiscal techniques, rather than the final success of the war financing.

Looking an other field to research the economic activity of the state (and the market) we can cast a glance at the regulation of the food supply during the war. The intervention of the government — maximising food-prices, regulating the grain trade by two, semi-state-owned companies — was earlier and more efficient in Austria-Hungary, than in Russia. What is extremely interesting in Russia, — partly an agrarian export country and partly that of famine — that during the war enormous reserves of food were accumulated in the grain producing areas. In this respect we can mention the old Austrian accusation against the Hungarian agriculture too, use of the Austrian food shortages during the war. "...in 1916 Hungary supplied no more than 100,000 tons of grain and flour to Austria, as against 2.1 million tons yearly before the war, and deliveries of other foodstuffs were likewise drastically reduced."[22]

More serious measures were taken in both empires only in the second half of 1916. In Hungary a decree of 24 August controlled the surplus product, and the possibility of requisitioning it.[23] After the weak yield of the grain-collection a new decree of 27 November 1916 ordered two more requisitions with a centrally determined contingent for every county. This measure was the first sign of the decisive change in the government's economic policy.

In Russia a decree of 29 November 1916 ordered the so called *"prodrazverstka,"* the collection of grain for national defence purposes.[24] The declaration of the State Monopoly of grain remained the duty of the Provisional Government in 25 March 1917, but was introduced only after the Bolshevik takeover.[25]

To sum up the points: during the war the economic activity of the state was weaker and more muted in the field of fiscal and food policy in Russia than in Austria-Hungary. It suggests to me, that in opposition to the Gerschenkron thesis in wartime not the difference of "relative backwardness" between the two empires was really the impetus for the state intervention. In Austria-Hungary, where the market and the economic infrastructure were deeply articulated this intervention could rather *substitute* during the war-time missing market factors.

According to some remarks, "by 1917 ... Austria-Hungary and Russia were racing each other to collapse."[26] This race was won undoubtedly by Russia in 1917. But the war was won by the Allies. Consequently the Habsburg-Monarchy disappeared from the scene of history and Russia received possibility once more to reorganize (for more than a half century) a new form of (soviet) empire.

Notes

1 Oscar Jászi, *The Dissolution of the Habsburg Monarchy* (Chicago, 1961), p. 202.
2 Krisztina Maria Fink, *Die österreichisch-ungarische Monarchie als Wirtschaftsgemeinschaft Ein historischer Beitrag zu aktuellen Integrationsproblem* (München, 1968), p. 35.
3 *Ibid.*, p. 45.
4 *Ibid.*, p. 58.
5 Galántai József, *A Habsburg-Monarchia alkonya* (Bp., 1985), pp. 154-155.
6 György Szabad, "Das Anwachsen der Ausgleichtendenz der Produktenpreise im Habsburgerreich um die Mitte des 19 Jahrhunderts," in V. Sándor & P. Hanák (eds.), *Studien zur Geschichte der österreichisch-ungarischen Monarchie* (Bp., 1961), pp. 123-137; David F. Good, *The Economic Rise of the Habsburg Empire 1750-1914* (Univ. of California Press, 1984), pp. 108-123.
7 There are two different interpretations: Leland B. Yeager, "Fluctuating Exchange Rates in the Nineteenth Century: The Experiences of Austria and Russia," in R. Mundell & A. Swoboda (eds.), *Monetary Problems of the International Economy* (Chicago, 1969), pp. 61-89; and John Komlos, "The Diffusion of Financial Technology into the Austro-Hungarian Monarchy toward the End of the Nineteenth Century," in J. Komlos (ed.), *Economic Development in the Habsburg Monarchy in the Nineteenth Century* (Boulder, New York, 1983), pp. 137-165.
8 Richard Pipes, *The Formation of the Soviet Union* (Atheneum, 1980), p. 3.

9 Richard Pipes, *Russia under the Old Regime* (Penguin, 1979), pp. 250-251; Istoriia SSSR, t. VI (Moscow, 1968), p. 360.

10 I.D. Koval'chenko & L.V. Milov, *Vserossiiskii agrarnyi rynok XVIII-nachalo XX veka* (Moscow, 1974), p. 239. According to an other research the equalisation of Russian and world grain prices came to the end only at the turn of the century. M.B. Mironov, "Faktory dinamiki khlebnykh tsen v evropeiskoi Rossii v 1801-1914 gg. i kolichestvennaia otsenka ikh vliiania," in *Matematicheskie metody v issledovaniiakh po sotsial'no-ekonomicheskoi istorii* (Moscow, 1975), p. 201.

11 Scott M. Eddie, "Economic Policy and Economic Development in Austria-Hungary 1867-1913," in P. Mathias & S. Pollard (eds.), *The Cambridge Economic History of Europe*, Vol. VIII (Cambridge Univ. Press, 1989) p. 838; Scott M. Eddie, "Mit bizonyítanak az 1882-1913-as export-statisztikai adatok: Magyarország valóban csak a Monarchia "éléskamrája" volt? [What Do the Export Statistics for 1882-1913 Prove: Was Hungary Really Only the "Pantry" of the Monarchy?]," *Történelmi Szemle*, No. 3 (1982), p. 424.

12 Eduard März, *Österreichische Bankpolitik in der Zeit der großen Wende 1913-1923 Verlag für Geschichte und Politik* (Wien, 1981), pp. 50-51; Fritz Bartsch, *Statistische Daten über die Zahlungsbilanz Österreich-Ungarns vor Ausbruch des Krieges Mitteilungen des K. K. Finanzministeriums XXII* (Wien, 1917).

13 Ludwig V. Mises, "The Foreign Exchange Policy of the Austro-Hungarian Bank," *The Economic Journal*, No. 6 (1909), p. 208.

14 Kövér György, "Az Osztrák-Magyar Bank 1878-1914," in T. Bácskai (ed.), *A Magyar Nemzeti Bank története I.* (Bp., 1993), p. 332.

15 B.R. Mitchell, *European Historical Statistics 1750-1970* (London, 1975), p. 496.

16 Paul Kennedy, *The Rise and Fall of the Great Powers Economic Change and Military Conflict from 1500 to 2000* (New York, 1989), p. 274.

17 Ivan T. Berend & György Ránki, *Economic Development in East-Central Europe in the 19th & 20th Centuries* (Columbia Univ. Press, 1974), p. 92.

18 Gerd Hardach, *The First World War 1914-1918* (Penguin, 1977), p. 150.

19 The weakness of infrastructural network was clear from military point of view too. P. Kennedy, *op. cit.*, p. 239.

20 Hardach, *op. cit.*, p. 153.

21 Teleszky János, *A magyar állam pénzügyei a háború alatt* (Bp., 1927), pp. 264-265; Eduard März, *Österreichische Bankpolitik in der Zeit der großen Wende 1913-1923* (Wien, 1981), pp. 198-199.

22 Hardach, *op. cit.*, p. 121.

23 Puskás Julianna, "Adatok a hadigazdálkodás kialakulásához és rendszeréhez Magyarországon az első világháború idején," *Történelmi Szemle,* Nos. 1-2 (1958), p. 140.

24 Rév István, "A nagy hisztéria, avagy az önmagát beteljesítő jóslat," *Medvetánc,* Nos. 3-4 (1987), p. 169.

25 E.G. Gimpel'son, *Voennyi kommunizm: Politika, Praktika, Ideologiia* (Moscow, 1973), pp. 56-57.

26 P. Kennedy, *op. cit.,* p. 263.

Chapter 6

The Development of the Russian State System in the Nineteenth and Early Twentieth Centuries

Pavel ZYRIANOV

The last *zemskii sobor* met in 1683-84. For over 200 years no general Russian representative assemblies were convened, if one does not count Catherine the Great's summoning of the "Great Commission," which had only a limited purpose. During that time a broad array of mutual misunderstandings and estrangements between society and the state developed. Many statesmen, public figures, and even a number of tsars understood how unnatural this situation was.

Alexander I, upon assuming the throne in 1801, considered abolishing serfdom, introducing a constitution, and convening a people's government. Above all else, however, he thought it important to strengthen the central government, which was then in a state of routine disarray. The colleges established by Peter the Great were clearly not working out. Widespread evasion of responsibility predominated in them, concealing the taking of bribes and the embezzling of public funds. The local authorities, taking advantage of the weakness of the central government, fostered lawlessness.

Alexander hoped to introduce order and to strengthen the state by introducing a ministerial system based on individual management. In 1802 eight ministries were created to replace the previous twelve colleges: the ministry of war, navy, foreign affairs, internal affairs, commerce, finance, public enlightenment, and justice. This measure strengthened the central government, but a decisive victory in the struggle against abuses of power was not achieved. The old defects were transplanted to the new ministries. It was obvious that it was impossible to solve the problem of creating a system of state authority that would actively contribute to the economic, social, and political development of the country and not devour its resources simply by making some rearrangements in the bureaucratic machine. A fundamentally new approach to the problem was needed.

In 1809, at the tsar's instruction, Secretary of State M.M. Speranskii put together a plan for radical reform. Speranskii placed the separation of power — legislative, executive, and judicial — at the foundation of his state structure. Each of these, from top to bottom, was supposed to act within a strictly outlined framework of law. Representative assemblies were created at several levels headed by the State Duma, a representative body for all of Russia. The Duma was supposed to pass judgment on bills presented for its examination and monitor the accounts of the ministers.

All power — legislative, executive, and judicial — was unified in a State Council, the members of which were appointed by the tsar. The opinions of the State Council, after confirmation by the tsar, became law. If a disagreement arose within the State Council, the tsar by his choice would confirm the view of the majority or the minority. No law could be promulgated without being discussed in both the State Duma and the State Council.

In Speranskii's plan real legislative power remained in the hands of the emperor and the upper-level bureaucracy. But Speranskii emphasized that the judgments of the Duma should be made freely and should express the "opinion of the people." This was the essence of Speranskii's fundamentally new approach: he wanted to subject the actions of both the central and local authorities to the control of public opinion.

Under Speranskii's plan voting rights would be enjoyed by all citizens of Russia who possessed land or capital, including state peasants. Workmen, domestic servants, and serfs would not participate in elections, but would enjoy important civil rights. The most important of these was that no one could be punished without a court sentence. If enacted, Speranskii's plan would have greatly limited the power that landowners held over the serfs.[1]

The implementation of the project began in 1810 when the State Council was created. But there things remained. The gentry, having heard of Speranskii's plans to grant civil rights to the serfs, openly expressed their dissatisfaction. All of the conservatives from N.M. Karamzin to A.A. Arakcheev joined together against Speranskii. "We don't need a constitution," Karamzin wrote in an note given to the emperor, "give us fifty intelligent and virtuous governors, and everything will turn out well." Speranskii was surrounded by hired and voluntary spies, who passed along to the tsar his every imprudent word. The proud and rancorous emperor would not allow any denunciation reaching his ears to go unnoticed. Further, in expectation of the inevitable war with Napoleon, Alexander I did not want to cloud his relations with the upper estate in any way. In March, 1812, Speranskii was arrested and exiled to Nizhnii Novgorod. Alexander said that he was "sacrificed to public opinion." And indeed, Speranskii's exile provoked loud rejoicing amongst the gentry.[2]

After the end of the war with Napoleon, Alexander I returned to his unrealized plans. In accordance with the decisions of the Congress of Vienna in 1814, a significant part of Polish lands, including Warsaw, were transferred to Russia. Poland was granted a constitution. In his speech at the opening of the Polish Diet on 15 March 1818, the emperor announced his intention to give a constitutional structure to all of Russia. Alexander then instructed his close friend, N.N. Novosil'tsov, to develop a plan for a Russian constitution. In order to carry out this request Novosil'tsov brought together a group of educated bureaucrats that included Prince P.A. Viazemskii, a poet and statesman. The Polish Constitution was taken as a model, and even Speranskii's plan was used. By 1821 work on the "Constitutional Charter of the Russian Empire" was completed.

Under the "Constitutional Charter" Russia was to receive a
federal structure that divided it into twelve regions, each of
which would have a representative body. The general Russian
representative assembly would consist of two chambers. The
upper chamber would be the Senate whose members were to be
appointed by the tsar. The members of the lower chamber
would be elected by local assemblies and confirmed by the tsar
(one deputy was to be chosen from three candidates). The part
of the "Constitutional Charter" that would guarantee personal
immunity was extremely important. No one would be arrested
without being charged. No one would be punished except by a
court and on the basis of law. Freedom of the press would be
established.[3]

If the "Constitutional Charter" had been put into effect,
Russia would have stepped on the path of a representative
system and civil freedoms. While a draft of the constitution
was being worked out, however, Alexander I lost the desire to
have it introduced. Upon receiving the final version of the
"Constitutional Charter," he familiarized himself with it, set it
down on the table, and never again returned to it.

The aggrieved Viazemskii, it seems, did not make a secret
of his work. Among those who became familiar with it was the
ideologue of the Decembrists, Nikita Murav'ev. He placed the
work of Novosil'tsov-Viazemskii at the foundation of a
constitution he developed. In Murav'ev's plan, however, the
rights of the representative body were significantly expanded
and those of the monarchy curtailed; Russia was to become a
constitutional monarchy. But the most profound difference
was that Murav'ev linked the introduction of a constitution to
the abolition of serfdom and estate privileges. "Villenage and
slavery are abolished," he wrote in his plan,

> The slave, tied to the land in Russia, will be free. The
> division between the noble and the common people is
> rejected in so far as it is contrary to Faith, by which all men
> are *brothers,* all are born *good* by the will of God, all are
> born *for the good* and all are *common people*: for everyone is
> weak and imperfect.[4]

Over the course of many years Soviet historians did all they could to transform the Decembrists into revolutionaries, to bring them closer to the Bolsheviks. The time has now come to revisit the Decembrists in the context of their time. A number of different social estates participated in the Decembrist movement (the landed gentry, provincial officers, the intelligentsia-*raznochintsy*), but the leading role, nonetheless, belonged to the upper gentry and aristocrats, both titled and untitled. In contrast to the revolutionary aristocrats of the following period (A.I. Herzen, P.A. Kropotkin, S.L. Perovskaia, etc.), the Decembrists did not break ties with their environment, but rather functioned as its representatives. The reason for this was that toward the end of Alexander I's reign the attitude of the gentry toward a constitution began to change. Further, a highly influential opposition to the autocratic system arose during the period between the tsars, which went well beyond the limits of the Northern and Southern Societies (one needs simply to mention the names of respected figures such as N. S. Mordvinov, A.P. Ermolov, M.A. Miloradovich, A.S. Griboedov, and also of Viazemskii to show this is so). The officers of the Guard came forward on 14 December 1825 to a large degree because they were counting on the support of the high-ranking opposition. These hopes were unwarranted, for Nicholas was able to win some of them over to his side and to neutralize others. Having broken up the Decembrists, he brought his anger down upon them directly. At the same time he decided not to punish other malcontents who had hesitated to act so that he would not spoil his relationship with the gentry. Of such men the Decembrists said with bitterness: "There are our friends from the fourteenth who granted us the favor of banishment."[5]

Nicholas I piously believed in the strength and righteousness of the autocratic system. Lacking trust in the public, the emperor saw his main foothold of support in the army and the bureaucracy. During Nicholas I's reign an unprecedented expansion of the bureaucratic apparatus took place. The most varied branches of human activity became the objects of bureaucratic regulation, including religion, art, literature, and science. The number of bureaucrats grew rapidly from 15-16,000 at the beginning of the nineteenth century to 61,500 in 1847 and 86,000 in 1857.[6]

Administrative centralism was reinforced beyond all reason. Practically everything was decided in Petersburg. Even the top institutions (the State Council and Senate) were overburdened with a mass of trivialities. This engendered a huge correspondence that quite often had a purely formal character (local bureaucrats would respond to papers from Petersburg without trying to grasp the essence of things and without collecting the necessary information).

The essence of bureaucratic administration, however, is not that it creates a large quantity of paper and official red tape. These are only its external signs. Its essence consists of decisions being made and carried out not by some collection of representatives and not individually by someone having supreme authority or by some responsible official (a minister, a governor), but rather by the entire administrative machine as a whole. The tsar himself, the ministers, the governors become nothing more than a parts of this machine, albeit very important ones.

Since all the information a minister receives flows through his administrative apparatus, it would seem that the minister is in the power of this apparatus. In addition, subordinate bureaucrats prepare draft decisions on various matters. Many matters, especially those in which the leadership has little interest, are in fact decided by the bureaucrats who prepare the draft documents. Under Nicholas I the leadership posts of civil departments were often filled with army generals who were poorly acquainted with their new assignments. Most often departments headed by such men turned out to be run by their subordinates.

If day after day subordinate bureaucrats methodically exert influence on the leadership of a given department in a certain direction, then in the end the policy of this department will be pushed in that direction. As a general rule sharp changes in the policies of a government are not introduced from without (for example, by the tsar, his advisors, or the public), but rather, over the course of many years they blossom little by little in the bureaucratic depths. Even if the idea comes from the outside, as it makes its way through various offices it will acquire a particularly bureaucratic interpretation.

Nicholas I, in a moment of insight, once said, "Russia is ruled by department heads." Indeed, middle bureaucrats (department heads) play a special role in directing the course of policy (in assessing information received from the provinces, in making decisions, and in interpreting how to implement them). If a particular decision leads to disastrous results, the minister or governor is deprived of his post. In an extreme case the tsar might even be overthrown. The department head, however, will stay in his previous job and at best add a new sauce to the same old policies. This is how an irresponsible bureaucratic administration operates.

To deal with the government's needs superficially, treating them narrowly and single-mindedly, is characteristic of bureaucracy and its narrowly grouped interests. The staffs of ministries and departments expand, especially for political investigations; foreign political ambitions grow and along with them, military expenditures. The bureaucratic caste and those social groups connected with it (in nineteenth-century Russia the landed gentry in particular) take advantage of the unnecessary paperwork. Literally nothing is done to improve the lives of the people, even though official propaganda never tires of repeating that this is the government's primary concern. Expenditures on education, science, and culture remain extremely meager and highly selective: first, a showcase is created for the outside world; next, preference is given to those branches of science from which militarily significant results can be expected. These are the fundamental properties of a bureaucratic system of administration.

The modern state can not get by without using the apparatus of bureaucrats. It should, however, function within the strict framework of law and under the supervision and control of representative bodies in both the center and the provinces. Only the introduction of a genuinely constitutional system permits the redistribution of the bureaucrats' absolute power. The experience of Russia in the nineteenth and twentieth centuries attests to the fact that bureaucracy is the most inveterate enemy of a constitutional system. It does not give up even when the circumstances are such that representative assemblies begin to operate. Bureaucracy makes every effort to free itself from parliamentary control, to transform the representative body into a decorative appendage of the state machine.

All of this leads to the idea that introducing a constitutional system would have been far easier, perhaps, under Alexander I than after the reign of Nicholas I, during which the bureaucracy grew, became stronger, and was transformed into an independent force.

In the scholarly world (with the exception, perhaps, of only Russia) ideas about bureaucracy carry the imprint of Max Weber's work on "ideal types." Although no "ideal" bureaucracy exists anywhere, Russia is even more difficult to evaluate in terms of Weberian types. By comparison, the works of the turn-of-the-century Russian political scientists N.M. Korkunov and N.I. Lazarevskii are considerably less well-known to the scholarly world (including in Russia).[7]

Knowledge of bureaucratic arbitrariness undoubtedly reached Nicholas I, but the tsar assumed that it could be curbed with the aid of a precisely composed system of laws. At the beginning of his reign complete confusion ruled this area. Since Alexis' Code of 1649 thousands of manifestos, instructions, and orders had accumulated that supplemented, replaced, and contradicted one another. The absence of a code of current laws made the work of the government more difficult and created fertile soil for bureaucratic abuses.

Nicholas I ordered that work on compiling a Code of Laws be concentrated in the Second Department of His Imperial Majesty's Own Chancery. The immediate direction of this project was given to Speranskii, who had returned to Petersburg at the end of Alexander I's reign. In the first stage of the work all of the laws passed after 1649 were dug out of the archives and arranged in chronological order. These were then published in the fifty-one volume *Complete Collection of the Laws of the Russian Empire*.

Then the more difficult part of the work began: all the current laws were selected, arranged according to a definite design, and revised. The revisions consisted mainly of eliminating the contradictions amongst the laws. Sometimes, however, the current laws were insufficient to complete the design, and Speranskii had to "finish writing" a law on the basis of the norms of Western law. By the end of 1832 all fifteen volumes of the *Code of Laws of the Russian Empire* had been prepared. The beginning of the first volume contained the "Fundamental Laws" in which the main principles of the state structure were consolidated. "The Emperor of all Russia," stated the first article of the Code of Laws, "is an autocratic and absolute monarch. God Himself commands us to obey his supreme authority not only out of fear, but also out of conscience."

The Code of Laws was approved by the State Council on 19 January 1833. Nicholas I, who was present at the meeting, took the Order of St. Apostle Andrew of the First-Called (the highest Russian award) from his chest and placed it on Speranskii. On 1 January 1835 the Code of Laws became the only official source of laws for the Russian empire.[8]

Soon after the Code of Laws was accepted, the Minister of State Domains, P.D. Kiselev, conducted a reform in the administration of state peasants. A little later the Minister of Finance, E.F. Kankrin, enacted monetary reform. All of these measures strengthened Emperor Nicholas I.

Under Nicholas I no one drew up constitutional plans, and no one created secret societies; everyone knew his place. Nicholas's Empire seemed to be unshakably secure. But it was unreceptive to changes. Nicholas I decided not to carry out even those reforms that he certainly knew were necessary. It is well known, for example, that from the very beginning of his reign he thought about abolishing serfdom and that he even took a number of steps in this direction. It became clear, however, that such a fundamental change would set all of the estates of the huge empire in motion and necessarily entail other changes as well. Having imagined all this and mentally shuddered, Nicholas I said, "There is no doubt that there is evil in serfdom as it exists amongst us today. This is perceptible and obvious to everyone, but to touch it *now* would be even more disastrous." In 1848 the idea of abolishing serfdom was decisively dropped.[9]

The Crimean War shattered the illusion that the Russian system was superior to that of Western Europe. It became obvious that Russia was in many respects falling behind the countries of Western Europe and that this backwardness was taking on dimensions that were dangerous for Russia's national sovereignty.

Alexander II's greatest service to his country consisted of his taking it upon himself to abolish serfdom, his persistence, and his seeing the affair through to the end. From the moment the laws were published on 19 February 1861, estate peasants stopped being considered property; from then on they could not be sold, bought, given as a gift, or resettled according to the whims of their owners. The government announced that the former serfs were "free rural inhabitants," and conferred upon them civil rights — the freedom to marry, the right to enter into contracts independently and to bring suits, the right to acquire property in their own name, etc.

Alexander II's government did not limit itself to the acts of 19 February 1861, but rather introduced a series of reforms, which are deservedly called the "Great Reforms." The creation of the zemstvos in 1864 restored local self-government to Russia in a new form and in accordance with the conditions of the nineteenth century. In 1870 city government was restructured according to non-estate principles. As a result of the judicial reform of 1864, Russia obtained an open court with jurors that was independent of the administration. Military reforms completed in 1874 eliminated the recruitment system and introduced general liability for military service. A secondary result of all these reforms was a slowdown of growth in the number of bureaucrats in the central government, while zemstvo reform allowed the staffs of local state institutions to be reduced.

The Great Reforms, however, did not touch upon all areas of the Russian state system. The estate system of local government remained inviolable. Government at the *guberniia* level was, for the most part, bureaucratic. At the *uezd* level of government the main figure was the marshal of the gentry (during the reform period the significance of the marshal even grew). The lower link (volost and rural society) was estate-peasant based. Local government of post-reform Russia was made up of three levels: the estate-peasant, the estate-nobility, and the bureaucratic. The bottom level was isolated from the other two and squeezed by them. No volost elder in history, most likely, ever managed to serve until he reached the position of governor. On the other hand, between the second and third levels — and even higher — there was a broad exchange of people and ideas.[10]

The Great Reforms also did not affect the upper levels of power. The Senate — the upper judicial-administrative instance, the interpreter of laws — was not reformed. But the most important thing over which Alexander II stumbled was the question of a constitution.

At the beginning of the nineteenth century, as we have seen, the gentry rancorously banished Speranskii and his constitutional plan. By 1861 the upper estate had, to a significant degree, changed its position. It would appear that the lessons of Nicholas I's long reign were not lost, for all the layers of the population, including the owners of serfs, suffered from the absolute power and self-rule of the bureaucracy. The danger also existed that once the bureaucracy had taken the management of the peasantry into its own hands it would become excessively powerful and utterly stop taking account of the gentry. Of course, there was no complete unanimity of opinion amongst the members of the upper estate, and the landowners of the southern and south-eastern provinces (the most peripheral and least enlightened part of the gentry) were largely indifferent to establishing a constitution and in the final analysis were satisfied with expanding their participation in local affairs. But the gentry in the capital and the surrounding provinces were decisively in favor of a constitution.

In February 1862 gentry from Tver province subjected the activity of the government to severe criticism at their provincial assembly and declared that the government was completely bankrupt. In an address to the tsar they emphasized: "Gathering together elected representatives from all the lands of Russia is the only way to solve satisfactorily the problems that have arisen, but have yet to be solved, as a result of the statute of 19 February." A few days later a meeting of peace negotiators from Tver province took place. In an even sharper form they repeated the basic points of the resolution from the gentry's assembly. All thirteen participants at the meeting were sent to the Peter-Paul fortress. After five months of confinement they were brought before a court, which sentenced them to a loss of freedom for periods of two to two and a half years. The harshest punishments were conferred on the main "ring-leaders," Aleksei and Nikolai Bakunin, brothers of the well-known revolutionary M.A. Bakunin. Although the Bakunins were quickly pardoned, they were prohibited from participating in any future elections.

In October of the same year a Petersburg provincial zemstvo assembly brought forth a petition calling for "a central zemstvo assembly to discuss the economic resources and needs common to the entire state."

In January 1865 the Moscow gentry addressed the following appeal to the tsar: "Complete, Sovereign, the state edifice founded by you by calling a general assembly of the elected people from all of the lands of Russia to discuss the needs common to the entire state." When the appeal was received a lively meeting took place in which quick-tempered speeches were made against the "oprichniks" surrounding the tsar.

Alexander II was extremely unhappy with this appeal, but, not wanting to spoil his relationship with the influential Moscow gentry, he did not resort to repression. Instead, he limited himself to a rescript issued in the name of the Ministry of Internal Affairs in which he announced, "No one may take it upon themselves to petition me on the general resources and needs of the state." In a private conversation with a member of the Moscow gentry he claimed that he would willingly give "some pleasant constitution if he were not afraid that on the following day Russia would fall to pieces."[11]

It would seem that Alexander II began to think that continuing the reforms would be dangerous. Both dignitaries and his closest ministers often repeated this, and under their influence Alexander II began to stop the reforms. At the same time discontent in the country was growing, left-radical groups were gathering momentum. The reign of Alexander II demonstrates just how difficult it is to *start* reforms and just how dangerous it is to *stop* them halfway, for once a country following a reformer has gathered the inertia of movement, it cannot suddenly stop. Once events began to taken on a dramatic character, Alexander II acceded to creating a certain prototype representative assembly, but this decision was incapable of averting a tragic outcome.

Alexander III was able to stabilize the situation in the country quickly, but he at once removed the question of a representative assembly from the agenda.

The liberation of the serfs in 1861 was built upon difficult compromises. The reform was too one-sided in taking into account the interests of the landowners and therefore, in technical terms, had a very short "resource time." At most, it had twenty years. After that it would be necessary to introduce new reforms in the same area, i.e., to expand the civil rights of the peasantry and return to it the land stripped away during the reform. After some wavering, however, Alexander III adopted the opposite policy. Zemstvo and urban counter-reforms limited the rights of the zemstvos and of the city dumas and strengthened bureaucratic control over them. Peasants were strained by their economic circumstances, and leaving the commune became extremely difficult.

In attempting to strengthen the estate structure and the power of the bureaucracy, Alexander III literally returned to the traditions of his grandfather's reign. But that reign was brought to an end by military defeat. As if to compensate for its conservative policies, therefore, the government under Alexander III adopted a course aimed at the rapid development of strategically important branches of industry. The initiator of this policy was the Minister of Finance, Sergei Witte. Having expanded railroad construction and set about rearming the army and navy, the government provided a market for metallurgic and machine-construction factories. In 1893 an enormous industrial expansion began in Russia. Unprecedented industrial monsters — what the writer A.I. Kuprin called "molochs" — grew out of Russian soil. The optimal ratio between heavy and light industry is approximately 1:4. On the eve of the industrial boom in Russia this ratio was about 1:5. Russian industry had a somewhat "light-weight" character. After years of expansion in favor of heavy industry, however, this ratio rose to 1:3.[12] A powerful heavy industry sector capable of overwhelming the economy was created in a country with a backward agriculture, impoverished villages, and a limited market. The urban population expanded rapidly. The number of inhabitants in Petersburg and Moscow nearly doubled in 30-35 years and towards the end of the century surpassed one million.

But while industrialization decisively ravaged the countryside, it failed to enrich the city. The created wealth was concentrated in the hands of a small group of industrialists and banking bigwigs, and the impoverished peasantry, in search of a better lot, began to flow into the cities. The traditional inhabitants of the city — the shopkeepers, the artisans, the petty proprietors, that "middle class" on which the movement for a constitution and for civil freedoms in nineteenth-century Europe relied — were lost amongst the thousands who migrated to the cities. In the contemporary developed countries the working class is organically inscribed in the social structure of society, and the workers' movement has become an important component part of the mechanism for supporting stability. In the West as well, however, the working class used to be a "difficult child."

In Russia the vast majority of the working class were peasants who retained their ties to the country. In the city they felt like foreigners; they were lost when left alone with city life and saw their salvation in mass action. The very difficult working and living conditions pushed them toward the most desperate forms of protest, all the more so since they had nothing to lose in the city and could always return to their native rural communities. The rural-oriented, simple-minded working masses eagerly believed the stories about how it was possible to improve their situation immediately and miraculously and were ready to follow any demagogue — Father Gapon, the leaders of the Black Hundreds, the Bolsheviks. Unfortunately, neither the official authorities, the liberal constitutionalists, nor the Church promised the masses much in this life, and they did even less.

Hardly had the first wave of arrivals (in the 1890s) settled and become urbanized before they were swallowed up by a second and third wave (in 1912-13 and during World War I). After each such wave enthusiasm for strikes increased, which was quickly taken advantage of by the various "well-wishers" of the common people.

The government soon came to pay a very dear price for the first successes of its industrialization policy. In 1900 an economic crisis developed that quickly became a political one as well. Soon thereafter began what for society and the people was an unfortunate and unpopular war with Japan. "How can a *muzhik* happily march off to battle to defend some leased piece of land in what to him is an unknown country?" asked P.A. Stolypin (at that time the Saratov governor) having in mind Port Arthur, which Russia leased from China. "A sacrificial impulse does not make this sad and difficult war more bearable."[13]

Before the war was over, revolution had arrived. At the height of the Revolution on 17 October 1905 a manifesto was published that promised to give the citizens of Russia political freedom and to create a legislative Duma. The elections to the Duma, while indirect and multilayered, nonetheless encompassed a fairly wide range of electors. The manifesto contained the proviso that the "further development of the principles of general electoral law" will remain with the newly established legislative order. At the same time a united government was created. Sergei Witte became the first chairman of the Council of Ministers.

At the beginning of 1906 a new edition of the "Fundamental Laws" was prepared. The word "absolute" was removed from the tsar's title. The State Council was reorganized into the upper legislative chamber. Half of its members were elected by the gentry societies, zemstvos, the orthodox clergy, industrialists, the universities, and the Academy of Sciences. The other half was appointed by the tsar. When the legislative chambers were not in session, the tsar could use his authority to enact any law that was urgently required, although he subsequently had to submit it to the legislature for approval. This was the infamous Article 87 of the Fundamental Laws. This power did not include the right to modify the laws governing elections to the Duma. Legal experts at the time pointed out that the 1906 edition of the Fundamental Laws partly resembled the Japanese constitution of that time.

The First Duma began its work on 27 April 1906. Contrary to prior predictions the creation of a parliament did not cause Russia to be "shattered to pieces." But the bureaucracy's lack of desire to work with the representative body quickly became apparent. The government, led in 1906 by I.L. Goremykin, cooperated with the Duma only begrudgingly, held up the introduction of legislative bills whenever possible (the first bill introduced by the government concerned the laundry at

Dorpat University),[14] and soon recommended dissolving the First Duma. After its dissolution P.A. Stolypin became the chairman of the Council of Ministers. He chose a different tactic. The government introduced an entire series of bills into the Second Duma, categorically insisting that the Duma preserve their basic provisions.

The majority of the members of the Duma rejected the government's ground rules, and consequently the government decided to change the electoral law to obtain a more subservient Duma. But it was illegal to make such a change without the Duma's consent; Article 87 in this case did not apply. On 3 June 1907, by dissolving the Second Duma and publishing a new Electoral Law, Stolypin's government violated the Fundamental Laws. This act went down in history as the June 3 *coup d'etat.* The government's coup did not immediately evoke any unpleasant consequences. The regime, however, had undermined its own legitimacy. This, in the end, sealed its fate.

The question of whether or not Russia was a constitutional state raised more than mere academic interest at that time; it was a pointed political question. Members of the government never used the word "constitution" in their official speeches. In an interview with the Saratov newspaper *Volga* in September 1909, Stolypin declared:

> The development of a purely Russian state structure, responsible to both the spirit of the people and to historic traditions, was foretold from the eminence of the throne by the Manifesto of October 17...
>
> The Sovereign gladly appealed to the people's representatives for cooperation. Is it possible to say after this that the people's representatives "snatched" something from the Tsar's power?[15]

In practice Stolypin's policy was to bring social "grassroots" local reforms to the forefront. His agrarian reform is by far the best known of all of his reforms. Far less well-known is that under Stolypin's leadership a series of reforms were developed for restructuring local government along non-estate principles. In place of the former volosts Stolypin suggested creating something like small zemstvo units. If previously the landowner was above the peasant, then Stolypin now wanted to place them side by side in the volost government. Power on the *uezd* level would be in the hands of an *uezd* official appointed by the government and responsible to it.

The situation for local reforms, however, became inauspicious. In the central non-black-earth provinces the amount of land owned by landowners dropped significantly for a variety of economic reasons. The enlightened and liberal gentry from the capital and adjacent provinces who lacked land poured into the ranks of the intelligentsia. In the gentry congresses, which took place regularly beginning in 1906, the prevailing tone was that of the southern gentry (from Kursk, Bessarabia, etc.), which was, on the whole, not so enlightened and not at all liberal. In any case, after the events of 1905-07 the gentry in general became much more conservative. Even in the non-black-earth provinces conservative elements emerged.

Beginning in 1907 at all the gentry congresses and at many of the gentry provincial assemblies sharp criticism of the local reforms proposed by the government could be heard. Encroachment upon the leadership role of the *uezd* marshal of the gentry evoked particular unhappiness. Representatives of the upper estate asserted that the government's plans would "destroy the institutions created by history and create new ones similar to the institutions of republican France that would democratize all local structures and annihilate the estate system." These plans, they argued, might "lead to the overthrow of the monarchy."[16] Energetic behind-the-scenes actions accompanied the public criticism. Many visible members of the gentry were present at court or became members of the State Council. The upper chamber was composed of an influential coalition of opponents to local reforms.

The State Council was reorganized in 1906 with the goal of creating a counter balance to the legislative Duma.

Accordingly, the government tried to expand the representation in the upper chamber of those groups of the population on whose support it believed it could rely. At the same time no mechanisms were envisaged that would allow a deadlock to be broken if irreconcilable differences of opinion arose between the two chambers of parliament. As a result a right-wing majority composed of aged bureaucrats and conservative landowners dominated the State Council. If they decided to be stubborn, neither the Duma nor the government could make them budge. Only the tsar, perhaps, could bring those members of the upper chamber whom he had appointed into line. Most often, however, the tsar's sympathies were on their side. Thus, the legislative machine was, in essence, unable to function. But no one really suspected this as long as the government and the Duma were fighting. Once this war was over the problem of the upper chamber came to light. Stolypin's government was unable to carry out a single major reform by a normal legislative path. The only reforms it was able to carry out were enacted under legislative emergency, according to Article 87, or through departmental instructions (as with the law of 29 May 1911 "On Land-Tenure Regulations").

The first bills in a series of local reforms that made their way through the Duma and were sent to the State Council bogged down there for a long time. At the height of the struggle with the upper chamber, in September 1911, Stolypin was killed. In May 1914 the State Council voted down a bill for volost reform, the first in a series of local reforms.

Russian historians have argued over the form and essence of the state structure of Russia in the final decades of the empire for a long time. The opinions expressed by E.D. Chermenskii and N.P. Eroshkin represent the most typical points of view.

In a very cautious way and with a number of reservations, Chermenskii leaned toward the idea that beginning in 1906 Russia had a constitutional structure, that a return to absolutism was impossible, and that the "evolution of autocracy toward a bourgeois monarchy" would have continued.[17] N.P. Eroshkin, on the other hand, believed that "the State Duma was literally not a legislative, but only a consultative institution that shielded the autocracy by pseudo-constitutional means."[18] Both points of view can be supported by a number of arguments. The first of them, however, seems to be too optimistic, while the second is somewhat oversimplistic. The Duma was a very poor "shield" when compared with the Supreme Soviet during the Bolshevik dictatorship, which always voted with unanimity. From a juridical point of view this question is indeed very difficult to resolve.

What is far clearer is that beginning with the Great Reforms, Russia set out on a path from the old estate-based society and an autocratic state toward a modern civil society and a state based on law. The process of modernization, as is well-known, also includes an industrial revolution, the introduction of market relations and of an advanced system of farming into the agricultural sector, and the widespread development of public education. In Russia the process of modernization proceeded at a slow pace and with breaks and stoppages. At times the temptation to develop a single facet of modernization (for example, creating large-scale industry) at the expense of all others won out. As a result the process of modernization in Russia was not confined to the optimal period of time — from the Crimean War to World War I. When Russia entered World War I some of its institutions had yet to acquire the necessary stability, while others had hopelessly decayed. Society was a mixture of former estates and new classes, and their interests and goals rarely coincided. This is why Russia was unable to endure the difficult ordeal of World War I and slid toward a national catastrophe that turned out to be long and arduous and whose consequences were extremely difficult to overcome.

In order to come closer to understanding the reasons for this change of events, one needs to examine the attitudes toward modernization of the most influential, active, or simply the most numerically significant classes, estates, and social groups. The most important of these was the gentry, next came the bureaucracy, then the peasantry, the working class, and the intelligentsia.

In Western Europe constitutionalism arose in the course of a struggle between the estates and royal power. Further, the aristocracy emerged at the head of the estates. The Russian gentry also played a part in the struggle for a constitutional limitation to autocracy. One needs only to recall the "Verkhovniki" of the eighteenth century, the Decembrists, or the gentry involved in the liberal movement from 1859 to 1904 to see that this was the case. The gentry in Russia, however, proved to be an inconsistent supporter of constitutionalism and the renewal of political institutions. From the beginning of the nineteenth century until the February Revolution, the gentry changed its position on this question three times (the last time was during the war when a gentry congress spoke out in favor of a Cabinet that would be responsible to the Duma). Moreover, the position of the gentry as a whole was highly conservative on the question of eliminating the estate system in the countryside. It seems that, for the most part, the gentry plays a positive role in modernization only during its earliest stages. To a significant degree this opportunity was lost in Russia.

I have already discussed the attitude of the bureaucracy towards a constitutional system. In general it should be said that of all the aspects of modernization the bureaucracy did advance the creation of modern large-scale industry. The attitude of the bureaucracy toward public education was highly contradictory (there was a pointed struggle on this question within the bureaucracy), but still more or less favorable. The accomplishments of the bureaucracy in the area of modernizing the countryside were not at all impressive, even keeping in mind Stolypin's agricultural reform. As far as the abolition of serfdom is concerned, it was the personal initiative of Alexander II, who relied on the most advanced part of the entire society, including a small group of liberal bureaucrats (who were shortly after joined by the bureaucracy itself). In general the modernization carried out at the hands of the bureaucracy was extremely one-sided, led to serious distortions in the social and political life of the country, and fostered a growing tension in society. The American investigator Tim McDaniel writes that "autocratic modernization in prerevolutionary Russia ... gave rise to class conflict more intense and persistent than in Western countries, where the contradictions of modernization were not so deep or unresolvable." One of the most important conclusions of McDaniel's book is:

> ... an autocratic regime's attempts to give birth to urban industrial society involve it and the society in a web of intractable contradictions. These contradictions, in turn, foster the emergence of revolutionary situations that, depending on the correlation of events, may culminate in revolutions.[19]

Ideas about the peasantry as a blind and ignorant force, the personification of the Acheron, are now to a large degree obsolete. McDaniel correctly points out that the peasantry did not play a leading role in the events of 1917.[20] At the beginning of the twentieth century the peasantry was ready to participate constructively in raising the level of Russia's agriculture. Literate peasants worked productively in the zemstvos and in their estate self-government. But not everything depended upon the peasants, and this was felt by the foremost representatives of this estate as well as by the ignorant and backward. The organization of relocations and of agricultural credit, equalizing the rights of all estates, solving the land problem (including limiting landowners latifundiums) — all this should have come from the outside. Years passed, the problems remained unresolved, life improved only marginally, and going to war made things even worse. The long passive expectation of "charity" from somewhere up above, from the city, could indeed give way to a spontaneous rebellion. It was usually the "urban" peasants who began to rebel, and then the sparks spread through the countryside. It was the factory worker, his brother-*muzhik*, whom the peasants trusted more than any of the other city dwellers. Thus, the "hegemony of the proletariat" was not just an invention of communist teleologists; it had a real underlying cause.

I have already spoken of the working class, which under the conditions in Russia was the offspring of industrial capitalism and the government bureaucracy. I pointed out its tendency to trust in any shrewd and conscientiously misleading demagogue. At the end of the nineteenth and beginning of the twentieth century the socialist intelligentsia very often and quite successfully assumed the role of such leaders of the blind.

The many judgments made of the Russian intelligentsia during its two-century history contain considerable criticism as well as praise, but very few sober evaluations. The intelligentsia was one of the main creators of the new Russian culture, which justly occupies a place in the family of European cultures. For a long time, however, the intelligentsia kept away from participating in politics. Their passive observation of how slowly things were going, of how discontinuous the process was, acted in a dispiriting way to push the intelligentsia toward an uncritical acceptance of utopian teachings, toward dogmatism, and toward developing a variety of plans for "saving humanity" in the full certainty of their right to implement them by any means. Even by the time of A.I. Herzen and N.G. Chernyshevskii a significant part of the Russian intelligentsia had become disillusioned with constitutionalism. Representative systems, from their point of view, worked too slowly and were too tedious; they wanted to solve all their problems in a single stroke with a social revolution. A dangerous infatuation for extremes developed in the Russian intelligentsia, which has not been overcome to this day. Herzen, who himself did not escape this infatuation, in the end made a very grim evaluation of it:

> We are exceedingly doctrinaire and argumentative. To this German propensity we add our own national, so to speak, *Arakcheevian* element — a mercilessness, an ardent

callousness, and an eagerness for butchery. Arakcheev flogged living peasants to death to satisfy his ideal of a grenadier guardsman; we flog to death ideas, the arts, humanity, former statesmen, anything we please. With a fearless front we march, step by step, *to the limit* and pass it by, never veering from our dialectical path, but only from the *truth*; unawares, we proceed further and further, forgetting that real sense and real understanding of life can only be found in stopping short of extremes....[21]

Of course, not all of the Russian intelligentsia held extreme views. At the beginning of the twentieth century, with the formation of the Kadet Party, centrist forces within the intelligentsia began to gain strength. But as before the left flank was too powerful. Its most decisive representatives played their part in pushing the country toward a national catastrophe, after which the people found themselves ruled by the same bureaucracy and bureaucratized revolutionaries.

It seems, then, that the constitutional idea in Russia in the nineteenth and early twentieth centuries lost two important battles: 14 December 1825, after which the bureaucracy grew and intensified, and 1 March 1881 when Alexander III came to power and then initiated a policy of narrow-minded industrialization, and consequently in the largest cities the working class became numerically dominant.

The Revolution, the Civil War, and subsequent events swept entire estates and classes out of Russian life, while others became unrecognizable. But the old problems returned. The process of modernization in Russia is far from over. The drama continues.

Translated from Russian by Gregory D. Crowe

Notes

1 S.V. Mironenko, *Samoderzhavie i reformy: politicheskaia bor'ba v Rossii v nachale XIX v.* (Moscow: Nauka, 1989), pp. 29-33.

2 N.K. Shil'der, *Imperator Aleksandr Pervyi: ego zhizn' i tsarstvovanie,* 2d ed., (St. Petersburg: A.S. Surovin, 1905), 3, pp. 34-48.

3 Mironenko, *Samoderzhavie i reformy*, pp. 184-197.
4 N.M. Druzhinin, *Revoliutsionnoe dvizhenie v Rossii v XIX v.* (Moscow: Nauka, 1985), p. 269. In an appendix to his monograph entitled "Dekabrist Nikita Murav'ev," Druzhinin includes the full text of Murav'ev's "Constitution." G.V. Vernadskii was the first to point out the close tie between the "Constitutional Charter" and Murav'ev's constitution (see *Izvestiia Tavricheskogo universiteta* (Simferopol') 1 (1919), pp. 140-141). In a monograph written in 1931 Druzhinin decisively rejects this view (see Druzhinin, *Revoliutsionnoe dvizhenie*, pp. 194-195). For some reason he believed that the primary influence on Murav'ev came from the state constitutions of North America. He did not include the "Constitutional Charter," which was born in government offices, in this circle of "bourgeois" constitutions out of the fear, it seems, that it might damage the reputation of the Decembrists. S.V. Mironenko, who contends that it is indisputable that Murav'ev was familiar with the Novosil'tsov-Viazemskii work, still leans toward Druzhinin's view on the fundamental difference between the two works (Mironenko, *Samoderzhavie i reformy*, p. 224). Just because Murav'ev introduced improvements into his version of the constitution, however, does not mean that the two works are unrelated.
5 A.E. Rozen, *Zapiski dekabrista* (Irkutsk: Vostochno-Sibirskoe knizhnoe izd.-vo, 1984), p. 138.
6 P.A. Zaionchkovskii, *Pravitel'stvennyi apparat samoderzhavnoi Rossii v XIX v.* (Moscow: Mysl', 1978), pp. 67-68.
7 See N.M. Korkunov, *Russkoe gosudarstvennoe pravo*, 2 volumes (St. Petersburg: Tsinzerling, 1893-97) and N.I. Lazarevskii, *Lektsii po russkomu gosudarstvennomu pravu*, 2 volumes (St. Petersburg: tip. "Slovo," 1910).
8 Marc Raeff, *Speransky: Statesman of Imperial Russia* (The Hague: M. Nijhoff, 1957), p. 325. See also M. Polievktov, *Imperator Nikolai I* (St. Petersburg, 1914).
9 P.A. Zaionchkovskii, *Pravitel'stvennyi apparat*, p. 109. See also M. Polievktov, *Imperator Nikolai I*.
10 For more detail see: P.N. Zyrianov, "Sotsial'naia struktura mestnogo upravleniia kapitalisticheskoi Rossii (1861 - 1914 gg.)," *Istoricheskie zapiski* (1982) 107, pp. 226-302.
11 A.A. Kornilov, *Obshchestvennoe dvizhenie pri Aleksandre II 1855-1881: istoricheskie ocherki* (Paris: Izd. red. "Osvobozhdeniia," 1905), pp. 91-94, 133-34, 141-42.
12 *Istoriia SSSR s drevneishikh vremen do nashikh dnei*, 12 volumes, first series, (Moscow: Nauka, 1968), 5, p. 312.
13 M.P. Bok, *Vospominaniia o moem ottse P.A. Stolypine* (New York: Izd. im. Chekhova, 1953), p. 128.

14 S.M. Sidel'nikov, *Obrazovanie i deiatel'nost' I Gosudarstvennoi dumy* (Moscow, 1962), p. 236.

15 *Volga* (Saratov), 1 October 1909.

16 *Moskovskie vedomosti*, 25 January 1908.

17 E.D. Chermenskii, *Istoriia SSSR, period imperializma* (Moscow: Prosveshchenie, 1965), pp. 250, 313; idem, *Burzhuaziia i tsarizm v pervoi russkoi revoliutsii*, 2d ed., (Moscow: Mysl', 1970), pp. 146, 410.

18 N.P. Eroshkin, *Istoriia gosudarstvennykh uchrezhdenii dorevoliutsionnoi Rossii*, 3d ed., (Moscow: Vysshaia shkola, 1983), p. 264.

19 Tim McDaniel, *Autocracy, Modernization and Revolution in Russia and Iran* (Princeton: Princeton University Press, 1991), pp. 223-224, 227.

20 Ibid., 223.

21 A.I. Gertsen, *Sobranie sochinenii v 30 tomakh* (Moscow: Izd. Akademii nauk SSSR, 1956), 10, p. 320.

Chapter 7

Land-Owning Nobles and Zemstvo Institutions: The Post-Reform Estate System in Political Perspective

Yutaka TAKENAKA

The Japanese Historiography of Russia in the Postwar Era

Japanese historians have devoted a great deal of energy to research in two major fields of Russian history; the first of those is agrarian and peasant history. In particular, the village commune of the late nineteenth and early twentieth centuries has attracted much attention in the postwar historiography of Russia. It would seem that for Japanese Russia specialists, the peasantry remains both the most mysterious and the most interesting social group. The radical intelligentsia and factory workers are also popular, but less than the peasantry. Indeed, other sectors of society have been neglected or ignored, and we have hardly any monographs about them.

The second major field that has commanded our attention is intellectual history. A variety of intellectual themes have intrigued many Japanese specialists of Russian history. One of the most likely reasons for this is that although we previously were not in an advantageous position with regard to access to original sources indispensable for research into political or social history, the disadvantage for intellectual historians was less severe. They could commence their work with only some well-revised books of the thinkers or social activists they were interested in. The revision of texts was seen as basically a job for Russian historians.

Japanese scholars of Russian intellectual history can be rightfully proud of quite a few excellent monographs on famous Russian thinkers and their writings. We should do some critical self-reflection here, however, in that there were some unfortunate consequences of our excessive preoccupation with intellectual history. We have tended to overestimate the significance of intellectual aspects in Russia's development, and possibly the role of the intelligentsia itself, in our attempts to understand the Imperial period of Russian history as a whole. We sometimes have confused pictures of these times drawn by the intelligentsia with historical reality, without submitting such perspectives to sufficiently rigorous analysis. We allowed the interpretations of the intelligentsia to shape our own interpretations of each era with few questions or modifications. Our analyses of the political process thus tended to be oversimplified, and everything was too easily explained as having been the result of ideological struggles between progressive and conservative forces.

As for our study of intellectual history itself, it must also be admitted that there has probably been some bias stemming from our own political ideologies. Naturally, Russian conservatives were unpopular in Japan, while Decembrists, revolutionary democrats, revolutionary populists, and others were regarded with some measure of sympathy. Certain great novelists and historians of conservative political persuasion, as well as (since the 1970s) Slavophiles and conservative Westernizers, have been accepted as worthy of serious research. However, unmistakable "ideologues of autocracy" such as M.N. Katkov and K.P. Pobedonostsev have not attracted much interest from historians, despite their sizable historical influence.

Another characteristic of Japanese studies of intellectual history is that it tends to be deeply moralistic. Great importance has been attached to the sincerity of subjects as human beings, their aloofness from material motivations and worldly fame, a critical and militant attitude against repressive policies of the tsarist government, and above all their sympathy for the common people and their miseries. Ethical purity has been preferred to accommodating pragmatism, the latter being seen as indicative of weakness rather than of political wisdom.

Consequently, revolutionary populists have been viewed as praiseworthy by every standard of evaluation which Japanese historians employed. Such populists were motivated by a high moralistic spirit even in the realm of politics. Their political action reflected their self-image of being agents of the people's will. As such, they aspired to realize the perfect embodiment of the people's will, rather than to achieve a stable political development which might have contributed more to the future welfare of the people.[1] Yet their ethical sincerity, reflected in their self-sacrifice and devotion to the cause of the people's salvation, deeply moved many intellectuals in post-war Japan.

Japanese historians generally looked upon the populist movement of the 1870s with respect and sympathy, and indeed they have done much to deepen our understanding of the populist ideas of the late nineteenth century.[2] Influenced as they were by the populist political thinking of that era, however, Japanese historians too readily granted the effectiveness and validity of political activism without fully considering the impact of such activity within the broader context of Russia's political development. The political thinking of that era in fact neglected the practical aspects of national development, and yet this has not been questioned by Japanese academics. It was apparently taken for granted that long-range, abstract ideals were superior to more mundane actions aimed at improving the concrete conditions of everyday life.

State-Society Relations and Local Administration

Japanese historians have tended to oversimplify explanations of the problems relating to Russia's political development, and some aspects have been completely overlooked in spite of their significance to the political modernization of Russia. One of great importance is the subject of public administration in the development of modern Russia, a subject which has not been much discussed by Japanese historians. Simple images of Russia's public administration have dominated the Japanese historiography.

For example, it is a widely accepted view (in Japan) that Imperial Russia was a bureaucratic society where every policy was dictated from above by administrative orders and police measures. This view reflects the traditional theory of the Russian state and society, which holds that in Russia everything was done from above (as contrasted with the West, where initiative for change often came from below).

This view now appears stereotypical and requires modification. Of course, in pre-modern societies there were virtually no active national organizations other than the state bureaucracy, the military, and religious institutions. It is not at all strange that these organizations should dominate "front stage" in public affairs. Any political regime cannot, however, survive without some sort of support from society. Governments need to institutionalize the voluntary support and cooperation of societies in some way or other; the Russian government was no exception.[3]

The necessity for cooperation from society was all the more urgent because the Russian bureaucracy was too inefficient to be called a modern bureaucracy *per se*, or to have accomplished its administrative functions entirely satisfactorily. In fact, it is considered to have frequently hindered rather than promoted social development. Therefore, Russian society in the Imperial period was in this sense extremely "under-governed," and the central government did not have adequate instruments at its disposal for effective policy-implementation.

Of course, we should not simply think that the Russian bureaucracy remained unchanged throughout the Imperial period. Significant changes in the first half of the nineteenth century should not be overlooked, such as the increasing importance that was being attached to higher education in the promotion of officials, and changes in the functional organization of the government through the development of the ministerial system.[4] Indeed, this process of bureaucratic development has attracted the interest of social historians; one of the conclusions they have reached through their study of Russian officialdom is that officials were being separated from the landed nobility (in terms of lifestyle, outlook, and consciousness) during the reign of Nicholas I. As the bureaucracy grew larger, the percentage of nobles in the bureaucracy as a whole decreased. Additionally, more officials came to depend upon their salaries, rather than income from fixed assets and property. As far as high officials were concerned, their educational background displayed a shift from home education (the traditional style of the landed nobility) to school education at universities, the Lyceum, and the Juridical School.[5] These salient facts suggest that officials of this era should not simply be regarded as agents of the land-owning estate. Neither should we, however, conclude that Russian officialdom of that period was exclusively oriented to public welfare. The state bureaucracy remained a sort of particularistic entity (*soslovie*), relatively closed and self-regenerating, even though it had undergone considerable institutionalization by the late nineteenth century.[6]

It is not at all strange that Imperial Russia did not have a genuine bureaucracy for a long time. Pre-modern society generally does not have the human resources necessary for efficient administration because of low living and educational standards which characterize that historical phase. It is virtually impossible to staff a bureaucracy with public-spirited and well-educated officials in a society which lacks a modern educational system, or to expect those officials to give priority to "national interest" or "public welfare."[7]

Nonetheless, each society must solve innumerable practical problems to achieve modern political life: convenient transportation and communication, primary education, a modicum social welfare, food supply, public safety, and so forth. Social and political stability depend upon the extent to

which these basic administrative tasks are carried out, and
these tasks often depend on administration, particularly at the
local level, for their realization. Therefore, efficient local
administration is vital for political development. Since the
Russian state bureaucracy did not have sufficient resources for
that purpose, it needed the assistance of an influential sector
of society to institutionalize state-society cooperation in the
last half of the nineteenth century.

It is not uncommon for a state bureaucracy to try to use or
rely on influential and loyal sectors of society in the process of
modernization. Japan also had similar institutions for so-
called "local self-government" in the Meiji era, formed under
the strong ideological influence of the famous German jurist R.
von Gneist and the direct guidance of his disciple A. Mosse.
Russia introduced a similar apparatus called zemstvo
institutions in 1864 three years after the abolishment of
serfdom.[8] The new administrative system introduced as part
of the Great Reforms was based on a dualistic principle,
consisting of the state bureaucracy and the zemstvo
institutions. The latter were established to complement the
former (since the state bureaucracy lacked both fiscal funds
and human resources for improving local conditions) and to
facilitate the bureaucracy's basic tasks by enlisting the help of
influential people of each estate (the landed nobility,
peasantry, clergy, and townspeople) without undermining
central government control over local society.[9]

In pre-reform Russia, only a small number of estate
representatives had been allowed to join local administrations.
Now, broader cooperation was required by the state
bureaucracy, and the situation in post-reform Russia required
special entities composed of estate representatives to
coordinate various conflicting interests. Even (ex-serf)
peasant representatives were expected to join these newly
established authorities. Indeed, this was not an attempt to
eliminate the traditional framework of social regimentation
— the estate (*soslovie*) system — but to make it more flexible
and efficient under the idea of "all-estateness." The state

bureaucracy and the zemstvo institutions each had their own unique functions and complemented each other. Both were integral parts of the whole administrative system.[10] The executive boards of zemstvo institutions played an important role in mediating between the state bureaucracy and the local representative assemblies. Some executive board chairmen were promoted to provincial governors, as were numerous marshals of the nobility.[11]

There were, of course, frequent conflicts between the zemstvos and the state bureaucracy, but these should not be interpreted in terms of the rather stale theory of local self-government being threatened by repressive government control.[12] This theory, attractive to those of liberal persuasion, needs to be revised on the basis of concrete historical analysis. The fact is that self-government as an ideal model was still little more than a dream in post-reform Russian society. The society still needed the authority of the central government and its local agents. That being the case, the dual system for local administration was well-suited to the reality of administrative capabilities then in existence. Internal friction should be understood more in view of the natural conflicts likely to arise when overlapping jurisdictions occurred, and examined in terms of the specific circumstances prevailing in each case.[13]

The administrative reforms of the 1860s brought about changes in the estate system as well. Originally, Russia's estate system was quite different from its Western counterparts. There were no cohesive groups with the clear collective consciousness and social basis to be called "estates" in a Western sense, but rather a number of different legal categorizations of the people for different administrative purposes. It is difficult to imagine that such estates in Russia would have been supporters of European-type constitutionalism.

The Great Reforms of the 1860s and early 1870s reorganized and simplified the estate system. Minor distinctions were eliminated and the barriers between estates became lower. Above all, the greatest prop of the old estate system — serfdom — was finally abolished. The *raison d'être* of the estate system came into question as the social structure grew too complex to provide each "estate" with a distinct social identity in the post-reform period.[14]

There can be no doubt that the estate system was a hindrance to efficient government, because it divided the nation into numerous categories having particular rights and obligations, thus making administration more complex than it might otherwise have been. Furthermore, the estate system prevented formation of the unified, cohesive national consciousness which is indispensable for a modern state, since it encouraged each estate to view itself as possessing a distinct identity.

On the other hand, the estate system was expected to deter the rapid development of excessive social mobility, and thus act as a bulwark against the social instability and disorder which social modernization and the development of capitalist production might cause. The new diversified social relationships produced a variety of new classes and other social groups, all of which heightened the government's fear of losing control over society. Social classes were a phenomenon which evolved naturally, without the help of any edicts or government circulars, and were much more difficult for the government to control than estates. Reinforcement of the estate system (which was basically a legal entity dependent on the government's will) could be seen as a rational means taken to cope with these difficulties, despite the conflicting wish to abolish the system in the interest of efficient government and the creation of a national ethos.

Special legal and administrative treatment of estates was considered indispensable to the control of rural society in particular. This in fact was the reason why the Ministry of Internal Affairs, responsible for keeping rural society peaceful, consistently supported the estate system until it became a matter of doubt whether the estate system was really suited for that purpose in the twentieth century.[15]

The Landed Nobility in the Post-reform Period

The most important estates in the post-reform era were the hereditary nobility and the peasantry. Each had their own estate institutions which helped them maintain their integrity. The other estates were much less significant in political and social terms than those two. It was therefore a task of vital importance to the tsarist regime itself to maintain a stable relationship between the hereditary nobles and the peasants.

The noble estate did not exactly coincide with the landowners as a social class. This is the reason the term "nobility" is more appropriate than "gentry" for the Russian *dvorianstvo*.[16] These essentially overlapped to a great extent, but were not completely identical; areas of divergence increased and broadened as the deep social changes which accompanied urbanization proceeded in the post-reform era.[17] The estate institutions, estate consciousness, and shared cultural tradition may have worked to enhance the cohesiveness of the noble estate, but the legal segmentation imposed by the state increasingly failed to reflect the social and economic diversity of a modernizing society. Certain conflicting elements were emerging within the noble estate.

The core of the noble estate was, however, still the middle-ranking landed nobility residing in the countryside. The crisis facing this sector of the nobility was serious from a conservative point of view; strengthening its social stature was seen as essential for the stability of the countryside. The objective of the counter-reforms of Alexander III's reign (introduction of land captains and the creation of the new zemstvo) was in effect to re-establish the estate system and the paternalistic authority of the noble estate in the countryside for administrative purposes. This was not being requested by the local nobility, but was motivated by bureaucratic considerations. This strategy entailed mobilization of the landed nobility to supervise peasant administration, along with the revitalization of stagnant zemstvos. The latter step it was hoped, would diminish the influence of the small number of political activists who might divert the zemstvos from their assigned tasks.[18] Politically, wealthy nobles were expected to form a faithful conservative bloc in the zemstvo institutions and lead them in the directions the government wanted. Even consistent supporters of bureaucratic control over zemstvos (such as D.A. Tolstoi) never believed that they could do without the zemstvo institutions as an instrument for obtaining the general cooperation of society.[19] From his point of view, this cooperation was not inconsistent with strict control by the Ministry of Internal Affairs.

In the 1880s, there appeared another program, put forth by V.P. Meshchersky and M.N. Katkov, which attempted to merge the two categories of nobles and landowners in an artificial way by keeping noble lands in noble hands, but this plan was not very realistic. Even the Noble Land Bank (established in 1885 to provide financial assistance to the landed nobility towards this end) was allotted a much more limited role than Meshchersky and Katkov had expected.[20]

The nobility was expected to be a rural estate from a liberal point of view as well. One popular idea regarding the future of the nobility in the early post-reform period was for it to become involved in leadership at the local level. Officials were not considered qualified for the demanding task of adjusting local society to the new conditions of the post-reform era. It was thus thought that this role should be exercised out by influential nobles who were public-spirited and wealthy enough to devote themselves to public affairs.[21] Indeed, in England the existence of such a thick social stratum comprised by an independent political class (the gentry) is thought to have been an important factor in modern English political development. Assignment of such a role to the nobility, it was expected, would erode the rigid estate system in the future.

B.N. Chicherin (the famous liberal professor) firmly insisted that the noble estate should be maintained. He did not expect the nobility to form a social class with particular economic interests, but rather to be an able and cultivated estate which could be responsible for local administration.[22] In his view, the well-educated, public-spirited, and politically moderate people in society would be powerless to check the arbitrary use of authority if they were dispersed. The estate system was thus convenient because it provided a structure for bringing such people together into coherent groups, even if in an artificial way. Chicherin believed that established institutions could serve liberal purposes, even though these had been invented by the government. In his views on the future of the country, he was not very far from the mainstream of reasoning current at that time.

To be public-spirited local leaders, however, proved to be a much heavier burden for the Russian nobles than had been anticipated. A number of necessary conditions had to be fulfilled in order for the nobles to be successful as social leaders. Among the most fundamental of these was that the nobility had to have social prestige and be politically active on the one hand, while retaining harmonious economic relations with various social groups on the other. As for social prestige, the Russian nobility was originally an estate for state service, and it had no other resource or means of generating social prestige. The increasingly urbanized lifestyle and consciousness of a large portion of the nobility, along with the subsequent decline in their interest in agrarian management and rural welfare (all brought about by the new economic conditions) more and more tended to undermine their sources of social prestige in the countryside.[23]

The nobles were not accustomed to political life, either. We should not overestimate the historical significance of the noble constitutional movement that took place after the abolishment of serfdom. Although most nobles were dissatisfied with the legislation of 1861, they did not know how to oppose it through political activity. Appeals for greater constitutional and political rights were too roundabout to save them from the immediate difficulty which was their real concern, and most nobles could not afford to seriously engage in politics.[24]

It was the zemstvo assemblies that might have served as the institutional base for the nobles' social leadership. In most provinces and districts, however, zemstvo assemblies were inactive until the 1890s.[25] Zemstvos were managed not by assemblies of estate representatives but by executive boards in close contact with the state bureaucracy. With the exception of a small number of political activists, most ordinary nobles tended to be indifferent to zemstvo activities and indeed to most political questions.[26] As a result, whether "zemstvo liberalism" was real or illusory is a question of secondary significance when taken in the context of this basic trend or situation. Each social group did not always have a clear-cut ideology, and the estate system itself was not a serious issue either, as long as the economic interests of the various groups were not threatened.

Most nobles were also indifferent to aristocratic ideologies in the post-reform era. Periodicals sympathetic to the privileged nobility, such as *Nashe Vremia* and *Vest'*, could not even obtain the support of ordinary nobles, these publications suffered financially and were short-lived.[27] This reflects the fact that aristocratic ideals did not resound beyond the small circle of aristocrats, so their influence on society at large was also limited. The last half of the nineteenth century was a period in which nationalism and populism were the dominant ideologies. The tension between and fusion of these two ideologies ultimately brought about what may be seen as uniquely Russian ideological dynamics. These dynamics, however, operated to the disadvantage of aristocratic ideals[28] because such ideals directly conflicted with populism, and were difficult to combine with nationalism given the cosmopolitan character of Russia's nobility and its responsibility for the long history of Westernization.[29]

In regard to harmonious economic relations with other social groups, the land problem (which framed the landed nobility-peasantry conflict and ultimately the fate of the noble estate itself) was still somewhat latent in the early post-reform period. Though there are different views about how firmly the landed nobility resisted the abolishment of serfdom, it is unquestionable that this reform created difficulties for most middle-ranking nobles. These difficulties were primarily due to a reduction in the labor force and the shortage of funds which resulted from the abolition. The land question was still secondary.

Nevertheless, land ownership did comprise the core of the nobles economic interests and this isolated them from the peasantry, who comprised the overwhelming majority of the rural population. Owing to the seriousness of the land question, the economic interests of peasants and land-owning nobles became more difficult to reconcile towards the end of the nineteenth century. Once that question became politicized in the late Imperial period, differences in political opinion lost their significance within the political activity of the landed nobility. They realized that they had to defend their economic interests by with all possible means. Both the corporate and zemstvo institutions should serve them.[30] The government had already abandoned any intention of maintaining their local hegemony at all costs. Nevertheless, confronted with the wave of democratization and land reform, the landed nobility could not depart from the old order based on autocracy and the estate system.

Comparisons of Russia and Japan

The Russian government attempted to use landed nobles to improve the poor situation of local administration and in peasant-control mechanisms, though the nobles proved incapable of performing such roles. The corporate institutions of the noble estate and zemstvo institutions were useful instruments for the government in its efforts to garner the support and cooperation of society in times of social mobilization. For the landed nobility, those institutions functioned as instruments for expressing their cohesiveness and power when their vital interests seemed endangered. These institutions did not, however, have the power to create a new stratum of independent social leaders in the countryside. The government did not wish to see formation of independent social forces in the early phase of modernization. Neither did landed nobles themselves appear willing or able to form a new political class; as they became increasingly preoccupied with their own narrow interests, their historical role deteriorated, and finally became completely submerged in the October Revolution.

Russia's nobility was too weak to emerge as a political class and coordinate conflicting interests in the countryside. They were really no less estranged from the peasantry than were state officials — too estranged to influence the peasantry for common local interests. To a considerable extent, this helps to explain some of the difficulties that Russian society experienced in the process of political development in this period.[31] And interestingly, this weakness and thinness of the rural elite class was a feature common to both Russia and Japan in the early phase of modernization. Neither had a strong land-owning class which could control rural society and assist the state bureaucracy. This is one area in which these two countries differed remarkably from England, and from Prussia, whose self-government of *Honoratioren* (notables) they took as their model.

This difficulty was, however, less serious in Japan than in Russia. A stratum of wealthy farmers had taken shape below the traditional ruling warrior class before the process of modernization really got underway in Japan. Land ownership by members of the warrior class had been so nominal that it was easily abolished by the government after the Meiji Restoration. There was not such a serious land question in Japan as that which Russian society had to confront, though it did become increasingly serious in the Taisho era (1912-1926). Furthermore, Japanese landowners had a more robust agrarian spirit than their Russian counterparts; in short, there were more reliable *Honoratioren* in Japan.[32] If this had not been the case, the government would not have established a parliamentary system on the basis of restricted suffrage as early as 1889, the year after local reforms had been carried out, and well before large-scale industrial development began (around the turn of the century). Japan was fortunate in that it completed its political reform well before industrialization got under way, and prior to the deep social changes brought about by the Russo-Japanese War.

Russian society experienced a rather different process of historical development. It was after the rapid industrialization and the First Revolution that Russia began a new phase of political life with the establishment of the Duma. This new political entity had to manage the abrasive conflicts of a society in great flux, a problem which Japan had only tackled after somewhat more practice and experience with representative government.

Of course, we cannot merely ascribe the different experiences of Japan and Russia to the differences between the latter's nobility and the former's land-owning class in economic, social, and political terms. It seems certain, however, that the study of the Russian nobility is useful in elucidating various aspects which have not been sufficiently treated in the history of Imperial Russia. It might be that we, Japanese historians, could use our knowledge of the Japanese modern period towards deepening the understanding of the Russian nobility and its role in political development.

The political development of Russia and Japan presents a variety of possibilities for comparative studies that have not yet been attempted. If we were to become more interested in considering the political and administrative aspects of Russia's modernization, we might contribute more to a deeper understanding of the history of Imperial Russia. Our past work in Russian history might also be seen in a new perspective and lead us towards a more fruitful historical interpretation of that period of Russia's development.

Notes

1 Samuel P. Huntington, "Political Development and Political Decay," *World Politics,* 17 (1965), pp. 411-412.

148   Yutaka Takenaka

2 Eiichi Hizen et al, "Japanische Forschungen zur russischen Geschichte in Vergangenheit und Gegenwart," *Jahrbücher für Geschichte Osteuropas,* 33 (1985), p. 552.

3 Views of the "police state" are closely connected with the question of state-society relations in Imperial Russia — see Richard Pipes, *Russia under the Old Regime* (Harmondsworth, Middlesex, 1977), chap. 11; and Marc Raeff, *The Well-Ordered Police State: Social and Institutional Change through Law in the Germanies and Russia, 1600-1880* (New Haven and London, 1983), pp. 251-257 (epilogue).

4 George L. Yaney, *The Systematization of Russian Government: Social Evolution in the Domestic Administration of Imperial Russia, 1711-1905* (Urbana, Illinois, 1973), chap. 5.

5 Walter M. Pintner, "The Russian Higher Civil Service on the Eve of the Great Reforms," *Journal of Social History,* 8 (1975), pp. 63-64; v. a., "The Social Characteristics of the Early Nineteenth Century Russian Bureaucracy," *Slavic Review,* 29 (1979), pp. 438-443; v. a., "Civil officialdom and the Nobility in the 1850s," in: Walter M. Pintner & Don K. Rowney (eds.), *Russian Officialdom: The Bureaucratization of Russian Society from the Seventeenth to the Twentieth Century* (Chapel Hill, 1980), pp. 245-249.

6 Hans J. Torke, "Continuity and Change in the Relations between Bureaucracy and Society in Russia, 1613-1861," *Canadian Slavic Studies,* 5 (1971), pp. 474-475; Richard G. Robbins, Jr., "Choosing the Russian Governors: The Professionalization of the Gubernatorial Corps," *Slavonic and East European Review,* 58 (1980), pp. 554-560.

7 Marc Raeff, "Russian Autocracy and Its Officials," *Harvard Slavic Studies,* 4 (1957), pp. 77-91; John P. LeDonne, *Absolutism and Ruling Class: The Formation of the Russian Political Order 1700-1825* (Oxford, 1991), pp. 42-60.

8 Some publicists of Russia were under the strong influence of Gneist's anglophilism when they considered the problem of self-government and took a great interest in the English model of self-government. See V.A. Kitaev, *Ot frondy k okhranitel'stvu: Iz istorii russkoi liberal'noi mysli 50-60-kh godov XIX veka* (Moscow, 1972), pp. 113-116, 141-145.

9 Yaney, *op. cit.,* p. 346; Thomas S. Pearson, *Russian Officialdom in Crisis: Autocracy and Local Self-Government, 1861-1900* (Cambridge, 1989), p. 246.

10 One effect of the zemstvo institutions upon Russia's estate-based society was the evolution of a new stratum of professional persons of differing social origins: teachers, physicians, agrarian experts, and statisticians. The zemstvo institutions developed human resources and provided public-spirited young people a place where they could do something useful for the people.

11 Roberta Thompson Manning, "The Zemstvo and Politics, 1864-1914," in: Terence Emmons and Wayne S. Vucinich (eds.), *The Zemstvo in Russia: An Experiment in Local Self-Government* (Cambridge, 1982), p. 138; Richard G. Robbins, Jr., *The Tsar's Viceroys: Russian Provincial Governors in the Last Years of the Empire* (Ithaca, New York, 1987), p. 35.

12 For example, see I.P. Belokonskii, *Zemstvo i konstitutsiia* (Moscow, 1910), pp. 5-38.

13 The situation changed remarkably in the mid-1890s. See Richard G. Robbins, Jr., *Famine in Russia 1891-1892: The Imperial Government Responds to a Crisis* (New York and London, 1975), pp. 180-183; Manning, op. cit., pp. 134-145. My understanding of the relations between the state bureaucracy and the zemstvos is generally based on Prof. Matsuzato's theory on Russian local government. See Kimitaka Matsuzato, "Typological Analysis of Tsarist Local Government: Governors and Zemstvos," in Osamu Ieda (ed.), *New Order in Post-Communist Eurasia* (Sapporo, 1993), pp. 68-74.

14 Gregory L. Freeze, "The *Soslovie* (Estate) Paradigm and Russian Social History," *American Historical Review*, 91 (1986), pp. 25-35.

15 Francis William Wcislo, *Reforming Rural Russia: State, Local Society, and National Politics, 1855-1914* (Princeton, New Jersey, 1990), pp. 306-309.

16 Daniel Field, *The End of Serfdom: Nobility and Bureaucracy in Russia, 1855-1861* (Cambridge, Mass., 1976), p. xi.

17 Earlier Soviet historiography has tended to overlook this difference and has not paid enough attention to diversity among the nobility or to the 'new breed' of nobles who embraced new political ideas and attitudes. The noble estate has often been simply identified with the land-owning class. The problem of defining the nobility is, however, more complicated because it involves not only economic interests, but also class consciousness, political inclinations, cultural preferences, and so forth.

18 James I. Mandel, "Paternalistic Authority in the Russian Countryside, 1856-1906," Ph.D. dissertation (Columbia University, 1978), pp. 5-6; George Yaney, *The Urge to Mobilize: Agrarian Reform in Russia, 1861-1930* (Urbana, 1982), pp. 70-75.

19 Pearson, *op. cit.*, pp. 211-212, 227-229.

20 G.M. Hamburg, *Politics of the Russian Nobility, 1881-1905* (New Brunswick, New Jersey, 1984), pp. 116-117.

21 K.D. Kavelin, "Dvorianstvo i osvobozhdenie krest'ian," in: *Sobranie sochinenii,* vol. II (Moscow, 1898), pp. 134-135; A.I. Koshelev, *Golos iz zemstva* (Moscow, 1869), pp. 44-47; Kitaev, *op. cit.*, pp. 160-163.

22 B.N. Chicherin, *Neskol'ko sovremennykh voprosov* (Moscow, 1862), pp. 257-258.

23 Dominic Lieven, *The Aristocracy in Europe, 1815-1914* (Houndmills and London, 1992), pp. 95-96.

24 N.I. Iordanskii, *Konstitutsionnoe dvizhenie 60-kh godov* (St. Petersburg, 1906), pp. 108-110.

25 B.B. Veselovskii, *K voprosu o klassovykh interesakh v zemstve* (St. Petersburg, 1905), pp. 1-4; Yaney, *The Systematization..*, pp. 349-351.

26 Manning, *op. cit.*, pp. 139-140.

27 V.G. Chernukha, *Pravitel'stvennaia politika v otnoshenii pechati. 60-70-e gody XIX veka* (Leningrad, 1989), pp. 105-106, 123-125.

28 Most advocates of aristocratic ideals justified the nobility's privileges on the grounds of legalism and its close relationship to the autocratic monarchy. See N.A. Bezobrazov, *Predlozheniia dvorianstvu* (Berlin, 1862), p. vi and *Sliianie soslovii ili dvorianstvo, drugie sostoianiia i zemstvo* (St. Petersburg, 1870), pp. 127-134. For an attempt to unite aristocratic ideals and nationalism, see R.A. Fadeev, *Russkoe obshchestvo v nastoiashchem i budushchem (Chem nam byt'?)* (St. Petersburg, 1874).

29 Alfred J. Rieber, "Interest-Group Politics in the Era of the Great Reforms," in: Ben Eklof et al. (eds.), *Russia's Great Reforms, 1855-1881* (Bloomington & Indianapolis, 1994), pp. 76-77.

30 Manning, *op. cit.*, pp. 160-168. But zemstvo institutions never became a simple instrument of the landed nobility. See Kimitaka Matsuzato, "Teisei Rosia no Tihou Seido (Local Government in Late Imperial Russia): 1889-1917," *Suravu Kenkyu (Slavic Studies)*, 40(1993), pp. 175-177.

31 Barrington Moore, Jr., *Social Origins of Dictatorship and Democracy* (Harmondsworth, Middlesex, 1977), pp. 459-460; Lieven, *op. cit.*, pp. 224-228.

32 Moore, *op. cit.*, pp. 280-285.

Chapter 8

Stalin, Politburo, and Its Commissions in the Soviet Decision-making Process in the 1930s

Takeshi TOMITA

More than two and a half years have passed since the Russian archives, especially those of the former CPSU (*RTsKhIDNI* and *TsKhSD*), were opened to the public. Many Russian and foreign scholars have since perused archival documents and published interesting articles and books about Collectivization, the mass deportations of peasants and nationalities, the Great Terror, and other subjects.[1]

However, as is well known, these documents contain their own "secrets," namely the descriptions *"Reshenie — osobaia papka* (decision — into the special file)" concerning the affairs of diplomacy, national defense, state security, and other sectors. Thus, even today, we cannot completely follow the Soviet top-level decision-making (and policy implementation) process.[2]

Here I would like to present a sketch of the general Soviet decision-making process in the 1930s, along with case studies based upon research into the protocols of meetings, part of the protocols of *Sovnarkom* (SNK) meetings, and protocols of meetings of the *Azov-Chernomore kraikom* (North Caucasus regional committee — until January 1934) bureau. The case study is limited to agricultural policy (see the SIPS papers of R.W. Davies' research group on the decision-making process via the Gosplan and the industrial ministries).[3]

1. The Soviet Decision-making Process in the 1930s

Needless to say, the Politburo of the Central Committee (CC) played a key role in the decision-making process under the conditions of a one-party state and democratic centralism. However, the manner in which the Politburo discussed and decided questions, especially after NEP, has remained almost unknown because of the confidentiality of archival documents.[4] We have received only fragments of information from the memoirs of Bazhanov (Stalin's personal secretary in the 1920s), Khrushchev, and some Soviet and foreign diplomats.[5]

Table 1: Attendance of principal Politburo and CC members at Politburo meetings

Periods and the number of sessions	33. 1. 16 ʃ (25 times) 34. 1. 20	34. 2. 20 ʃ (18 times) 35. 1. 3	35. 2. 22 ʃ (21 times) 36. 7. 19	36. 9. 1 ʃ (15 times) 39. 1. 29
Stalin	18	14	19	13
Molotov	24	15	20	15
Kaganovich, L.	23	16	18	12
Voroshilov	20	14	18	13
Mikoian	22	16	20	11
Andreev	20	13	15	8
Ordzhonikidze	18	11	14	3
Kirov	5	4	-	-
Zhdanov	2	12	12	9
Yezhov	-	7	17	15
Krupskaia	18	12	17	11
Litvinov	-	7	10	8
Mekhlis	-	16	15	9
Poskrebyshev	-	14	17	9
Piatakov	21	12	12	-
Khrushchev	-	14	20	7
Iagoda	19	14	16	1

*Kirov died in December 1934, and Ordzhonikidze in February 1937. Piatakov was arrested and Iagoda was discharged from people's commissar of internal affairs in September 1936.

According to Khrushchev's memoirs, Politburo meetings were held at fixed times on set days (he did not list these, but noted their length: 1-2 or more hours). In these participated, but only listening quietly, members of the CC and the Central Inspection Commission, according to a custom which originated during the Lenin period. There also were closed meetings, which only Politburo members could attend. Decisions were recorded in a special file; CC members could read them with special permission in the secret department of the CC. Molotov presided over Politburo meetings (Stalin himself presided after the War ended) and L. Kaganovich served as the *de facto* second secretary. The attendees discussed some questions still furiously, despite the monolithic image of Politburo in the 1930s. There even occurred such an extreme case that Ordzhonikidze nearly hit Rozengol'ts.[6] Khrushchev, elected a full member of the CC at the 17th Party Congress, participated in Politburo meetings as often as the principal Politburo members, until he was dispatched to Ukraine (cf. Table 1).[7]

The protocols of Politburo meetings prove the accuracy of Khrushchev's memoirs. Meetings were to be held regularly three times a month (on the 5th, 15th, and 25th), but in fact they were held irregularly and less often (24 times in 1933, 17 in 1934, 16 in 1935, 9 in 1936, 7 in 1937, 4 in 1938, 2 in 1939, and 2 in 1940). Participants in these meetings were full and candidate members of the Politburo (10 and 5, respectively, after the 17th Congress), some full and candidate members of the CC, and members of the Presidium of the Central Control Commission, for a grand total of 60-70 persons. They discussed questions of diplomacy, defense, security, trade and economy, labor and social insurance, education and culture, and other subjects. They also discussed party activities (management of the party itself, leadership of the soviets, trade unions, and the like) and cadre problems (recruitment, distribution, training, etc.). The agendas usually contained 20-40 points for discussion.[8]

Commissions were established to prepare the proposals for Politburo meetings, which were rarely held but attended by many persons. Commissions usually consisted of 5-15 members, including a full or candidate Politburo member (who served chairman) and some chiefs or deputies of government ministries (*narodnye komissariaty*) concerned.[9] Unfortunately, protocols of their meetings remain classified even at present, except for a few. However, there is no doubt that the commissions, especially the standing ones, played important roles in the Politburo discussions and decisions. Among the standing commissions were those on foreign affairs and foreign trade (both chaired by Molotov), defense (by Voroshilov), and legal affairs (by Kaganovich).[10] For example, the Politburo discussed and decided such an important question as the establishment of diplomatic relations with the USA only four times and interrogatorily (*oprosom* on 14, 17, 20, and 25 October 1933 / *Reshenie* — *osobaia papka*).[11] The commission on foreign affairs doubtlessly was held beforehand and *de facto* made the decision. In addition, the departments of the CC, except that of agriculture, did not have such a function of preparing proposals as they later did.[12]

In addition to having the commissions prepare proposals, the Politburo entrusted the SNK with leadership in some sectors of the national economy. It only ratified to or amended proposals by the SNK concerning routine matters such as drafting the plan of national economy and the state budget each year. The SNK consisted of fewer members (no more than 20) and its meetings were held about once a week.[13] Moreover, it had already established bureaucracies of the ministries and the standing subordinate organs (Gosplan and STO).

However, the Politburo led agricultural policy via the local party organs (*obkom, kraikom,* and the CC of each republic CP) rather than via the organs of agricultural ministries. It controlled the military, the transport sector, and the *sovkhoz* sector through *politotdely.* The Politburo committed itself to deciding the construction and management of important projects (mining and industrial *kombinaty*, main railway lines, giant canals, etc.) and even important mines and factories (the Moscow Automobile Factory, the Stalingrad Tractor Factory, etc.). Last but not least, the Politburo was engaged in deciding policies in spheres where there were no union-level ministries (education, internal affairs until July 1934, and legal affairs and health until July 1936).[14]

Chart 1:
Organizational Structure (after the 17th Congress)

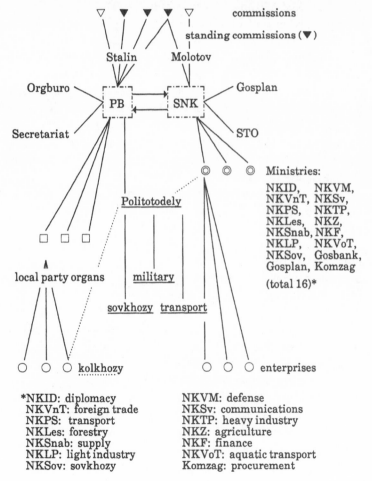

*NKID: diplomacy   NKVM: defense
NKVnT: foreign trade   NKSv: communications
NKPS: transport   NKTP: heavy industry
NKLes: forestry   NKZ: agriculture
NKSnab: supply   NKF: finance
NKLP: light industry   NKVoT: aquatic transport
NKSov: sovkhozy   Komzag: procurement

The Politburo administered larger policy spheres than the SNK and placed its members in leading posts of the SNK (Molotov: chairman of the SNK and STO; Kuibyshev: chairman of Gosplan and deputy chairman of the SNK; Ordzhonikidze: people's commissar of heavy industry; Andreev, succeeded by Kaganovich: people's commissar of transport; Voroshilov: people's commissar of national defense). Therefore, the Politburo was superior to the SNK in decision-making power. The relationship between the Politburo and the SNK involved a kind of division of labor as well as an overlap of membership and functions. For example, the commission for rail transport was a standing one of the SNK and the CC (*de facto* the Politburo).[15] Some decrees were promulgated in the name of the SNK and the CC. This was the logical consequeence of the one-party state, but we can find therein a certain balance which ensured both double-checking and efficiency (cf. Chart 1).

Here I refer to individual roles of the principal Politburo and CC members to some extent, by showing the record of their attendance at Politburo meetings (cf. Table 1). Molotov attended almost all meetings as chairman of both the Politburo and SNK. Kaganovich was the second best in attendance as *ex officio* second secretary. General Secretary Stalin took a long holiday each summer, but controlled the meetings through the second secretary and his personal secretary (Poskrebyshev). Such principal ministers as Mikoian (supply, then food industry), Ordzhonikidze, Voroshilov, Iagoda and Yezhov (internal affairs) naturally attended Politburo meetings. Iagoda was only a candidate member of the CC until the 17th Congress. Piatakov, a full member of the CC and deputy people's commissar of heavy industry, attended more often than infirm Ordzhonikidze until the Great Terror, despite his Trotskyist past. Stalin's favorite *apparatchiki*, i.e. Khrushchev, Mekhlis, and Poskrebyshev, came to be invited to Politburo meetings after the 17th Congress.

However, the forementioned balance under the suzerainty of the Politburo seemed to be destroyed during the Great Terror. D. Volkogonov pointed out in his recent book that decisions were made within a limited circle — Stalin, Molotov, Kaganovich, Voroshilov, and later with Zhdanov or Beria; then Stalin established various Politburo commissions, so-called 'the five,''the six,' etc.[16] According to archival documents, two standing commissions of the Politburo took the place of the Politburo itself after April 1937: that for "urgent problems of confidential nature" consisted of Stalin, Molotov, Voroshilov, Kaganovich, and Yezhov; another for "the urgent problems of economic nature" consisted of Molotov, Stalin, Chubar', Mikoian, and Kaganovich.[17] Immediately afterward, the Committee of Defense was founded as the 'inner cabinet' of the SNK in accordance with the perception of an increasing threat to the USSR. Its full members were Molotov (chairman), Stalin, Kaganovich, Voroshilov, Chubar' (deputy chairman of the SNK), Rukhimovich (people's commissar of defense industry), and Mezhlauk (chairman of Gosplan); the candidate members were Gamarnik (head of the Political Administration of the Red Army), Mikoian, Zhdanov (secretary of the CC), and Yezhov.[18]

Both protocols of the meetings of Politburo standing commissions and the Committee of Defense, regrettably, remain confidential even at present. The party, which had many core cadres liquidated during the Great Terror, restricted its role to leading the state and economic organs, the social organizations ideologically and through cadre policies, giving up taking the place of them. The Committee of Defense became a more important decision-making entity as the danger of war increased (Stalin officially replaced Molotov as chairman of the SNK in May 1941). Immediately after the outbreak of the "Great Patriotic War," the Committee of Defense was reorganized into the State Committee of Defense as the supreme organ (its members were Stalin, Molotov,

Voroshilov, Malenkov, and Beria;   Kaganovich and Voznesenskii were soon added).[19]

2. Decision-making in the Critical Period of 1932-1933

As is well known, the Great Famine occurred in the winter of 1932-1933 due to the severe grain procurement policy and the peasants' resistance to it. The period from the beginning of November 1932, when the Politburo dispatched a special commission headed by Kaganovich to the North Caucasus region, until the beginning of May 1933, when Stalin and Molotov issued a secret instruction banning mass repression against the peasants, was one of the most critical periods of the Stalinist regime. The CC plenum in January 1933, though taking a more flexible line in industrial policy (a slow-down of the high-tempo production of the First Five-Year Plan), approved harsher policies towards peasants and *kolkhozy*, i.e. the establishment of *politotdely* attached to MTS and *sovkhozy*, prohibition of peasant migration into the cities (the introduction of a domestic passport system), and others. The Stalinist leadership not only permitted local party organs to take whatever measures necessary to enforce grain procurement, but also intervened directly in local affairs by promulgating special decisions. At the same time, such direct interventions provided the Stalinist leadership with much local information and allowed them to reconsider their policies. The Veshenskii affair, revealed by Khrushchev exclusively as a typical case of Stalin's repression of peasants,[20] is such a case.

Here the decision-making process via *ad hoc* commissions and Stalin's personal initiative will be analyzed in two sections. The first concerns repression directed by the Kaganovich Commission, and the second concerns the Veshenskii affair (The Veshenskii district belonged to the North Caucasus region).

(1) The Kaganovich Commission

Grain procurement in 1932 proceeded with more difficulty than in 1930 and 1931. The fulfillment level of the year plan was only 52.7% at the end of October (as compared with to 64.8% in 1930, and 55.3% in 1931). In particular, the level in the North Caucasus region was only 37.8% on 25 October.[21] The *kraikom* secretary Sheboldaev fell into difficulties, being under pressure from both above and below. On 22 October, the Politburo decided to dispatch two commissions, one led by Molotov to Ukraine (the largest grain region) and another led by Kaganovich to North Caucasus.[22] On the same day, Stalin invited Sheboldaev to Moscow and persuaded him to resort to repression against the "sabotage" of grain procurement, while rejecting his request for a seed loan.[23]

On 1 November 1932, a meeting of the *kraikom* bureau together with the Kaganovich Commission was held and adopted a decision on the basis of the latter's proposal (*Reshenie — osobaia papka*).[24] The next day the commission, confronted with resistance at a meeting of rural *raikom* secretaries, had to reduce the year plan amount of grain procurement, while at the same time declaring war against "sabotage."[25] Then the *kraikom* bureau adopted three decisions: on grain procurement in the whole region, in the Kuban districts, and on the purge (*chistka*) of rural party organizations. Repressive measures taken in order to hasten grain procurement and punish "saboteurs" were called the "black list" (*chornaia doska*). To villages (*stanitsy*) listed on the "black list" commodities and credits were not to be offered, *kolkhozy*, cooperatives, and state apparatuses were to be purged, and inhabitants were to be deported to northern regions if they continued "sabotage."[26] These measures were essentially a revival of the emergency measures previously taken in the midst of Collectivization.

The commission apparently remained in the region for three weeks. In fact, Kaganovich made a report at the meeting of the *kraikom* bureau on 23-24 November, which decided to add two villages to the "black list" (five in total).[27]

The Stalinist leadership, apparently dissatisfied with the results of these measures, took a more drastic step. Stalin began to revise the official view of *kolkhozy* at the joint meeting of the Politburo and the Presidium of the CCC on 27 November, saying that the party must not idealize *kolkhozy* and must not hesitate to resort to repression against sabotaging *kolkhozy*.[28] On 10 December, the Politburo heard reports by S. Kosior and Sheboldaev on the grain procurement and entrusted a commission (Molotov, Stalin, Kaganovich, Kosior, Sheboldaev, and others) to prepare a draft of the decision.[29] The Politburo on 14 December adopted (*oprosom*) the secret decision of the CC and the SNK on grain procurement in Ukraine, North Caucasus, and the Western region. It specified each time-limit for grain procurement and mandated repressive measures against "the worst counter-revolutionary elements" which included arrest, long-term imprisonment in *lager'* (concentration camp), and shooting. It also provided for wholesale deportation of a village (Poltavskaia *stanitsa*) population to northern regions.[30]

The *kraikom* bureau on 16-17 December approved the deportation of Poltavskaia *stanitsa*, though removing two other villages from the "black list."[31] On 19 December, the Politburo decided (*oprosom*) to dispatch Kaganovich (the new head of the CC agricultural department just established on 15 December) to Ukraine, the second most troubled region for grain procurement.[32]

The joint plenum of the *Kraikom* and the *KraiKK* (Control Commission) on 26-29 January 1933 sent a telegram to Stalin, reporting complete fulfillment of the year plan of grain procurement.[33] But the toll of victims was enormous — 15 villages "blacklisted", 2 villages deported, more than 63,500 inhabitants deported, and 16,000 peasants arrested by OGPU in Kuban alone.[34]

In this way, the Politburo initiated a breakthrough in the crisis and took emergency measures through *ad hoc* commissions. The commissions put Politburo decisions into effect on the spot, imposing them upon the local party organs, while partly taking their conditions into account. Assumably, two *ad hoc* commissions were reorganized into the CC agricultural department on one hand, and into the *politotdely* on the other. The latter was a revival of the plenipotentiaries dispatched to the fronts of Collectivization. In this sense, there were two inconsistent tendencies of leadership in the agricultural policy sphere: normalization on the basis of traditional party rule and institutionalization of emergency measures.

(2) The Veshenskii Affair

Mikhail Sholokhov, one of the most famous and influential Soviet writers, sent a letter to the editorial board of *Pravda*. The letter, which pointed out that seed transfer from Veshenskii district (where he lived) to neighboring Millerovskii district had been delayed, was published on it on 23 March 1933.[35] Then Sholokhov, dissatisfied with the decision of the *kraikom* bureau (*oprosom*, on 27 March),[36] sent a letter to Stalin on 4 April. He pointed out the very fact of famine and criticized the *kraikom* leadership for imposing too heavy a burden of grain procurement and overlooking its plenipotentiary's repressive measures for grain procurement (fines, expulsions from *kolkhozy*, evictions from households, arrests, etc.).[37] Stalin, in his reply of 16 April, promised to help the Veshenskii district and asked how many poods of grain should be sent.[38] Sholokhov, receiving the reply, immediately sent a follow-up letter to Stalin on the same day. He set out the necessary quantities of grain and once again criticized the *kraikom* bureau for ascribing the delay to the unwillingness of the districts. He pointed out that the *kraikom* had kept silent, though it had collected through its instructors evidence of repressive measures.[39]

As for the relationship between the Politburo and the *kraikom* bureau, I could find only the following information in the protocols of Politburo meetings. The Politburo made one decision concerning the *kraikom* (*oprosom, Reshenie — osobaia papka*, on 1 April) and another demanding that the *kraikom* bureau should reconsider its decision on the norm of grain procurement from individual peasants (on 2 April).[40] In any case, the *kraikom* bureau adopted a decision admitting its own mistake on 21 April.[41] Two days later the Politburo adopted a decision, on the basis of Stalin's proposal, to dispatch Shkiriatov to the district in order to investigate the "excesses" in grain procurement.[42] Stalin seemed to be consistently supporting Sholokhov after his letter to *Pravda*, in his proposal for supplementary grain (on 22 April), but he pointed out in his letter to Sholokhov (on 6 May) that the Veshenskii peasants had to be accused of sabotage ("Italian strike"), and their "quiet" war against the soviet authorities.[43]

It is not accidental that the same Politburo meeting (on 23 April) decided to convene a meeting of OGPU plenipotentiaries on 3 May; following that, on 7 May, the Politburo decided (*oprosom*) to stop mass repression against peasants taken since the beginning of wholesale collectivization, i.e. since the end of 1929.[44] The secret instruction signed by Stalin and Molotov was issued on 8 May.[45] The Politburo, perhaps hearing about Shkiriatov's report, decided on 4 July (*oprosom*) to discharge Zimin (second secretary of the *kraikom*) and Ovchinnikov (secretary of Rostov *gorkom*, former plenipotentiary of Veshenskii district), saying that "the completely correct and absolutely necessary policy of pressure against *kolkhozniki* who sabotaged grain procurement was distorted in Veshenskii district because of insufficient control by the *kraikom*."[46] The *kraikom* bureau approved the Politburo decision, and additionally discharged the secretary of Veshenskii *raikom* and the chairman of the *raiKK* (*oprosom*, on 10 July).[47] Then the *kraikom* bureau took steps for relief of the repressed peasants, setting up a commission in order to examine their appeals (on 22 July).[48]

Thus the Politburo directly controlled agricultural policies, i.e. not through the agricultural-administrative organs (People's Commissariat of Agriculture, *Komzag*, *Zagotzerno*), and not even through the CC agricultural department. The more critical the situation became, the more deeply the

Politburo, and first of all Stalin, intervened in local affairs. Stalin, who caught the signals from correspondents or contributors to the central or local newspapers, dispatched his plenipotentiaries to investigate the facts and restrain the "excesses" of agricultural policies (collectivization, grain procurement, and others), ascribing them to local officials. In this Veshenskii case, Sholokhov played the role of correspondent, and Zimin and Ovchinnikov that of scapegoats.

These case studies show important roles of the Politburo, particularly decisive roles of Stalin in decision-making. However it does not mean that the Politburo was a decorative organ and Stalin could dictate everything without an approval of the Politburo. The legitimatizing function of the Politburo was very important for a party of ideology and democratic centralism, at least until the Great Terror. As for the relationship between the Politburo and local party organs (here the *kraikom* bureau), the former seems absolutely superior in power to the latter, but I found in the protocols evidence that the *kraikom* often insisted on its claims. For example, the *kraikom*, dissatisfied with the draft of the 1933 state budget, demanded an increase in its share from the Commissariat of Finance (7 December 1932).[49] The *kraikom*, against the plan of the Commissariat of Supply to decrease the grain supply in February, appealed to the CC (*de facto* the Politburo) to preserve the former level of supply (25 January 1933).[50] These both happened at the very time the *kraikom* had fallen into its weakest position vis-a-vis the Politburo due to the failure of grain procurement.

Notes

1 V. N. Zemskov, " 'Kulatskaia ssylka' v 30-e gody," *Sotsiologicheskie issledovaniia,* No. 10 (1991); V. N. Zemskov, "Sud'ba 'kulatskoi ssylki' (1930-1954 gg.), *Otechestvennaia istoriia,* No. 1 (1994); N. F. Bugai, "K voprosu o deportatsii narodov SSSR v 30-40-kh godakh," *Istoriia SSSR,* No. 6 (1989); N. F. Bugai, "Vyselenie sovetskikh koreitsev s Dal'nego Vostoka," *Voprosy istorii,* No. 5 (1994); O. V.

Khlevniuk, *Stalin i Ordzhonikidze. Konflikty v Politbiuro v 30-e gody* (M., 1993); R. Davis, O. V. Khlevniuk, "Vtoraia piatiletka: mekhanizm smeny ekonomicheskoi politiki," *Otechestvennaia istoriia,* No. 3 (1994); J. Arch Getty, Roberta T. Manning (eds.), *Stalinist Terror: New Perspectives* (Cambridge University Press, 1993); Sheila Fitzpatrick, *Stalin's Peasants. Resistance and Survival in the Russian Village after Collectivization* (Oxford University Press, 1994); Edwin Bacon, *The Gulag at War. Stalin's Forced Labour System in the Light of the Archives* (Macmillan, 1994); E. A. Rees, *Stalinism and Soviet Rail Transport, 1928-41* (Macmillan, 1995).

2 The special file has been kept in the so-called Kremlin or Presidential Archiv. It is nearly impossible to obtain access to the Archiv. Only D. Volkogonov (as a supervisor) and a few other people — e.g. S. Shakhrai as one of the prosecutors in the so-called GKChP trial — could use those documents. However, some articles based on those documents have recently appeared.

3 R. W. Davies, O. V. Khlevnyuk, "The Role of Gosplan in Economic Decision-making in the 1930s," *CREES D. P., SIPS,* No. 36 (University of Birmingham, 1993).

4 G. Gill provided much useful information about the central organs (including the Politburo) on the basis of the published data — e.g. at the 12th Congress it was reported that the Politburo had met on 60 occasions in the 12 months since the previous Congress and, together with 19 meetings of the CC, had dealt with 1,322 questions. Graeme Gill, *The Origins of the Stalinist Political System* (Cambridge University Press, 1990), p. 156.

5 Boris Bazhanov, *Vospominaniia byvshego sekretaria Stalina* (Paris-New York, 1983; St.Petersburg, 1992); "Memuary Nikita Sergeevicha Khrushcheva," *Voprosy istorii,* No. 2, 3, 4 (1990); Evgenii Gnedin, *Katastrofa i vtoroe rozhdenie* (Amsterdam, 1977), etc.

6 "Memuary...," *Voprosy istorii,* No. 2, pp. 105-108; No. 3, pp. 63, 72-73. Kaganovich, in his last interview, acknowledged his role as the second secretary. Feliks Chuev, *Tak govorit Kaganovich* (Moscow, 1992), p. 73.

7 Khrushchev was elected a candidate member of the Politburo as well as first secretary of the CC of the Ukrainian CP in January 1938.

8 *RTsKhIDNI,* f. 17, op. 3, d. 901-1028. These cover the period from October 1932 to October 1940.

9 *Ibid.*

10 *Ibid.*

11 *RTsKhIDNI,* f. 17, op. 3, d. 933, l. 6, 12, 20. Diplomatic relations between the USSR and USA were established on 16 November 1933. For an aspect of the process of policy-making towards the USA, see G. N. Sevost'ianov, "Posly vruchaiut veritel'nye gramoty.

Ustanovlenie sovetsko-amerikanskikh diplomaticheskikh otnoshenii v svete novykh dokumentov," *Novaia i noveishaia istoriia*, No. 6 (1993), pp. 16-35.

12 The CC had 8 departments and 2 sections after the 17th Congress: (1) plan-finance-commerce, (2) industry, (3) transport, (4) agriculture, (5) political-administrative, (6) ORPO (department of the leading party organs), (7) culture-propaganda, (8) IMEL (Institute of Marx-Engels-Lenin) (9) special section, and (10) Chancellory. These fell under the supervision of the Orgburo and the Secretariat; (1)-(6) were mainly engaged in organizational and cadre questions; (5) controlled the military, security, and judicial organs.

13 *RTsKhIDNI*, f. 17, op. 3, d. 901-1028. *GARF*, f. 5446, op. 1, d. 82-87 (These cover the period from January to June 1934).

14 *RTsKhIDNI*, f. 17, op. 3, d. 901-1028.

15 The commission was established by a Politburo decision (*oprosom*, on 18 August 1933) as "a type of commission of national defense." It seems to mean the commission of both the Politburo and SNK. *RTsKhIDNI*, f. 17, op. 3, d. 929, l. 11.

16 D. A. Volkogonov, *Triumf i tragediia. Politicheskii portret I. V. Stalina*, kn. 1, ch. 2, p. 109.

17 *RTsKhIDNI*, f. 17, op. 3, d. 986, l. 16-17.

18 *GARF*, f. 5446, op. 1, d. 130, l. 235.

19 The documents of the State Committee of Defense (GKO) have been preserved in *RTsKhIDNI* and remain closed to historians at present, but some articles based on some of those documents have recently appeared.

20 *Pravda*, 10 March 1963.

21 T. Tomita, "Kokumotuchoutatu to koluhozu [Grain procurement and *kolkhozy* in 1932-1933]," *Rekishi-gaku Kenkyu* [*Historical Studies*], No. 505 (June 1982), p. 1, 9.

22 *RTsKhIDNI*, f. 17, op. 3, d. 904, l. 11.

23 E. N. Oskolkov, *Golod 1932/1933. Khlebozagotovki i golod 1932/1933 goda v Severo-Kavkazkom krae* (Rostov-na-Donu, 1991), pp. 37-38.

24 *RTsKhIDNI*, f. 17, op. 21, d. 3377, l. 82.

25 Oskolkov, pp. 31-35.

26 *RTsKhIDNI*, f. 17, op. 21, d. 3377, l. 83-87.

27 *RTsKhIDNI*, f. 17, op. 21, d. 3377, l. 93, 104.

28 *Bol'shevik*, No. 1-2 (1933), p. 19.

29 *RTsKhIDNI*, f. 17, op. 3, d. 910, l. 3.

30 *RTsKhIDNI*, f. 17, op. 3, d. 911, l. 42.

31 *RTsKhIDNI*, f. 17, op. 21, d. 3377, l. 115-116.

32 *RTsKhIDNI*, f. 17, op. 3, d. 912, l. 11; d. 911, l. 12.

33 *Partrabotnik*, No. 4 (1933), p. 29.

34 Oskolkov, pp. 52, 55, 56, 50.

35 *Pravda*, 20 March 1933.

36 *RTsKhIDNI*, f. 17, op. 21, d. 3378, l. 63.
37 "Sholokhov i Stalin. Perepiska nachala 30-kh godov," *Voprosy istorii*, No. 3 (1993), pp. 7-18.
38 *Ibid.*, p. 18.
39 *Ibid.*, p. 18-21.
40 *RTsKhIDNI*, f. 17, op. 3, d. 919, l. 25, 27.
41 *RTsKhIDNI*, f. 17, op. 21, d. 3378, l. 79.
42 *RTsKhIDNI*, f. 17, op. 3, d. 921, l. 4.
43 "Sholokhov i Stalin...," p. 22.
44 *RTsKhIDNI*, f. 17, op. 3, d. 922, l. 16.
45 The secret instruction was addressed to all party and soviet activists, all the OGPU, judicial, and prosecutor organs. *RTsKhIDNI*, f. 17, op. 3, d. 922, l. 58-59. This has been known to Western historians who investigated the so-called Smolensk Archiv (S.A., WKP 231).
46 *RTsKhIDNI*, f. 17, op. 3, d. 926, l. 5.
47 *RTsKhIDNI*, f. 17, op. 21, d. 3379, l. 4.
48 *RTsKhIDNI*, f. 17, op. 21, d. 3379, l. 24.
49 *RTsKhIDNI*, f. 17, op. 21, d. 3377, l. 105.
50 *RTsKhIDNI*, f. 17, op. 21, d. 3378, l. 21.

Chapter 9

The Making of Foreign Policy
under Stalin

Jonathan HASLAM

1. The Inherent Flaw in Biography

The issue as to how Soviet foreign policy was made during
the period of Stalin's dictatorship will seem a trifle redundant.
Surely the dictator decided upon foreign policy and that was
that? This has certainly been the view conventionally adopted
by the dictator's biographers. But those biographers have not
generally specialised in any one area of Soviet policy and have
therefore not actually seen policy-making in any detail.
Theirs is all too often the view from on high rather than that at
eye level. This approach makes certain assumptions about
Stalin's position within the structure and about Stalin himself:
for example, that the Stalin of 1929 to 1939 was exactly the
same man as the supremely self-confident and apparently very
well informed "generalissimo" who sat with Churchill and
Roosevelt to carve up the world; that Stalin was always
interested in international relations; that from the outset he
always had his own ideas about the conduct of foreign policy;
that he would not allow others to influence the course of
events. This mythical Stalin is unchanging, by all accounts a
most exceptional man who escaped the impact of experience
unlike almost everyone else in history; a man never given to
doubt, a man who never acted on advice, a man who never
gained confidence in spheres that originally lay far beyond his
own limited realm. But perhaps we should not be too

surprised. This is the Stalin recreated by political scientists rather than historians; and if there is one obvious weakness in western social science, it is that it is static and insensible to the changing impact of events. But why not pause to reconsider the nature of Stalin's dictatorship and the mechanisms other than pure terror by which Stalin assured his predominance?

Because of the somewhat sensational claims made by Professor Getty[1] from the United States about Stalin's place within the structure of power, which in my view falsely eliminate Stalin from full responsibility for the terror unleashed from 1936, it is best to state from the outset that although the case to be made with respect to foreign policy decision-making calls for a more open-minded and enquiring view onto the functioning of the entire dictatorship, this writer is unalterably convinced that Stalin *was* directly and personally responsible for the terror campaign in those years; as all the evidence so far released from the newly opened Russian archives testifies. He was plainly an evil man. Having established that much, however, is it really necessary to insist that all policies carried out by the Soviet regime from 1929 to 1953 were products of *his* thinking, were *his* personal inspiration; that there was no significant contribution of others? To read his biographers, one would indeed assume so. And it seems to me that this line of reasoning — unsupported by evidence and taken for granted — is fundamentally flawed with respect to the way Stalin operated; and betrays a fundamental misunderstanding about the manner in which any political system makes policy, whether totalitarian or democratic.

2. The Inadequacy of Political Science

Perhaps the most baffling characterisation of foreign policy making by a prominent sovietologist can be found in a piece by Leonard Schapiro, who emerged in 1980 with a new discovery: "Totalitarianism in Foreign Policy."[2] Whatever the merits of his treatment of the Brezhnev era — and what we now know is that it certainly was not Brezhnev alone who made foreign policy — his discussion pays no attention whatever to how foreign policy is normally made in the West; had he done so, certainly with respect to Britain, and France under the fifth republic, he may have found at least as much in common between the processes of totalitarian states and their democratic counterparts as their differences, not least because public opinion has traditionally been excluded or manipulated (as over Irangate and British arms sales to Iraq), Ministers lie to Parliament, and decisions have been concentrated into the hands of very few: this makes any notion of effective democracy in foreign policy somewhat tenuous, in Europe at least, and therefore the notion of totalitarianism in foreign policy making a matter of degree, not absolutes. What is also worrying about this characterisaiton of the processes in Moscow is the naive assumption that in day-to-day matters one can simply conduct policy without delegating power; yet this is definitely not like working a machine, for even the most lowly official has to interpret the policy laid down in what is often a rapidly changing context.

Schapiro gave us a general conception of Soviet foreign policy making. Robert C. Tucker gives us an eloquent but flawed portrait of Stalin and Stalin's methods both in his early essays and more recently in his full length biography, most importantly in volume two: *Stalin in Power: The Revolution from Above, 1928-1941.*[3] His approach to Stalin is clearly marked out from that adopted by E.H. Carr and Isaac Deutscher who, borrowing from Trotsky, see Stalin largely in impersonal terms: not a man of ideas but a man almost devoid of original thought, and a politician who was the product of his times rather than the *deus ex machina* that others have usually presented.[4] Under Trotsky's persuasive influence, these historians undoubtedly underrated the impact of Stalin's personality. But — and this is where Tucker marches rather too far out ahead of the evidence — having established that Stalin was less the product of, than the maker of, the system, he goes on to assert that the system created was nothing but a blind creature of Stalin's.

This position has its roots far back into the past, in Tucker's personal experience of Stalin's dictatorship while serving at the US embassy in Moscow during the early Cold War. Haunted by this bitter experience, he formulated this conception of the dictatorship not many years later. It is in an essay on "The Politics of Soviet De-Stalinisation" published in *World Politics* in October 1959 that he makes the classic formulation of the Soviet regime as a totalitarian structure:

> Every true totalitarianism is a one-man system and comes to power through the subversion of a pre-existing political regime...after Stalin's blood purges of the middle 1930s, there was no longer in any real sense a ruling party, just as there was no real ruling class; there was at most a privileged stratum of bureaucratic serving-men who lived well and wore medals but who were instrumentalities rather than real holders or sharers of power.[5]

Tucker thus insists that from 1936 no one *shared* power with Stalin. How, then, did Stalin rule? Through the so-called Special Sector, Tucker tells us:

> All directives for trials and purges were funneled through it. All information was channelled into it. It had a foreign section through which Stalin conducted foreign policy, and so on... It was, as it were, a little gear box through which the massive machinery of Soviet rule of over nearly 900 million human beings on about one-third of the earth's surface was operated. By manipulating the levers in the control panel, Stalin could cause all kinds of things to happen. He could play politics as though playing a piano, touching a key here and striking a chord there, with results as diverse as a blast in *Pravda* against Churchill, a purge in the Ukraine, a plan for a new power station on the Volga, a propaganda campaign about germ warfare, a re-evaluation of Einstein, or a government change in Bulgaria.[6]

It would be idle to deny that this portrayal does, of course, provide an explanation for much that happened. But one has to ask how complete it is as an explanation. The image is surely too simplistic. Stalin alone seems to do everything in relation to policy; others merely execute it. This claim is not new. It is the Stalin that was presented to us daily through the adulatory organs of the Soviet press from 1929 to 1953. It is also the Stalin that Khrushchev describes as the sole villain of the piece in his secret speech of 1956. As the leader of the Italian Communist Party Palmiro Togliatti put it: "At first, all that was good was put down to the superhumanpositive qualities of one man; now, all that was bad comes to be attributed to the as many exceptional and even astonishing of his defects."[7] The adulation and the condemnation both served useful political purposes, both suspect, though perhaps not equally so; but was this approach ever adequate as an explanation as to how the system really worked?

It is striking to note that the view of the Stalinist system presented by Merle Fainsod was a more nuanced and sophisticated one:

> The formula of totalitarian rule as it took shape under Stalin's ministrations was a complex one. It represented, in one aspect, a drive to safeguard his own security by obliterating all actual or competing centers of power... In this system of institutionalized mutual suspicion, the competing hierarchies of Party, police, army, and administration were kept in purposeful conflict and provided with no point of final resolution short of Stalin and his trusted henchmen in the Politburo. The concentration of power in Stalin's hands rested on the dispersal of power among his subordinates.[8]

This general comment with respect to "Stalin's Totalitarian Formula" seems much closer to reality than that presented by Tucker. For in Tucker there is no "dispersal of power"; there are not really any henchmen, either — at least, after 1929-30. Stalin's closest associates are mentioned without being discussed: Litvinov and Molotov, Dimitrov and Radek, all

appear and disappear from the pages of the text without any
serious attention to their personalities, their power and their
true influence. Since Stalin knows what he is going to do from
the outset in every sphere of Soviet life and politics, what is
the point of discussing the role of mere subordinates whose job
it was just to execute policy, not think about it and guide
Stalin's judgements?

For the characterisation given in *World Politics* in 1959, a
good six years after Fainsod's portrayal of the system but with
no reference to the alternative view he presents, is fully
consonant with the Stalin presented in volume two of the
biography. We are soon informed that Stalin "had his own
distinctive orientation and... during the 1920s he worked out a
policy program that gave concrete expression to it."[9] In respect
of foreign policy, Tucker claims Stalin had a peculiarly
"German orientation."[10] To make clear what his orientation
was, whether in foreign or domestic policy, Tucker lack any
direct evidence. What we "can" do, he suggests, is to "piece it
together from various statements that he made during that
decade."[11] This, it has to be said, is rather dubious
methodologically. For he *assumes* that Stalin knew from the
outset what he would do; he does not prove it. He then
attempts to illustrate this assumption by means of very
selective quotation. With respect to foreign policy this has an
odd, but not altogether unexpected, result. Since the general
line laid down by Lenin in foreign policy was that of an
orientation towards Weimar Germany — the so-called Rapallo
relationship — based on a common hostility to the Versailles
peace settlement, it is as easy to find pro-German statements
by Stalin as it is by everyone else; and extremely difficult to
find anything said in public which contradicts it. The
quotations from Stalin's public statements of the 1920s are
therefore worthless as evidence of a personal orientation.

The Rapallo relationship underpinned the Soviet priority of
keeping the capitalist camp divided; there is nothing odd in
the fact that Stalin continued that line after he achieved
personal supremacy in 1929. There is, however, no evidence to

suggest any particular personal attachment to that line or any other orientation in foreign policy. Indeed, what is most noticeable throughout the period of Stalin's supremacy is a marked reluctance to say anything coherent about foreign policy in public and an equally marked reluctance to meet foreign ambassadors, leaders or journalists, for discussions on the subject, with the notable exception of the period 1941-45. It is that image of the generalissimo taken from World War II projected back into the past which is so misleading.

3. Stalin's Immediate Entourage

The evidence of Stalin's own predetermined orientation lacking, what of those around him? It is, in my view, here that we find the sources of Stalin's position on any given question. First there is the issue of the strategy of collective security which Litvinov originated. Tucker informs us that "in the new atmosphere following January 1933, Litvinov and others were bound to be attracted to the idea of a new diplomacy of cooperation with those European states that had cause to fear Hitler's Germany. Stalin, however, had other ideas..."[12] But if Stalin had supreme power, how was it that the policy was adopted in December 1933? And statements Stalin made in support of the policy — most notably to Kollontai, the Soviet ambassador to Sweden — are ignored.[13] There is also the adoption of the Popular Front policy by the Comintern. Tucker passes by the evidence concerning major disputes over the direction Comintern should take and the fact that Stalin had favoured a continuation of the old line of class against class without comment.[14] Then there is the role of Vyacheslav Molotov. Born on 9 March 1890 Molotov joined the Bolsheviks at only sixteen years of age. Like Stalin he formed part of the internal emigration and therefore lost the opportunity to know what the outside world was really like. He became closely associated with Stalin in 1921 and Politburo member in January 1926. Stalin felt he could count on Molotov's political loyalty and it was for this reason and certainly no other that he charged him with responsibility for the Comintern after Bukharin's removal in 1928-29. Then in 1930 he took over from Rykov as chairman of the Council of People's Commissars. Traditionary Molotov has always been assumed to have been a mere mouthpiece of Stalin's. New evidence has come to light that this was not so. We have Molotov's own testimony, for example. In conversation with Felix Chuyev in June 1977, he said the following with reference to his relationship with Stalin which had broken down after 1949:

> I criticised certain views of Stalin's even before, and I told him in person. I consider that a Communist, a member of the Politburo, thirty years there but with no opinions of his own, is a chatterbox. Thus I consider that Stalin valued me, the fact that I had some kind of opinion, some understanding of the issues. Well, he did not always agree with me, but I have to say that he largely agreed with me. Otherwise we could not have worked together for 30 years.[15]

Yet when he considers a statement by Molotov on policy towards Germany that contradicts the basic line of Soviet foreign policy — notably when in 1936 Molotov tells a French journalist that "the chief tendency, and the one determining the Soviet Government's policy, thinks an improvements in Soviet-German relations possible" — Tucker immediately leaps to the conclusion that "Stalin made his position public via Molotov."[16] But this is an assumption, not a statement of fact. Why is it not equally possible that Molotov held to a strongly pro-German line, and that he had managed to convince an agnostic Stalin that now was the time to make it more public? This would, of course, flatly contradict Tucker's assumption that from the outset Stalin had a strategy of dragging the West into a war with Germany.[17] This is exactly what Stalin feared the West might be contemplating with respect to Russia and Germany. Nonetheless Litvinov had persuaded him to take a forward position in favour of the containment of Germany even at the risk of provoking Berlin.[18] And in this writer's view it was only in August 1939 that Stalin finally gave up that option and switched decisively to the other side.[19]

There is other testimony that Molotov had open disagreements with Stalin over policy. "I would say," recalls Khrushchev, "that he [Molotov] was the only person in the Politburo who opposed Stalin on this or that question for the second time."[20] In the opinion of Marshal Zhukov, who observed Molotov and Stalin at close quarters for the first time in 1940-41, Molotov "exerted serious influence over Stalin, particularly in questions of foreign policy, in which Stalin then, until the war, considered him [Molotov] competent." When attacked by Stalin, "Molotov by no means always remained silent." Indeed, "at times it reached the point where Stalin raised his voice and even lost all self-control, and Molotov, smiling, rose from behind the table and held firm to his point of view."[21]

There is evidence that Stalin was indecisive on matters of foreign policy. This emerges most clearly in respect of relations with Japan. The Japanese assault on manchuria from September 1931 threatened to evolve into a campaign against the Soviet Far East. In Moscow this jeopardised completion of the first five-year plan and forced the speeding-up of preparations for war. The thorny question was: should the Russians appease the Japanese until they were ready for war or should they make a show of standing firm and risk war even though defence preparations were far from adequate? There is no evidence that Stalin took a decisive position either way. And there is abundant evidence that his subordinates were bickering with one another over the right path to take; in itself an unambiguous sign that Stalin found it difficult to make up his mind. The issue was further complicated when Hitler took power in January 1933. Those who argued that Germany now presented a threat to Soviet security — as Litvinov predicted it would when Hitler took power — pressed for continued appeasement of Japan; those who were more rabidly anti-Japanese found a further reason for continuing to sustain close relations with Germany. The Soviet Union did not have the power to contemplate a war on two fronts; so a decision was required between the two orientations. Early in 1932 the French ambassador to Moscow reported a clash of opinion between those advocating a forward policy in the East, including the Deputy Commissar for Foreign Affairs Lev Karakhan, and those advocating a more passive line, first and foremost Litvinov. Thereafter foreign embassies picked up frequent signs of discord among leading officials.[22]

4. The Postwar Period

We have spoken entirely about pre-war Stalin and emphasised here and elsewhere that he may well have been rather a different figure in relation to foreign policy than the Stalin of the war and after, in that it took time for him to take a direct grip on all aspects of foreign policy; and that partly from lack of interest and partly also from lack of direct knowledge, he diffused control among his immediate entourage, adopted policies proposed by others on a trial and error basis, and ultimately only took more operational control after the dismissal of Litvinov in May 1939. On this view the difference between pre-war and postwar Stalin was one of degree. He appears never to have handed over a degree of operational control to Molotov and Vyshinsky to the same extent that he did to Litvinov. On the other hand, the signs are that debates over policy continued — indeed intensified — into the early Cold War; and that the great battles of the 1950s over whether to pursue detente with the West and, if so, how far to go, fought out between Malenkov and Molotov, and then Khrushchev and Molotov, were to some extent prefigured in these earlier debates.

Much of this will, of course, remain speculative until the Politburo papers on the foreign policy issues of the period are opened.[23] But then Stalin's biographers have not shunned speculation, even if it is presented as hard fact. The evidence in US diplomatic archives is that there were, indeed, some intense debates in Moscow over the line to take from 1945.

Walter Bedell-Smith, who served as US ambassador to the Soviet Union from 1946-1949 before heading the newly formed Central Intelligence Agency, wrote memoirs which appeared in 1950. There he had some interesting reflections on the structure of power and decision in the Kremlin. He describes Stalin thus: "Courageous but cautious; suspicious, revengeful and quick to anger, but coldly ruthless and pitilessly realistic; decisive and swift in the execution of his plans when the objective is clear, but patient, deceptive and Fabian in his tactics when the situation is obscure..."[24] Because he centralised power, and because the officials down below dare not communicate the unadorned truth, even if their indoctrination allowed them to see it, "Stalin must be by character, experience and environment, almost completely dependent on a few close friends and advisers within the walls of the Kremlin." Bedell-Smith continues: "It is not only in authoritarian states that the continuous struggle for access to the Chief of State, and for control of his sources of information, is a major factor in political life. In the Soviet Union, where secrecy and suspicion are rife, this must be particularly intense. Because of Stalin's ignorance of the West, his suspicious Georgian character and his isolation, the power of his few political intimates must be very great. It is in the character of these advisers, and in their relationship with Stalin, that we must seek the answers to many of the perplexing manifestations of Soviet foreign policy and of the Soviet attitude toward the United States and Western Europe."[25] "My own impression," wrote Bedell-Smith, "is that there really was a decided difference of opinion in the Politburo concerning relations with the West."[26] Interestingly he saw opinions cluster around two distinct group within Stalin's entourage: the "Moderates," who believed the Soviet Union needed to buy more time before confronting the West and should therefore required a "closer understanding" with the United States and its allies; and the hardliners, who favoured a more pro-active policy of "constant pressure, aggressive action and intransigence." The more militant group

he saw clustered around Molotov and included Zhdanov —
"one of the most anti-Western and anti-foreign members of the
upper Soviet hierarchy"[27] — and Beria; the more moderate
element he saw grouped around Malenkov. When set against
what we know of the events that followed Stalin's death and
the struggle over the direction of Soviet foreign policy between
Molotov and Malenkov from 1953-55 (and then between
Molotov and Khrushchev from 1955-56 and later), Bedell-
Smith's conclusions carry an undeniable authority. And his
conclusions were not mere speculation. Some concrete
evidence had come to his notice with respect to the "events
which preceded Zhdanov's death [31 August 1948]," which
"reflected some discord in the ranks of the Politburo."[28] And
the continuation of the debate concerning the thesis by Eugene
Varga that the capitalist world was entering a new period of
stabilisation gives added support to the notion of a clash of
views on the future direction of foreign policy. For if the West
was restabilising and unlikely to re-divide in further
internecine warfare, then the Soviet Union would be wiser to
come to terms with it in the spirit of compromise; if the
opposite were true, as Varga's opponents argued, then the
Russians could afford to pursue their goals entirely
unilaterally confident that a Western bloc could not come into
being and confident that capitalism would sooner rather than
later collapse. As Bedell-Smith noted in 1948: the ultimate
fate of the Varga group "may therefore well serve as a
weathercock of party attitudes toward [the] western world..."[29]

Of course, these internal differences were never permitted
except as Stalin's own peculiar means of ensuring that he
never received a monolithic set of advice on important
questions; and by setting his entourage at loggerheads, he
could also ultimately ensure that they would always require
him to reach a neutral decision. The means of making
decisions was thus in a fundamental sense intimately
connected with the means of assuring continued supremacy;
the terror was too blunt a tool to serve all purposes and might
in the end ensure he never had alternative options presented

from which he could, in his more Fabian moods, select the right course. Perhaps this is the least misleading way in which to view the operations of the Soviet dictatorship under Stalin; certainly it is a hypothesis that fits the known facts more adequately than the alternatives presented. But above all we should not be intimidated into thinking that any reformulation of our ideas on this subject is somehow tantamount to Stalin's rehabilitation; for if we are to work in fear of this, we might as well be living in a totalitarian system ourselves.

Notes

1 J.A. Getty, *Origins of the Great Purges: the Soviet Communist Party Reconsidered, 1933-1938* (Cambridge University Press, 1985).

2 K. London (ed.), *The soviet Union in World Politics* (Westview and Croom Helm, Boulder and London, 1980), pp. 3-24.

3 Robert C. Tucker, *Stalin in Power: The Revolution from Above 1928-1941* (Norton, New York and London, 1990).

4 For Carr's portrayal: E.H. Carr, *Socialism in One Country 1924-1926*, Vol. 1 (Macmillan, London, 1958), pp. 174-186. For Deutscher's: I. Deutscher, *Stalin: A Political Biography* (Oxford University Press, London, 1949), pp. 273, 295, 318, 322 and 326. And for Tucker's criticism of this approach: Tucker, *The Soviet Political Mind*, pp. 108-112. This criticism is repeated in Tucker's biography of Stalin: *Stalin in Power*, p. 145.

5 Reprinted in R.C. Tucker, The Soviet Political Mind: Stalinism and Post-Stalin Change (revised edition, Norton, London, 1972), pp. 178-179.

6 Ibid., p. 182.

7 Intervista a Nuovi argomenti, No. 20, May-June 1956: reprinted in P.Togliatti, G. Santomassimo (ed.), *Opere scelte* (Editori Riuniti, Rome, 1974), p. 716.

8 M. Fainsod, *How RUSSIA is Ruled* (Revised edition, Oxford University Press, 1963), p. 109.

9 Tucker, *Stalin in Power,* p. 40.

10 Ibid., p. 226.

11 Ibid., p. 40.

12 Tucker, *Stalin in Power,* p. 233.

13 Haslam, The Soviet Union and the Struggle for Collective Security in Europe, 1933-39 (Macmillan, London; St. Martin's Press, New York, 1984), p. 41.

14 For the disputes: Haslam, "The Comintern and the Origins of the Popular Front 1934-1935," *The Historical Journal,* 22, 3 (1979), pp. 673-691.

15 Interview, 16 June 1977: *Sto sorok besed s Molotvym* (Terra, Moscow, 1991), p. 370.

16 Tucker, *Stalin in Power,* p. 350.

17 Ibid., pp. 342 and 345.

18 See Haslam, *The Soviet Union and the Struggle for Collective Security in Europe 1933-39* (Macmillan, London and St. Martin's Press, New York, 1984).

19 The latest evidence on this supports that view: see the documents recently published from the Narkomindel files and now open to readers in the archives – V. Komplektov et al. (eds.), *Dokumenty Vneshnei Politiki 1939 god,* Vol. 1 (Mezhdunarodnaia otnosheniia, Moscow, 1992).

20 Quoted in Haslam, *The Soviet Union and the Threat from the East, 1933-41: Moscow, Tokyo and the Prelude to the Pacific War* (Macmillan, London, and Pittsburgh University Press, 1992), p. 17.

21 Ibid.

22 Ibid., pp. 18-19 and 21-22.

23 The decisions on foreign, defence and intelligence policies are not recorded in the regular minutes, but in another category – osobaia papka (special file). The category is apparently being released to readers only for the pre-war period; moreover, it is said that the supporting position papers that underlay the final decisions are to remain closed. That files of the Foreign Ministry for the early Cold War are now declassified (1945-49) with the exception – an important and extremely frustrating exception – of the ciphered correspondence, which remains closed. It is said that the ciphered correspondence for the years 1917-41 will now be declassified. But we have no promises with regard to the subsequent period.

24 W. Bedell-Smith, *Moscow Mission 1946-1949* (Heinemann, London, 1950), p. 51.

25 Ibid., pp. 51-52.

26 Ibid., p. 64.

27 Ibid., p. 65.

28 Ibid., p. 64.

29 Bedell-Smith (Moscow) to Marshall (Washington), 6 December 1948: *Foreign Relations of the United States,* 1948, Vol. IV: Eastern Europe; The Soviet Union (USGPO, Washington, 1974), p. 942.

Chapter 10

The Concept of "Space" in Russian History

— Regionalization from the Late Imperial Period to the Present —

Kimitaka MATSUZATO

1. Why Is Russian Historical Geography Not Developed?

This chapter is aimed at contributing to the development of Russian historical geography, perhaps the weakest area of our studies, by analyzing the history of territorial reform in Russia and the Soviet Union.*

"In most countries where geography is a well-established and vigorous academic discipline, historical geography is similarly well-established and vigorous." In this sense, however, the Soviet Union was an exception.[1] Likewise, Western historians of Russia have generally paid little attention to geographic factors.

It is true that some groups of Western historians (for example, specialists in pre-modern Russia, its colonial expansion, and ethnic questions) have been much more disciplined in including geographic factors. Certain studies offer indisputable evidence of this: *Russian Colonial Expansion to 1917* (1988) edited by Michael Rywkin, and one recent article by John P. LeDonne.[2] Moreover, *Domination of Eastern Europe* (1986) by Orest Subtelny is not only an excellent example of historical geography but also of a combination of comparative and causal analyses.

---

* As this chapter is aimed at analyzing administrative-territorial division itself, the names of territorial units (guberniia, uezd, volost, raion, etc.) will be neither translated into English, nor italicized.

Unfortunately, however, specialists in the modern and Soviet periods are still obliged to put up with such studies as combine into one paragraph several examples picked up from the Urals, Belorussia, and Crimea. Such a negligent attitude to the relevance of geographic factors can be termed *geographic nihilism.* Apparently, recent dramatic changes in the former Soviet Union in allowing access to historical materials, local (state and party) archive materials in particular, have not thus far affected our geographic nihilism. This should prompt us to consider what was wrong with our approaches, and what is to be done.

The underdevelopment of historical geography in the Soviet Union is demonstrated by the fact that throughout the 74 years under Soviet Power not a single historical atlas for professional historians was published. Only in the final years of the Soviet Union was an editing commission for a historical atlas organized in the Institute of USSR History of the Soviet Academy of Sciences. It is known that this commission prepared a draft of a highly accurate and detailed historical atlas, but due to the recent economic situation of the country, the draft has been shelved.

Russian historians seem to enjoy publishing chronicles, but do not seem to like drawing maps. As a result, foreign historians are confronted with a staggering array of place names whose locations cannot be identified. We have no choice but to depend on guberniia maps appended to the Encyclopedia *Brokgauz and Efron,* or a relatively accessible atlas *Geograficheskii atlas Rossiiskoi imperii, Tsarstva Pol'skogo i Velikogo kniazhestva Finliandskogo; Raspolozhennyi po guberniiam*, published in 1823. Regrettably, these maps, with scales of one inch to 30, 60, or even 160 *verstas* (1 *versta* = 1.067 km), cannot show locations of all villages, or sometimes even of volosts. Such maps are inappropriate, for example, to study peasant movements. While specialists in the French Revolution enjoy opportunities to study the paths along which peasant insurgence spread as well as its methods (by rumors, sending couriers, etc.), students of Russian history do not even know the locations of villages!

To the best of my knowledge, the most detailed Russian historical atlas is *Podrobnaia karta Rossiiskoi imperii i bliz' lezhashchikh zagranichnykh vladenii,* prepared by the "Imperial Depot of Maps" and presented to Alexander I around 1810. This is a collection of 107 maps drawn to a scale of 100 mm to 70 *verstas.* This scale enables us to identify each village, road, and church, and to gain a rough indication of land use. What is important is that the maps show the significance of each church and, consequently, the significance of the village where the church was located. Although this atlas is highly useful, it is rare. The British Museum, for example, holds one copy, but the Library of Congress in the United States does not.

The development of historical geography in the Soviet Union was hampered by its academic structure. In general, professional historians working in Russian and Ukrainian local universities or institutes specialize in their own regions (the Urals, the Central Industrial Region, the Central Black-Soil Region, Right-Bank Ukraine, etc.), selecting them as the subjects of their life-work. Russian and Ukrainian historians often say that four guberniias are to be analyzed in preparing a doctoral candidate's dissertation. Since the present oblasts are, as a rule, smaller than the former guberniias, it means that he needs to visit between five and ten oblast state archives, not counting party ones.

These requirements enriched Soviet historiography by *intra*regional typology (in Soviet dissertations we can often find such questions as "why did it happen in Tambovskaia but not in Orlovskaia guberniia?") but hampered the development of *inter*regional typology. A survey trip entailing long-distance travel has not been affordable for Russian and Ukrainian historians, let alone the difficulties caused in recent years by regional conflicts in the area of the former Soviet Union.

In this sense, Moscow and St.Petersburg historians are patently privileged. They have opportunities to select regions more freely than do their hinterland colleagues. Strangely enough, however, it seems that they are more hesitant to visit Russian and Ukrainian provinces than we (foreign historians) are. Perhaps Muscovites and Petersburgers fear that they will become the prey of tigers and wolves in outlying Russian and Ukrainian provinces. Regrettably, it is also the case that sometimes we are better informed about able, young historians working in Russian and Ukrainian provinces than are their colleagues in Moscow and St. Petersburg.

For our part, a serious obstacle to the development of studies of Russian historical geography had been the restrictions imposed by the Soviet regime on foreigners wishing to travel to Soviet provinces. Up to the end of the 1980s, substantial areas of the Urals, the Mid-Volga Region, and Ukraine were "closed" areas for foreigners. It is difficult to share a sense of space and location with historical figures if you yourself have never been there.

However, the negative effects of these "totalitarian" restrictions should not be exaggerated. A significant number of prominent scholars who have contributed to the study of Russian historical geography (J.P. LeDonne for example) belong to a generation which was unable to enjoy opportunities to work in Soviet local archives. On the other hand, most Western historians, as mentioned above, have not escaped geographic nihilism despite the greater access to historical sources in the last years. Therefore, our faults should be seen as mainly methodological.

2. "Space" and Public Administration

Some 30 years ago, J.P. LeDonne pointed out that "France, a close relative of Russia in the family of over-centralized states, had in 1901, 86 *départements* and 36,192 communes, each with an elected mayor subject to dismissal by the *préfect* of the *département* appointed by the Ministry of the Interior,

and European Russia with nearly four times the population
and five times the territory of France had only 51 guberniias,
511 uezds and 10,257 volosts."[3]

However, how could a French-style state exist in a country
where the population density was only one-twelfth of France
(as a whole)?[4] Even at the present time, professional police
force is almost non-existent in rural Russia. Local enterprises
(collective farms and factories) regularly supply a few of their
laborers for this purpose. They are organized into *druzhiny*
(militia units) and patrol their areas. Administrative
Commissions attached to village district administrations
(former selsovets, i.e., village Soviets) deal with minor
offenses. Members of the Commissions work "on social
principles" (without pay). If a case is too serious for the
Commission, the latter transfer it to the professional
policeman who visits the village district, as a rule, once a
week. It must be noted that given the conditions of the
Russian countryside, such a non-professional police system is
rational and feasible. It would be unaffordable for each village
district to hire even one professional policeman.

In Western countries, care for bedridden old people requires
only to organize a system of "home helpers." If a home helper
finds something wrong with an old person's health, the helper
calls an ambulance. In the Russian countryside, this service is
one of the duties of *zhensovety* (Women's Soviets), whose
members serve without pay. Heads of village district
administrations (former chairmen of selsovets) convene
skhody (assemblies) in each "population place" (*naselennyi
punkt*) to organize a system of mutual care. If someone finds a
suffering elderly person, he informs the head of the village
district administration, who in turn negotiates with the
collective farm office in the district so that the farm's truck
may take the person to the nearest hospital. It happens that
the collective farm's truck is the only automobile in the
district.

Working in such an environment, heads of village district
administrations are required to be sturdy bosses (*krepkie*

khoziaeva) but neither democratic representatives nor efficient bureaucrats. Here there are scant possibilities for the development of a Weberian bureaucracy.

Specifics of socialist public administration, such as amateurism, the absence of a solid financial system, and the direct mobilization of popular service, have been regarded as unique to Communism or Soviet idealism. The situation after the downfall of Communism, however, revealed that these had in fact been feasible forms of public administration under Russian (Eurasian) geographic conditions. The origin of predominance of direct mobilization of popular service should not be sought in War Communism but in *natural'naia povinnost'* (levy in kind or *corvée* labor) in pre-revolutionary Russia.

This is symbolized by reintroduction of the *Subbotnik* (formerly called the *Leninskii subbotnik*). Late in April throughout Russia, after the spring thaw, someone must clean up the streets. If Russian local authorities were to forego the *Subbotnik* and hire street-cleaners, it would surely be more costly *for taxpayers*. In Western countries also, *corvée* labor remains in some spheres of public administration which are unsuited for the professional (hire) principle. An excellent example is the system of volunteer (amateur) fire-fighting brigades in Japan, organized in almost all villages, towns, and urban districts. Since the ideal of fire-fighting is to minimize the dispatch of fire brigades, it would be unprofitable to organize them only with professional firemen. Notwithstanding, Russia (its countryside in particular) can be distinguished from Western countries by an abundance of public duties which can be accomplished less expensively and more effectively by the population themselves than by professional officials.

Historians studying administrative reforms in late Imperial Russia have not been accustomed to evaluating such factors as available manpower, financial resources, territorial optimality, all of which however are definitely important for analyses of public administration. For example, some Western and Soviet historians have argued that the lack of volost zemstvos was the fatal flaw of the tsarist regime. If we, however, compare the available rural manpower at that time (physicians, agronomists, veterinarians, and others) with the average size of volosts, it is indisputable that in most volosts, zemstvos would have been founded without intellectual workers and, therefore, could not have played the role of modernizing institutions. This was actually proved at the time of the Provisional Government.[5] In short, some historians' anti-realism is caused not only by their liberal/leftist orientation, but also by the lack of spatial sensitivity.

3. Territorial Units in Imperial Russia and the USSR

(1) Significance of the question

The issue of administrative-territorial division (*raioni-rovanie* = regionalization) is very important not only because it is one of the basic frameworks for historical geography but also because it reflects chronic requirements which impose various conditions on the politics and government of the country (or region) concerned.

For example, Russian raions and American counties are considerably similar in character, while English counties correspond to Russian oblasts or Japanese *ken* (prefectures). In this author's opinion, the former resemblance results from low population densities in Russian and American rural areas which atomize the countryside and prevent effective township or village self-government. While Japanese *gun* (counties) have degenerated to be strictly territorial units without any administrative function, Russian raions and American counties continue to play a vital role in rural administration.

Every modern state inherited small villages (communes) from its feudal predecessor. In countries with high population densities such as Japan, England, and Germany, these small villages have been consolidated and enlarged to the extent that made stable township self-government possible. This, however, did not occur in Russia. Even after Nikita Khrushchev's amalgamation of small villages, a significant number of selsovets in the RSFSR had populations of only several hundred persons. Although the United States did not inherit small villages from feudalism, this country experienced a similar difficulties in effecting strong township government. Thus, the raion continues to be a vital link in Russian local government. This author was surprised that Western political scientists were not surprised at the abolition of representative organs at the raion level after the Presidential *coup d'etat* in October, 1993 — which no one had dreamed of after Alexander II's introduction of uezd zemstvos.

According to Yuzuru Taniuchi, debates on territorial reform in the 1920s focused on achieving a balance between democracy and administrative efficiency. Enlargement of lower territorial units (selsovets, volosts and the newly established raions) was aimed at cutting administrative costs, while utilizing cadres muximumly and ensuring their political obedience. On the other hand, the division of administrative units was regarded as desirable in order to "bring Soviets closer to the population."[6] Since rural Soviets suffered from a chronic insufficiency in manpower and financial resources, the dominant tendency in their territorial reform was the enlargement of their areas, which eventually culminated in Khrushchev's amalgamation of villages. However, enlargement was checked and even temporarily overturned when limited experiments in "revitalizing Soviets" were made in the mid-1920s, in 1929,[7] in the mid-1930s,[8] and over the past twenty years.

(2) A short history of Soviet regionalization

In common with other absolutist states, the administrative division of the Russian empire was based on purely demographic principles. Moreover, even from a demographic point of view, the tsarist government was unable to adapt itself to the situation created by Russia's rapid industrialization in the second half of the nineteenth century.

One striking example which has been a favorite of Soviet historians is that Ivanovo-Voznesensk, containing about 30,000 textile and printing laborers, was only one of the "cities" in Shuimskii uezd (Vladimirskaia guberniia), the capital of which had a much smaller population.[9]

The Communist Revolution ensued two new criteria to the issue: the ethnic composition of the population and the economic affinity or cohesion (*economicheskoe tiagotenie*) of the region.[10] As a result, Soviet regionalization became much more dynamic than that in tsarist period. This can be shown by comparing Map 1 with Map 2. Territorial division in the European portion of the contemporary CIS is most significantly distinguished from its pre-revolutionary counterpart in such regions as northern Russia, Ukraine, the Mid-Volga, and the northern Caucasus. Territorial changes in northern Russia, the Mid-Volga, and the northern Caucasus resulted from the Soviet government's endeavors to reflect the ethnic composition of the people there. Oblasts in Ukraine, as a rule, are much smaller than its pre-revolutionary guberniias. Due to the rapid development of its economy in the nineteenth century, Ukraine at the beginning of this century suffered from contradictions between administrative units and spatial economic affinity more deeply than did other regions of the Russian empire. Although the territorial division in the Soviet Ukraine underwent numerous changes, we can see a long-term trend toward adaptation of administrative units to realities of the economic situation. The same can be said for the partition of several large guberniias in Russia, namely Tambovskaia, Orlovskaia and Permskaia which even at that time suffered from a lack of internal cohesion.

As Tables 1 - 6 show, Soviet administrative regionalization passed through several critical junctions. First, the numbers of territorial units at all tiers (selsovets, volosts, uezds, and guberniias) increased between 1917 and 1922, and consequently their average area decreased. Second, from 1923 to 1929 the "guberniia/uezd/volost" system was replaced with

the new "oblast (or krai)/okrug/raion" framework.[11] Oblasts
and krais were broad-area units similar to *general-
gubernatorstvo* in pre-revolutionary Russia. As a rule, okrugs
were smaller than guberniias but larger than uezds. Raions
were smaller than uezds but larger than volosts.

The third critical juncture of Soviet regionalization was
reached when okrugs were abolished at the height of
Collectivization (June 1930).[12] The fourth came in the mid-
1930s when, as a logical consequence of the abolition of
okrugs, oblasts were redivided down to the size of the former
guberniias, or even smaller.

The fifth critical juncture was Khrushchev's amalgamation
of villages in the mid-1950s, which sharply reduced the
number of selsovets. The final juncture was the amalgamation
of raions decided by the Central Committee of the CPSU in
November, 1962. The consequences of this action revealed a
geographical contrast. The Russian SFSR redivided raions
soon after Khrushchev's fall from power, while in the
Ukrainian SSR, enlarged raions have been maintained up to
the present (see Tables 3 and 4). As a result, Russia and
Ukraine today display a remarkable contrast in rural
administrative structures. In Russia, rural population places
are less populous than in Ukraine (see Table 7), but on the
average, selsovets contain a higher number of population
places than their Ukrainian counterparts do. Instead, in
Russia on the average, a raion has fewer selsovets than a raion
does in Ukraine. Thus, each Ukrainian raion has a
comparatively larger number of selsovets and each selsovet
contains only a few population places but these population
places are much more populous than in Russia. As is
suggested by Tables 5, 6, and 7, the Belorussian SSR followed
the example of Russia (in even more extreme fashion), while
the Moldavian SSR took the Ukrainian course.

(3) Selsovets: peasant communes or volosts?

Peasant life in pre-revolutionary Russia took place within
three territorial categories: peasant communes (*sel'skie*

obshchestva) as administrative units; land communes (*pozemel'nye obshchestva*) as land-use units; and purely geographical units (*sela* and *derevni*). The formation of selsovets was a process to integrate these three categories into a single territorial unit.

"Selo" means a big village with a church, while "derevnia" means a small village without one. "Selenie" is a general term which embraces both "selo" and "derevnia." Usually, selos were located near road junctions, and had marketplaces (bazaars), post offices, sanatoria, and other public facilities.[13] A selo had several (sometimes, more than ten) "satellite" derevnias. As Aleksandr Chaianov observed,[14] the average radius from the center of selos to their outlying derevnias was about 5 *verstas* (5.3km). This was a distance within which peasants could walk to church and carry grain to the bazaar. For convenience, let us term this sort of territory a "selo-derevnias" unit. It was here that peasants were born, worked, bought and sold, prayed, married and, finally, were buried.

Of the three territorial categories, the "selo-derevnias" units were the most important in peasants' daily life. This fact is often ignored by historians, who have exaggerated the significance of the other two units (peasant and land communes). In this author's opinion, historians' excessive fascination for communes is also symptomatic of an ignorance of spatial factors. Undoubtedly, it was impossible for peasants to support themselves in a commune which had a male population of only 100 - 600 persons (See Table 1).

One of the greatest obstacles to the study of Russian peasant life is the lack of records for the total number of land communes nationwide, as contrasted with our knowledge of the national total of peasant communes and population places.[15] Scholars of the pre-revolutionary Russia did not count the number of land communes, for indeed they were almost impossible to count.

Reformers under Alexander II intended that the area of peasant communes should be the same as that of land communes. However, this principle was soon abandoned, because if peasants in a village had formerly belonged to more than one serf owners and each group had been allotted differing amount of land, after the Emancipation, peasants with larger allotments did not wish to merge into the same land commune with neighboring "poorer peasants." On the other hand, there were also land communes consisting of several peasant communes.

Table 9 and Map 3 show the remarkable variety of guberniias in European Russia with regard to population structures, namely population densities and correlations between selenies and peasant communes.[16]

According to the census of 1897, there were 6,330 volosts, 78,361 peasant communes and 185,025 population places (selenies) within the territory corresponding to the European part of the present Russian Federation (see Table 1). In 1917, there were 10,606 volosts [a] and about 110,000 peasant communes [b] in the territory corresponding to the Russian SFSR as a whole (not to its European part). By 1922, this had increased to 12,363 volosts [a'] and 120,200 selsovets [b'] in the Russian SFSR (see Table 3).

The increases from [a] to [a'] and from [b] to [b'] reveals the spontaneous division of territorial units during the Revolution. Moreover, the increase from [b] to [b'] demonstrates that selsovets were often born out of selenies but not out of peasant communes (former administrative units). In other words, selsovets were often organized on a purely spatial basis.

As Table 3 shows, the number of selsovets in the Russian SFSR had already decreased to one-third of the 1922 figure even before Khrushchev's amalgamation, which reduced the number again by half. The Statute of Selsovets of the Russian SFSR (1931), which ordered that selsovets be organized in all selenies or within areas with a radius of 3 km,[17] could not stem this decline. As a result, there were only 16,358 selsovets (or 15,540 if we exclude oblasts for which former guberniias are omitted from Table 1 because of their substantial nomad and

Cossack territories) in the European part of the Russian Federation in 1993.

Referring to Tables 1 - 6, let us compare the correlations between the numbers of present selsovets (village districts), pre-revolutionary volosts, and peasant communes in the European Soviet Republics.

	ratio of the number of selsovets to that of volosts	ratio of the number of former communes to that of selsovets
European Russia*	2.5	5.0
Ukraine**	3.6	2.8
Byelorussia	2.0	4.6
Moldavia	3.9	1.5

* Excluding the former Orenburgskaia and Astrakhanskaia guberniias.
** Excluding Western Ukraine.

Here we can find the same sort of grouping as shown in the Republics' responses toward the amalgamation of raions decided by the Central Committee of the CPSU in 1962: in the Republics with low population densities (Russia and Byelorussia), the amalgamation of villages during the Soviet period was much more drastic than in densely populated Ukraine and Moldavia. It is common to all four Republics, however, that current village districts (selsovets) are larger than pre-revolutionary peasant communes but smaller than volosts, and they seem to most resemble the former "selo-derevnias" units.

A significant number of the present core settlements (*tsentral'nye usad'by*) of village districts are in fact former selos. Scenes in these core settlements remind us of the former selos because various administrative and social facilities are concentrated there: the office of the village administration (former selsovet office), the collective farm office, school, hospital, "palace of culture" and the like. The transition from selos to the present core settlements is ironically marked by the sight (often seen in central Russia) of a selsovet office standing beside a ruined church.

* * *

Strictly speaking, pre-revolutionary peasant and land communes were corporative-estate (but not territorial) entities, and the tsarist regime was based, in principle, on the former.[18] The 1917 Revolution rejected the corporative structure of the state. At the same time, the territorial holdings of land communes, as a general rule, approached those of selenies, and the former took over a significant part of the administrative functions of pre-revolutionary peasant communes. However, the legal status of land communes, especially their relationship with selsovets, was dubious throughout the 1920s. E.H. Carr remarked that "as the village Soviet approached, both in size and in the nature of its functions, the initial design of the rural district (volost - K.M.) executive committee, so the *skhod* (commune assembly - K.M.) rose up from below to assume the initial form of a village Soviet. It was paradoxical that the institution in the countryside which most closely conformed to the original Bolshevik conception of a Soviet should have been one which did not bear the name."[19]

The Collectivization abolished land communes. At the same time, however, the Statute of Selsovets of the Russian SFSR in 1931 introduced a system of plenipotentiary agents (*upolnomochennye*) of selenies elected by the latter's assemblies (*skhody*).[20] "Paradoxically" again, it was precisely when the Soviet government abolished the communes that a solid legal relationship was established for the first time between selsovets and selenies. Villagers often called plenipotentiary agents of selenies "*starosta*" (the head of a peasant commune in pre-revolutionary Russia). *Skhody* continued to "be alive" (*zhivy*) as fundamental organs of selsovets even after the Collectivization.

The "*skhod-sel'kii starosta*" system as a basic link between village administrations and the population was officially restored in the course of local reforms after the Presidential coup in October, 1993. The *"skhod-starosta"* system took the place of selsovets.

Originally, this system was proposed by local Soviet leaders as early as the autumn of 1991.[21] Their proposal was directed against idealistic tendencies of the Law of Local Government of the RSFSR adopted in July, 1991 by the RSFSR Supreme Soviet. This was the first comprehensive law concerning local government in the Russian Republic since 1917. The main concept of this law was the "separation of legislative and executive branches of power" at the local levels, from which even the articles for selsovets were not immune. As the introduction of volost zemstvos in 1917 had confused Russian local government, so did this prescription in 1991, both of which were, according to the legislators' goodwill, designed to introduce a Western-style democracy to Russia. It is necessary to note here that in most "democratic" countries, except for Japan, legislative and administrative powers at the local levels are not separate, with the latter being elected by the former. In the same way, in "democratic" countries there have never been such a strong township self-government as had been imagined by the proponents of volost zemstvos. Fortunately, the confusion caused by the 1991 Law was much less than had occurred in the case of volost zemstvos, since the separation of village executives from selsovets was seldom achieved because of the insufficient rural manpower. Nevertheless, the idealism of the 1991 Law dissatisfied some Soviet leaders who, in their turn, sought their own model in the traditional system which was *de facto* functioning then.

After the October coup in 1993, this idea was plagiarized by the President. One head of a village administration in Staritskii raion in Tverskaia oblast remarked in an interview with this writer that one merit of the *"skhod-starosta"* system is that *starostas,* conscious that they are bosses (*khoziaeva*), not only propose courses of action but also see them through, whereas the previous selsovet deputies generally performed only the former function.[22] "Paradoxically" once again, "the original Bolshevik conception of a Soviet" revived when the Soviet itself was abolished.

To sum up, regionalization policy at the lower Soviet level from the Revolution of 1917 to the present brought about two changes: (1) it integrated three kinds of territorial units into a single administrative, economic, and social unit — namely the village district based upon the former "selo-derevnias" unit; and (2) it created a system for "pumping out" administrative resources from local enterprises (collective farms and factories). It is necessary to bear in mind that one of the most serious issues the selsovet management faced in the 1920s was how to pump out administrative resources from land communes. To this end, the Collectivization provided a solid foundation.

These achievements, however, were Pyrrhic in nature. Khrushchev's amalgamation of villages delivered the final blow to derevnias and made the hegemony of selos over derevnias Gulliver-like. In most village districts in contemporary Russia, nearly all persons capable of working live in the core settlements (selos), whereas only pensioners live in derevnias.

(4) Raions: volosts or uezds?

Raions were, formally, declared to be the successors of volosts. As already mentioned, however, volosts on the eve of their abolition were not the size of pre-revolutionary volosts, but much larger (See Table 8).

	ratio of the number of raions to former uezds	ratio of the number of the former volosts to raions
European Russia*	3.7	5.8
Ukraine**	4.1	4.5
Byelorussia	2.9	6.2
Moldavia	5.0	5.3

* Excluding the former Orenburgskaia and Astrakhanskaia guberniias.
** Excluding Western Ukraine.

While referring to Tables 1 - 6, let us proceed to compare the correlations between the numbers of present raions, pre-revolutionary uezds, and volosts in the European Soviet Republics.

Here we can discern the same trend as is found in the correlations between selsovets and communes. In the Republics with low population densities (Russia and Byelorussia), the consolidation of volosts (and early raions) into larger raions was more drastic than in other Republics. Generally speaking, however, the current raions are larger than pre-revolutionary volosts but smaller than uezds. They seem to most resemble the former uchastoks.

In fact, based on evidence for the Ural regions, where territorial reforms were carried out as early as 1923, J.P. LeDonne observed that the formation of raions was designed to "make the borders of the lower school, agronomic, financial, and other uchastoks coincide with those of the raion in order to avoid recreating the 'capricious intermingling of departmental jurisdictions and local institutions' which characterized the pre-revolutionary volost."[23] Y. Taniuchi quoted A. Rykov's speech at the 12th Congress of the CPSU (1923), which demanded the enlargement of volosts in order to make volost boundaries coincide with those of various uchastoks such as agronomic, veterinary, land-settlement, forestry, judicial, and others.[24]

It seems strange that, despite these remarks, neither LeDonne nor Taniuchi trace the origin of raions to pre-revolutionary uchastoks. Perhaps it is not they but specialists in late Imperial Russia who are to blame, since latter have not supplied available materials on pre-revolutionary uchastoks.

Due to the insufficiency of intellectual manpower in rural Russia, the volost could function only as a unit of peasant estate self-government, but not as a base for modernization. The latter role was played by uchastoks, which acted as links between uezds and volosts. Roughly speaking, there were four kinds of uchastoks in late Imperial Russia. Among them, the uchastoks of land captains (*zemskie nachal'niki*) is most well-known. With regard to zemstvos, there were medical, veterinary, and agronomic uchastoks. In 1913, there were 2,866 medical uchastoks,[25] and 1,005 uchastok agronomists worked in 34 "old zemstvo" guberniias,[26] while there were 360 uezds in the same territory.

The introduction of volost zemstvos by the Provisional Government did not improve administrative efficiency but only caused financial crises and geographic diffusion of intellectual manpower. Confronting this situation, during the final stage of the "bourgeois democracy" (up to March 1918) and in White-held territories during the Civil War, zemstvo activists tried to consolidate volost zemstvos to form larger ones. If peasants in a volost were "completely illiterate," it was inevitable to amalgamate it with a neighboring volost to obtain candidates for volost zemstvo councillors.[27]

On the other hand, there were certain centrifugal forces which resulted in the partition of volost zemstvos. One of these was land distribution. If peasants after the Emancipation did not wish to merge into a land commune with poorer neighbors, "revolutionary" communes enriched by confiscating landowners' land similarly did not wish to share it with neighboring communes, and tried to form independent volosts.[28] Another centrifugal force was caused by ethnic factors. One example may be cited in Samarskaia guberniia: in September 1918, ethnic German "colonists" wanted to separate from the Bashkir volost, the cultural level of which was considered to be lower than that of the Germans.[29]

The increase in the numbers of volosts and selsovets (former peasant communes) between 1917 and 1922 suggests that Bolsheviks relied upon these centrifugal forces in order to win the Civil War. Therefore, it was natural that in 1922, they (as victors and rulers) resumed the zemstvo activists' work for the consolidation of volosts, a process which ended in the substitution of raions for volosts.

Bolsheviks were seemingly more conscious of the vital importance of raion organs than zemstvo liberals were of uchastoks, although the latter also did not demean the importance of uchastoks. Raions (uchastoks) were the scattered footholds of "progress" in the hostile surrounding world. One of the main motives behind the abolition of okrugs in 1930 was redeployment of okrug cadres by the raion party and Soviet organs in order to reinforce the latter.[30]

If raions (uchastoks) could be distinguished from volosts by their relative abundance of available manpower, then the difference between raions (uchastoks) and uezds was that the former were purely executive organs of higher tiers of government, irrespective of the existence of representative organs at the raion level. As zemstvo uchastok workers served as functionaries of uezd zemstvos, so raion Soviet (party) leaders were, in fact, only functionaries of oblast Soviet (party) organs, while the latter enjoyed a certain *de facto* independence from Moscow.

However, over the past twenty years, the characteristics of raion Soviets changed significantly, due to an increase in the number of qualified leaders. Until the 1960s, it was possible that a chairman of a collective farm who had graduated from a Higher Party School by "home education (*zaochnoe*)" won rapid promotion up to the position of first secretary of a raion committee of the CPSU, for instance, within three years.[31] It was the professionalization of party and Soviet duties during the Brezhnev era that made such ridiculous things impossible.

Improvement in the quality of raion leadership made the relationship between oblast and raion Soviets similar to that between guberniia and uezd zemstvos: oblast Soviets (party committees) worked out strategic objectives, and raion Soviets (party committees) gave them shape and put them into effect. The raion became an independent unit of policy-making and, consequently, of self-government. As the Soviet regime abandoned policies which had provoked the hostility of the population and as raion organs overcame the chronic insufficiency in intellectual manpower, raions were steadily *uezdized*. Ironically, it was then that the Presidential coup abolished the raion representative organs. This was the first time that Russian "uezds" lost their organs of representation since the time of Alexander II.

IV. Conclusion

Since Russian historical geography is in an underdeveloped state, we must, if quoting again Bater and French, try to "illuminate certain directions in which one can advance... like street lamps spaced out along roads."[32]

As for the question of regionalization, the conclusion reached in this chapter is quite simple. Three pre-revolutionary territorial categories of peasant life were consolidated into the present village district. Raions succeeded uchastoks, but steadily became "uezdized."

Methodologically, what "directions" can this chapter "illuminate"? Generally speaking, it is impossible to share mentalities, emotions, and ways of thinking with historical figures if we do not feel their sense of space. Moreover, this chapter has tried to prove that spatial sensitivity prevents historians from a dogmatic conceptualization of phenomena and precludes the mechanical transplantation of European concepts such as "parliamentary democracy," the "sovereign state," and "Weberian bureaucracy" to Russia. Spatial sensitivity provides criteria for ascertaining what was feasible in the past. In brief, a sense of "space" is one of the bases for historical realism.

Notes

1 J.H. Bater and R.A. French (eds.), *Studies in Russian Historical Geography*, 2 vols. (London, 1983), p. 2.

2 J.P. LeDonne, "The Geopolitical Context of Russian Foreign Policy: 1700-1917," *Acta Slavica Iaponica*, tomus XII (1994), pp. 1-23.

3 J.P. LeDonne, "From Guberniia to Oblast: Soviet Territorial-Administrative Reform 1917-1923," Ph. D. dissertation, Columbia University, 1962, p. 112.

4 The population density of France was 71.8 person/km² according to the 1896 Census (*Entsiklopedicheskii slovar', Brokgauz i Efron*, vol.

XXXVI^, 1902, pp. 550-551). The figure for Russia was 6.0 according to the 1897 Census (*Ibid.*, vol. XXVII^, 1899, p. 115).

5 See this author's "Teisei Rosia no Chiho Seido 1889-1917 [Local Government in Late Imperial Russia: 1889-1917]," *Suravu kenkyu (Slavic Studies)*, No. 40 (1993), pp. 167-183; Idem, "Zemusutovo no Saigo: Rosia niokeru Shiminteki Minshushugi no Kanousei [The End of Zemstvos: A Possibility of Burgerlich Democracy in Russia]," *Surabu no sekai* [The Slavic World] series, vol. 3 (1995); Idem, "Konets zemstva," *Istoriia zemstva i perspektivy razvitiia mestnogo samoupravleniia v Rossii* (forthcoming).

6 Y. Taniuchi, *Sutarin Seiji Taisei no Seiritsu [The Formation of the Stalinist Political Regime]*, vol. 2 (Tokyo, 1972), pp. 489-502.

7 Ibid., pp. 494-502.

8 The scaling down of selsovets and raions territories in the mid-1930s was one component of "Spring of the Soviets" at that time. See: K. Uchida, "Sutarin Seiji Taiseika no Nouson niokeru Touch Taisei no Saihen: 1931-34 [The Reorganization of Rural Government under the Stalinist Political Regime: 1931-34," *Suravu kenkyu*, No. 29 (1982), pp. 115-116 (for its English summary, see, pp. 117-121).

9 *Sovetskaia istoricheskaia entsiklopediia*, vol. 5 (1964), pp. 738-739.

10 J.P. LeDonne traced the origin of the concept of "economic affinity" to several things in pre-revolutionary Russia: a project for economic regionalization prepared by the Ministry of Commerce and Industry; the activities of regional unions of zemstvos; and, the establishment of the Standing Commission for the Study of the Natural Productive Forces of Russia (*Kommissiia po izucheniiu estestvennykh proizvoditel'nykh sil Rossii*) created in the Academy of Sciences in May, 1915 in order to mobilize Russian industry for war management (LeDonne, "From gubernia...," pp. 31-42, 52 and 66-68). Since not only this Academy Commission but also various regional unions of zemstvos emerged during World War I, it must be noted that the concept of "economic affinity" was brought to the forefront not only by Russia's industrial development but also by the necessities for the total-war management. In other words, attempts at economic regionalization in Russia were, from the very beginning, connected with the idea of public control of the national economy.

11 With regard to discussion about regionalization in the 1920s, both Y. Taniuchi and J.P. LeDonne focused on the confrontation between the Administrative Commission organized under the leadership of the Commissariat of Internal Affairs and the Goerlo-Gosplan block. Taniuchi explained this as an expression of the agrarian-industrial conflict (*Sobieto Seijishi: Kenryoku to Noumin [A Soviet Political History: Power and Peasants]*, (Tokyo, 1962), pp. 189-195 and 212-214). LeDonne explains it as a conflict dating back to pre-revolutionary Russia. In his opinion, pre-revolutionary attempts at

territorial reform tried to satisfy two requirements: the adaptation of
territorial units to economic affinity, and the improvement of
administrative effectiveness in local government. The former
demanded, as a rule, enlargement of territorial units, whereas the
latter could be achieved "by granting smaller territories the
authority of larger ones" ("From Guberniia...," p. 127), namely by
downscaling the territories. Therefore, the replacement of volosts by
raions had dual significance – the introduction of larger volosts for
the first purpose; and for the second, introduction of smaller uezds.
Similarly, okrugs were enlarged uezds for the first purpose, but for
the second, reduced guberniias.

12 Taniuchi, *Sutarin...*, vol. 4 (1986), pp. 752-770.

13 Hiroshi Okuda provides an excellent description of "selo-derevnias"
    units in his book *Soveto Keizai Seisakushi* [*A History of Soviet
    Economic Policy*] (Tokyo, 1979), pp. 1-6. Let us glance at one example
    of Voronezhskaia guberniia presented by Okuda. There were 136
    "commercial-bazaar selos" in the guberniia. The radius of their
    economic influence (*tiagotenie*) was roughly 10 to 13 km. However,
    on the average, satellite derevnias were located within 5 km from the
    selos. Since Voronezhskaia guberniia did not experience a drastic
    territorial change during the Soviet era, we can make a long-term
    comparison.

Pre-Revolutionary Voronezhskaia guberniia (65,900 sq. km)

Selenies	... 2,358
Peasant communes	... 2,099
Volosts	... 232 (Average radius 9.5km)
"Commercial-bazaar selos" ...	136 (Average radius 10-13km)
Zemstvo agronomic districts (uchastoks) ... 58	
Uezds	... 12

Voronezhskaia oblast in 1993 (52,400 sq. km)

Selsovets	... 490
Raions	... 32

Apparently, the "commercial-bazaar selo" is narrower concept
than the usual "selo." As a result, the evidence used by Okuda
indicates that "commercial-bazaar selos" were more sparsely
distributed than volost centers. Except for this, the example of
Voronezhskaia guberniia does not contradict the statistics analyzed
below.

The specified number of agronomic uchastoks applies for 1916
(Departament zemledeliia, *Mestnyi agronomicheskii personal,
sostoiavshii na pravitel'stvennoi i obshchestvennoi sluzhbe, 1 ianvaria
1916*, Petrograd, 1917, pp. 48-59). The number of agronomic

uchastoks in a uezd reflected the level of the uezd zemstvo's agricultural policy. For example, in Voronezhskii uezd (where the uezd zemstvo was very active in agricultural assistance) each uchastok agronomist was responsible for only 1-3 volosts. On the other hand, in Biriuchenskii and Pavlovskii uezds, agronomic uchastoks consisted of 6-7 volosts.

14 A. Chaianov, *Metody izlozheniia predmetov* (Moscow, 1916), p. 4.

15 In this paper, only official records for selenies could be used. If we survey rural churches, schools, bazaars, and taverns, we would be able to present a much more vivid picture of the relationship between selos, derevnias, and those categories falling between the two (polselos, etc.).

16 Among the eight zones indicated, we can elucidate four basic categories. Zone A with very low population densities can be termed "northern peripheral type"; here, as a rule, a large peasant commune consisted of numerous small selenies. Zone D with low or medium population densities can be termed "northern peasant type"; here, a medium-sized commune consisted of many small selenies. Zone F with medium or high population densities can be termed "southern peasant type"; here, a large commune consisted almost entirely of a large selenie (or the size of the latter might even exceed the former). Zone H with low population densities can be termed "southern peripheral type"; here, a large commune consisted of several large selenies.

Zone B, where the relationship between communes and selenies continues to be the same as in Zone A, can be regarded as intermediate between A and D. Zone E falls between D and F not only spatially but also typologically. In the same way, Zone G lies between F and H. Thus, only the C group cannot be categorized.

17 Taniuchi, *Sutarin...*, vol. 2, p. 500.

18 Sometimes the tsarist government was forced to to intrude into the purely geographical demarcation. For example, the Provisional Statute of Food Administration in 1901 afforded the opportunity to divide volosts into food precincts. This was designed to bring public food management closer to the people, mobilize rural intelligentsia (irrespective of the estate to which they belonged), and release volost officials from this tiresome duty. However, according to a survey made by the Ministry of Internal Affairs in 1904, the local authorities' responses to this Statute were not positive. Volosts were divided into food precincts in some uezds in Bessarabskaia, Vilenskaia, Voronezhskaia, Viatskaia, Kovenskaia, Mogilevskaia, Nizhegorodskaia, Olonetskaia, Orenburgskaia, Orlovskaia, Permskaia, Samarskaia, Saratovskaia, and Tambovskaia guberniias. However, in most cases, smaller precincts emerged only

temporarily due to the famine of 1901-02 (RGIA, f. 1291, op. 130-1902 g., d. 106-a, 6 and в).

19 E.H. Carr, *Socialism in One Country 1924-1926,* vol. 2 (London, 1959), p. 356.

20 Taniuchi, *Sutarin...,* vol. 2, pp. 500-501.

21 N. Smirnova, "Sokhraniatsia li sel'sovety?" *Tverskie vedomosti* (October 18 1991), p. 2.

22 Interview with A.V. Baranov, the Head of the village administration of the "Stantsiia Staritsa" district (Staritskii raion, Tverskaia oblast), April 15, 1994.

23 LeDonne, "From Guberniia...," p. 140.

24 Taniuchi, *Sobieto...,* p. 195.

25 *Izvestiia Moskovskoi gubernskoi zemskoi upravy,* 1914, No. 1, p. 4.

26 *Mestnyi agronomicheskii personal...1 ianvaria 1913* (St. Petersburg, 1913). The total number was calculated by this author.

27 For example, see: Gosudarstvennyi arkhiv Tambovskoi oblasti, f. 24, op. 1, d. 698, ll. 14-15.

28 For example, see: Gosudarstvennyi arkhiv Samarskoi oblasti, f. 5, op. 11, d. 226, l. 10.

29 Ibid., l. 15.

30 Taniuchi, *Sutarin...,* vol. 4 (Tokyo, 1986), pp. 754-757.

31 Personal list (*lichnoe delo*) included in f. 147 of *Tsentr dokumentatsii noveishei istorii Tverskoi oblasti* (the former Party archive of Tverskaia oblast). This "personal lists" have neither been classified nor numbered, since it is part of a huge complex of archival materials transferred to the Party archive after the Tver oblast committee of the CPSU was liquidated.

32 Bater and French, op. cit., vol. 2, p. 483.

⟨Map 1⟩ *Administrative Territorial Division of Late Imperoal Russia*

⟨*Map 2*⟩ *Administrative Territorial Division of Present European CIS*

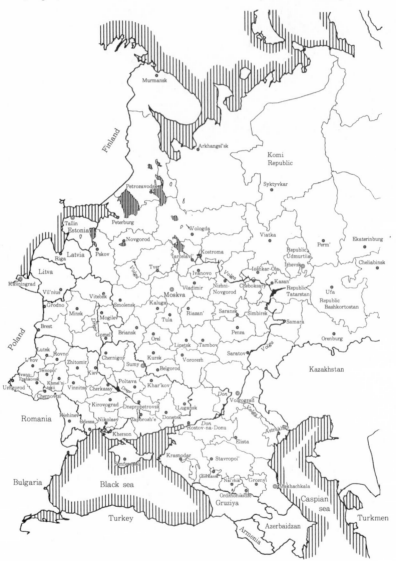

⟨*Map 3*⟩ *Population Structures, in Guberniias
of Pre-Revolutionary European Russia*

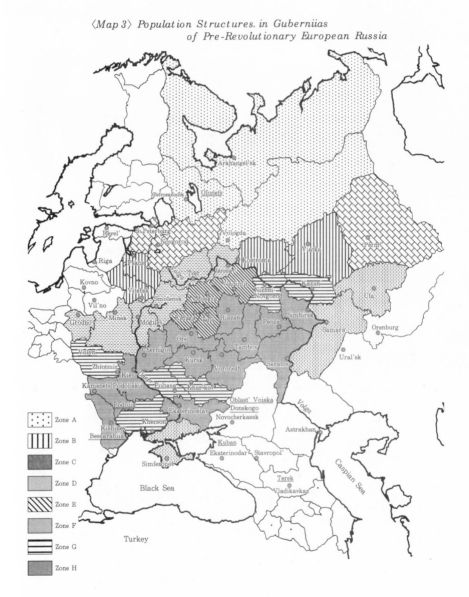

Table 1 Numbers and Areas of Administrative-Territorial Units in Pre-Revolutionary European Russia

Guberniia	Areas (sq.verst)	Areas (sq.km)	Population including urban area	population density	Number of uezds	Number of volosts	Number of sel'skie o-vos	Number of selenies
1 Arkhangel'skaia	748,051	851,282	347,509	0.4	8	100	306	3,006
2 Vologodskaia	353,349	402,111	1,365,587	3.4	10	225	1,630	12,677
3 S-Peterburgskaia	39,203	44,613	2,107,691	47.2	8	126	1,460	4,033
4 Novgorodskaia	104,163	118,537	1,392,933	11.8	11	238	4,890	9,631
5 Olonetskaia	112,322	127,822	366,715	2.9	7	80	354	4,223
6 Pskovskaia	37,956	43,194	1,136,540	26.3	8	144	1,833	15,997
subtotal/average	1,395,043	1,587,559	6,716,975	4.2	52	913	10,473	49,567
7 Vladimirskaia	42,832	48,743	1,570,733	32.2	13	222	4,159	6,252
8 Kaluzhskaia	27,178	30,928	1,185,726	38.3	11	205	2,776	4,175
9 Kostromskaia	73,809	83,995	1,429,228	17.0	12	263	2,038	12,515
10 Moskovskaia	29,236	33,271	2,433,356	73.1	13	166	3,594	5,514
11 Riazanskaia	36,845	41,929	1,827,539	43.6	12	248	4,848	3,362
12 Smolenskaia	49,212	56,003	1,551,068	27.7	12	266	4,144	11,015
13 Tverskaia	56,837	64,681	1,812,825	28.0	12	244	4,042	10,809
14 Tul'skaia	27,204	30,958	1,432,743	46.3	12	279	4,433	4,207
15 Iaroslavskaia	31,231	35,541	1,072,478	30.2	10	165	1,810	9,530
subtotal/average	374,383	426,048	14,315,696	33.6	107	2,058	31,844	67,379
16 Voronezhskaia	57,902	65,892	2,546,255	38.6	12	232	2,099	2,358
17 Kurskaia	40,821	46,454	2,396,577	51.6	15	214	3,646	3,410
18 Orlovskaia	41,058	46,724	2,054,749	44.0	12	198	3,943	4,154
19 Tambovskaia	58,511	66,586	2,715,453	40.8	12	331	3,627	3,365
subtotal/average	198,292	225,656	9,713,034	43.0	51	975	13,315	13,287
20 Nizhegorodskaia	45,037	51,252	1,600,304	31.2	11	258	2,927	3,798
21 Kazanskaia	55,955	63,677	2,191,058	34.4	12	182	3,003	4,224
22 Samarskaia	136,714	155,580	2,763,478	17.8	7	305	2,121	3,047
23 Simbirskaia	43,491	49,493	1,549,461	31.3	8	155	2,277	1,809
24 Penzenskaia	34,129	38,839	1,491,215	38.4	10	240	2,337	1,840
25 Saratovskaia	74,245	84,491	2,419,884	28.6	10	281	2,289	2,135
subtotal/average	389,570	443,330	12,015,400	27.1	58	1,421	14,954	16,853
26 Viatskaia	135,020	153,652	3,082,788	20.1	11	306	2,725	21,711
27 Permskaia	290,169	330,212	3,003,208	9.1	12	482	3,141	12,759
28 Ufimskaia	107,210	122,005	2,220,497	18.2	6	175	1,909	3,469
subtotal/average	532,398	605,869	8,306,493	13.7	29	963	7,775	37,939
Total/average 1-28	2,889,686	3,288,463	51,067,598	15.5	297	6,330	78,361	185,025
29 Ekaterinoslavskaia	55,706	63,393	2,112,651	33.3	8	225	1,630	1,756
30 Poltavskaia	43,844	49,894	2,794,727	56.0	15	263	2,885	5,403
31 Tavricheskaia	53,054	60,375	1,443,566	23.9	8	89	583	1,616
32 Khar'kovskaia	47,885	54,493	2,509,811	46.1	11	264	1,683	3,313
33 Khersonskaia	62,213	70,798	2,732,832	38.6	6	233	2,009	3,539
34 Chernigovskaia	46,042	52,396	2,321,900	44.3	15	175	3,134	3,345
subtotal/average	308,744	351,350	13,915,487	39.6	63	1,249	11,924	18,972
35 Volynskaia	63,037	71,736	2,997,902	41.8	12	207	2,718	6,180
36 Kievskaia	44,778	50,957	3,576,125	70.2	12	202	1,985	2,357
37 Podol'skaia	36,922	42,017	3,031,513	72.1	12	153	1,887	1,986
subtotal/average	144,736	164,710	9,605,540	58.3	36	562	6,590	10,523
Total/average 29-37	453,480	516,060	23,521,027	45.6	99	1,811	18,514	29,495
38 Vitebskaia	38,650	43,983	1,502,916	34.7	11	197	995	15,096
39 Grodnenskaia	33,901	38,579	1,617,859	41.9	9	185	2,225	7,992
40 Minskaia	80,152	91,213	2,156,123	23.6	9	202	1,634	10,634
41 Mogilevskaia	42,135	47,949	1,708,041	35.6	11	145	1,903	7,880
subtotal/average	194,837	221,725	6,984,939	31.5	40	729	6,757	41,602
42 Bessarabskaia	39,015	44,399	1,933,436	43.5	8	213	1,241	1,514
TOTAL AND AVERAGE 1-42	3,577,019	4,070,647	83,507,000	20.5	444	9,083	104,873	257,636

According to the Census in 1897. Baltic guberniias (Vilenskaia, Kovenskaia, Kurliandskaia, Liflandskaia and Estliandskaia) and the guberniias containing nomad and Cossack territories (Astrakhanskaia, Orenburgskaia and Oblast Voiska Donskogo) are excluded.

Average number of volosts in an uezd	Average number of sel.o-vos in a vol.	Average number of selenies in an o-vo	Average area of an uezd (sq.km)	Average area of a volost (sq.km)	Average radius of a volost (km)	Average male population belonging to o-vos	Average number of males in an o-vo	Average number of males in a selenie	Guberniia	
12.5	3.1	9.8	106,410	8,513	52.1	148,551	485.5	49.4	Arkhangel'skaia	1
22.5	7.2	7.8	40,211	1,787	23.9	585,102	359.0	46.2	Vologodskaia	2
15.8	11.6	2.8	5,577	354	10.6	270,518	185.3	67.1	S-Peterburgskaia	3
21.6	20.5	2.0	10,776	498	12.6	542,920	111.0	56.4	Novgorodskaia	4
11.4	4.4	11.9	18,260	1,598	22.6	158,567	447.9	37.5	Olonetskaia	5
18.0	12.7	8.7	5,399	300	9.8	448,397	244.6	28.0	Pskovskaia	6
17.6	**11.5**	**4.7**	**30,530**	**1,739**	**23.5**	**2,154,055**	**205.7**	**43.5**	subtotal/average	
17.1	18.7	1.5	3,749	220	8.4	606,766	145.9	97.1	Vladimirskaia	7
18.6	13.5	1.5	2,812	151	6.9	517,405	186.4	123.9	Kaluzhskaia	8
21.9	7.7	6.1	7,000	319	10.1	557,951	273.8	44.6	Kostromskaia	9
12.8	21.7	1.5	2,559	200	8.0	576,894	160.5	104.6	Moskovskaia	10
20.7	19.5	0.7	3,494	169	7.3	837,232	172.7	249.0	Riazanskaia	11
22.2	15.6	2.7	4,667	211	8.2	627,976	151.5	57.0	Smolenskaia	12
20.3	16.6	2.7	5,390	265	9.2	770,182	190.5	71.3	Tverskaia	13
23.3	15.9	0.9	2,580	111	5.9	633,020	142.8	150.5	Tul'skaia	14
16.5	11.0	5.3	3,554	215	8.3	432,615	239.0	45.4	Iaroslavskaia	15
19.2	**15.5**	**2.1**	**3,982**	**207**	**8.1**	**5,560,041**	**174.6**	**82.5**	subtotal/average	
19.3	9.0	1.1	5,491	284	9.5	1,170,652	557.7	496.5	Voronezhskaia	16
14.3	17.0	0.9	3,097	217	8.3	1,048,156	287.5	307.4	Kurskaia	17
16.5	19.9	1.1	3,894	236	8.7	864,732	219.3	208.2	Orlovskaia	18
27.6	11.0	0.9	5,549	201	8.0	1,195,572	329.6	355.3	Tambovskaia	19
19.1	**13.7**	**1.0**	**4,425**	**231**	**8.6**	**4,279,112**	**321.4**	**322.1**	subtotal/average	
23.5	11.3	1.3	4,659	199	8.0	653,117	223.1	172.0	Nizhegorodskaia	20
15.2	16.5	1.4	5,306	350	10.6	967,348	322.1	229.0	Kazanskaia	21
43.6	7.0	1.4	22,226	510	12.7	1,118,162	527.2	367.0	Samarskaia	22
19.4	14.7	0.8	6,187	319	10.1	679,332	298.3	375.5	Simbirskaia	23
24.0	9.7	0.8	3,884	162	7.2	690,863	295.6	375.5	Penzenskaia	24
28.1	8.1	0.9	8,449	301	9.8	967,560	422.7	453.2	Saratovskaia	25
24.5	**10.5**	**1.1**	**7,644**	**312**	**10.0**	**5,076,382**	**339.5**	**301.2**	subtotal/average	
27.8	8.9	8.0	13,968	502	12.6	1,365,993	501.3	62.9	Viatskaia	26
40.2	6.5	4.1	27,518	685	14.8	1,239,198	394.5	97.1	Permskaia	27
29.2	10.9	1.8	20,334	697	14.9	846,960	443.7	244.2	Ufimskaia	28
33.2	**8.1**	**4.9**	**20,892**	**629**	**14.2**	**3,452,151**	**444.0**	**91.0**	subtotal/average	
21.3	**12.4**	**2.4**	**11,072**	**520**	**12.9**	**20,521,741**	**261.9**	**110.9**	Total/average 1-28	
28.1	7.2	1.1	7,924	282	9.5	713,251	437.6	406.2	Ekaterinoslavskaia	29
17.5	11.0	1.9	3,326	190	7.8	1,091,041	378.2	201.9	Poltavskaia	30
11.1	6.6	2.8	7,547	678	14.7	422,443	724.6	261.4	Tavricheskaia	31
24.0	6.4	2.0	4,954	206	8.1	989,236	587.8	298.6	Khar'kovskaia	32
38.8	8.6	1.8	11,800	304	9.8	676,698	336.8	191.2	Khersonskaia	33
11.7	17.9	1.1	3,493	299	9.8	849,198	271.0	253.9	Chernigovskaia	34
19.8	**9.5**	**1.6**	**5,577**	**281**	**9.5**	**4,741,867**	**397.7**	**249.9**	subtotal/average	
17.3	13.1	2.3	5,978	347	10.5	816,533	300.4	132.1	Volynskaia	35
16.8	9.8	1.2	4,246	252	9.0	1,193,448	601.2	506.3	Kievskaia	36
12.8	12.3	1.1	3,501	275	9.4	997,327	528.5	502.2	Podol'skaia	37
15.6	**11.7**	**1.6**	**4,575**	**293**	**9.7**	**3,007,308**	**456.3**	**285.8**	subtotal/average	
18.3	**10.2**	**1.6**	**5,213**	**285**	**9.5**	**7,749,175**	**418.6**	**262.7**	Total/average 29-37	
17.9	5.1	15.2	3,998	223	8.4	491,937	494.4	32.6	Vitebskaia	38
20.6	12.0	3.6	4,287	209	8.1	471,541	211.9	59.0	Grodnenskaia	39
22.4	8.1	6.5	10,135	452	12.0	643,532	393.8	60.5	Minskaia	40
13.2	13.1	4.1	4,359	331	10.3	558,824	293.7	70.9	Mogilevskaia	41
18.2	**9.3**	**6.2**	**5,543**	**304**	**9.8**	**2,165,834**	**320.5**	**52.1**	subtotal/average	
26.6	5.8	1.2	5,550	208	8.1	587,210	473.2	387.9	Bessarabskaia	42
20.5	**11.5**	**2.5**	**9,168**	**448**	**11.9**	**31,023,960**	**295.8**	**120.4**	**TOTAL/AVERAGE 1-42**	

Table 2 The Areas and Numbers of Administrative-Territorial Units in the Provinces of the RSFSR, USSR and the BSSR

European Part of the RSFSR (excluding Kaliningradskaia oblast' and Karel'skaia ASSR)

	Areas (sq.km)	Areas of former guberniias (sq.km)	raions (1963	1972	1993)	selsovets (1963	1972	1993)	Average number of selsovets in a raion (1963	1972	1993)
North-Western Region	1662.8		103	137	144	1799	1733	1658	17.5	12.6	11.5
1 Arkhangel'skaia oblast	587.3	851.3	21	19	20	241	235	240	11.5	12.4	12.0
2 Vologodskaia oblast	145.8	402.1	19	26	26	372	382	376	19.6	14.7	14.5
3 Leningradskaia oblast	85.9	44.6	10	16	17	314	250	212	31.4	15.6	12.5
4 Murmanskaia oblast	144.9		4	4	5	28	19	21	7.0	4.8	4.2
5 Novgorodskaia oblast	55.3	118.5	12	20	21	340	327	275	28.3	16.4	13.1
6 Pskovskaia oblast	55.3	43.2	16	24	24	238	247	247	14.9	10.3	10.3
7 Karel'skaia ASSR	172.4		10	15	15	114	112	99	11.4	7.5	6.6
8 Komi ASSR	415.9		11	13	16	152	161	188	13.8	12.4	11.8
Central Region	460.5		148	256	278	4143	4146	4016	28.0	16.2	14.4
9 Brianskaia oblast	34.9		14	22	27	387	385	411	27.6	17.5	15.2
10 Vladimirskaia oblast	28.9	48.7	14	16	16	223	228	222	15.9	14.3	13.9
11 Ivanovskaia oblast	24.0		11	19	22	235	230	216	21.4	12.1	9.8
12 Kalininskaia oblast	84.2	64.7	17	33	36	646	637	617	38.0	19.3	17.1
13 Kaluzhskaia oblast	29.8	30.9	13	23	24	316	338	339	24.3	14.7	14.1
14 Kostromskaia oblast	60.2	84.0	14	24	24	244	248	267	17.4	10.3	11.1
15 Moskovskaia oblast	47.0	33.3	12	39	39	582	556	474	48.5	14.3	12.2
16 Riazanskaia oblast	39.6	41.9	17	24	25	520	509	484	30.6	21.2	19.4
17 Smolenskaia oblast	49.9	56.0	14	20	25	404	400	415	28.9	20.0	16.6
18 Tul'skaia oblast	25.7	31.0	12	23	23	346	375	345	28.8	16.3	15.0
19 Iaroslavskaia oblast	36.3	35.5	10	13	17	240	240	226	24.0	18.5	13.3
Volga-Viatska Region	263.2		68	141	143	1743	1943	2040	25.6	13.8	14.3
20 Gor'kovskaia oblast	74.8	51.3	18	47	47	519	527	519	28.8	11.2	11.0
21 Kirovskaia oblast	120.7	153.7	20	39	39	423	548	586	21.2	14.1	15.0
22 Mariiskaia ASSR	23.2		8	13	14	127	154	176	15.9	11.8	12.6
23 Mordovskaia ASSR	26.2		11	21	22	373	395	413	33.9	18.8	18.8
24 Chuvashskaia ASSR	18.3		11	21	21	301	319	346	27.4	15.2	16.5
Central Black-Soil Region	192.4		75	131	146	2091	2069	2110	27.9	15.8	14.5
25 Belgorodskaia oblast	27.1		12	18	21	346	330	324	28.8	18.3	15.4
26 Voronezhskaia oblast	52.4	65.9	16	29	32	479	479	490	29.9	16.5	15.3
27 Kurskaia oblast	29.8	46.5	12	25	28	434	434	474	36.2	17.4	16.9
28 Lipetskaia oblast	24.1		10	18	18	307	296	297	30.7	16.4	16.5
29 Orlovskaia oblast	24.7	46.7	12	19	24	222	224	221	18.5	11.8	9.2
30 Tambovskaia oblast	34.3	66.6	13	22	23	303	306	304	23.3	13.9	13.2
Volga Region	536.5		107	198	214	2660	2771	3112	24.9	14.0	14.5
31 Astrakhanskaia oblast	44.1	235.8	7	10	11	119	121	141	17.0	12.1	12.8
32 Volgogradskaia oblast	114.1		19	32	33	396	394	442	20.8	12.3	13.4
33 Kuibyshevskaia oblast	53.7	155.6	13	25	27	275	277	309	21.2	11.1	11.4
34 Penzenskaia oblast	43.2	38.8	15	27	28	263	317	375	17.5	11.7	13.4
35 Saratovskaia oblast	100.2	84.5	18	36	38	517	525	587	28.7	14.6	15.4
36 Ul'ianovskaia oblast	37.3	49.5	12	20	21	263	267	311	21.9	13.4	14.8
37 Kalmytskaia ASSR	75.9		6	12	13	61	83	104	10.2	6.9	8.0
38 Tatarskaia ASSR	68.0	63.7	17	36	43	766	787	843	45.1	21.9	19.6
Ural Region	823.9		109	225	229	2994	3116	3422	27.5	13.8	14.9
39 Kurganskaia oblast	71.0		11	22	24	380	361	417	34.5	16.4	17.4
40 Orenburugskaia oblast	123.9	189.7	17	34	35	489	520	573	28.8	15.3	16.4
41 Permskaia oblast	160.7	330.2	20	37	37	491	496	512	24.6	13.4	13.8
42 Sverdlovskaia oblast	194.7		16	30	30	428	440	429	26.8	14.7	14.3
43 Cheliabinskaia oblast	87.9		12	24	24	173	218	264	14.4	9.1	11.0
44 Bashkirskaia ASSR	143.6	122.0	21	53	54	777	832	922	37.0	15.7	17.1
45 Udmurtskaia ASSR	42.1		12	25	25	256	249	305	21.3	10.0	12.2
TOTAL	3939.3		610	1088	1154	15430	15778	16358	25.3	14.5	14.2
Total minus 31, 37 and 40	3695.4		580	1032	1095	14761	15054	15540	25.5	14.6	14.2

Ukrainian SSR (1982)

	Areas (sq.km)	Areas of former guberniias (sq.km)	raions	selsovets	Average number of selsovets in a raion
Vinitskaia oblast	26.5		26	588	22.6
Volynskaia oblast	20.2	71.7	15	309	20.6
Voroshilovgradskaia oblast	26.7		18	170	9.4
Dnepropetrovskaia oblast	31.9	63.4	20	232	11.6
Donetskaia oblast	26.5		18	208	11.6
Zhitomirovskaia oblast	29.9		22	531	24.1
Zakarpatskaia oblast	12.8		13	257	19.8
Zaporozhskaia oblast	27.2		18	228	12.7
Ivanovo-Frankovskaia obl.	13.9		14	350	25.0
Kievskaia oblast	28.9	51.0	25	558	22.3
Kirovogradskaia oblast	24.6		21	297	14.1
Krymskaia oblast	27.0	60.4	15	231	15.4
L'vovskaia oblast	21.8		20	485	24.3
Nikolaevskaia oblast	24.6		19	223	11.7
Odesskaia oblst'	33.3		26	353	13.6
Poltavskaia oblast	28.8	49.9	25	375	15.0
Rovenskaia oblast	20.1		15	303	20.2
Sumskaia oblast	23.8		18	341	18.9
Ternopol'skaia oblast	13.8		16	424	26.5
Khar'kovskaia oblast	31.4	54.5	25	327	13.1
Khersonskaia oblast	28.5	70.8	18	217	12.1
Khmel'nitskaia oblast	20.6		20	465	23.3
Cherkasskaia oblast	20.9		20	412	20.6
Chernovitskaia oblast	8.1		10	204	20.4
Chernigovskaia oblast	31.9	35.5	22	460	20.9
Total	**603.7**		**479**	**8548**	**17.8**
minus					
Zakarpatskaia obl.	12.8		13	257	19.8
Ivanovo-Frankovskaia obl.	13.9		14	350	25.0
Ternopol'skaia obl.	13.8		16	424	26.5
L'vovskaia obl.	21.8		20	485	24.3
Chernovitskaia obl.	8.1		10	204	20.4
Total without Wst.Ukraina	**533.3**		**406**	**6828**	**16.8**

Belorussian SSR (1989)

	Areas (sq.km)	Areas of former guberniias (sq.km)	raions	selsovets	Average number of selsovets in a raion
Brestskaia oblast	32.3		16	225	14.1
Vitebskaia oblast	40.1	44.0	21	249	11.9
Gomel'skaia oblast	40.4		21	299	14.2
Grodonenskaia oblast	25.0	38.6	17	195	11.5
Minskaia oblast	40.8	91.2	22	307	14.0
Mogilevskaia oblast	29.0	47.9	20	207	10.4
Total	**207.6**		**117**	**1482**	**12.7**

Table 3   The Number of Administrative-territorial Units in the
Russian Soviet Federated Socialist Republic

	1917	1922	1923	1924	1925	1926	1927	1928	1929	1935	1941
Territory (millions of km²)	20.8				20.0					19.6	16.8
Autonomous republics	-	7	11	12	9	11	11	11	2	15	16
Autonomous oblasts	-	8	14	12	15	12	12	12	12	10	6
Krais	-	-	-	-	1	1	1	3	5	12	6
Oblasts	-	-	-	1	1	2	3	2	8	27	35
Guberniias and oblasts with the right of guberniias	56	72	63	61	51	40	38	33	-	-	-
Okrugs	-	-	-	15	28	58	59	67	125	12	7
National okrugs	-	-	-	-	-	?	?	1	-	9	10
Uezds	476	601	607	551	435	359	366	308	-	-	-
Raions	-	-	-	132	353	769	779	986	1,576	2,365	2,339
Volosts	10,606	12,363	10,972	8,556	4,491	3,479	3,341	2,791	-	-	-
Sel'skie sovets	-	120,200	96,700	76,456	45,170	50,000	?	55,858	43,744	45,601	41,105
Sel'skie ob-vos	110,000	-	-	-	-	-	-	-	-	-	-
volosts/a uezd*	22.3	20.5	/	/	/	/	/	/	-	-	-
selsovets/a raion (or a volost)**	-	9.7	/	/	/	/	/	/	27.8	19.3	17.6

	1950	1954	1957	1959	1962	1963	1966	1971	1979	1989	1992
Territory (millions of km²)	16.9	16.9	17.1	17.1	17.1	17.1	17.1	17.1	17.1	17.1	17.1
Autonomous republics	12	12	14	15	16	16	16	16	16	16	21
Autonomous oblasts	6	6	7	6	5	5	5	5	5	5	1
Krais	6	6	6	6	6	6	6	6	6	6	5
Oblasts	50	51	53	49	49	49	49	49	49	49	49
National okrugs	10	10	10	10	10	10	10	10	10	10	10
Raions	2,529	2,476	2,321	2,237	1,967	1,049	1,627	1,750	1,800	1,839	1,863
Sel'skie sovets	41,195	40,671	27,439	26,770	22,412	22,132	21,987	22,587	22,683	23,223	24,084
Population places	?	?	?	?	?	?	?	?	177.0	152.9	?
selsovets/a raion	16.3	16.4	11.8	12.0	11.4	21.1	13.5	12.9	12.6	12.6	12.9
pop. places/a selsovet***	/	/	/	/	/	/	/	/	7.8	6.6	/

*   Average number of volosts in a uezd.
**   Average number of selsovets in a raion (or a volost).
***   Average number of population places in a selsovet.

Sources: Tsentral'noe upravlenie narodnokhoziaistvennogo ucheta gosplana SSSR,
Sotsialisticheskoe stroitel'stvo SSSR (*Statisticheskii ezhegodnik*), 1936, XLVI-XLIX;
Statisticheskoe upravlenie RSFSR, *Narodnoe khoziaistvo RSFSR* (*Statisticheskii
sbornik*), 1957, pp. 5-6; Tsentral'noe statisticheskoe upravlenie pri sovete ministrov
RSFSR, *Narodnoe khoziaistvo RSFSR v 1962 godu* (*Statisticheskii ezhegodnik*), 1963, p.
7; Tsentral'noe statisticheskoe upravlenie pri sovete ministrov RSFSR, *Narodnoe
khoziaistvo RSFSR v 1971 godu* (*Statisticheskii ezhegodnik*), 1972, p. 7; Tsentral'noe
statisticheskoe upravlenie RSFSR, *Narodnoe khoziaistvo RSFSR v 1978 godu*
(*Statisticheskii ezhegodnik*), 1979, pp. 13-15; Gosudarstvennyi komitet RSFSR po
statistike, *Narodnoe khoziaistvo RSFSR v 1988 godu* (*Statisticheskii ezhegodnik*),
1989,pp. 22-24; Goskomstat Rossii, *Rossiiskaia federatsiia v 1992 godu* (*Statisticheskii
ezhegodnik*), 1993, pp. 5-10; Y.Taniuchi, *Sutarin Seiji Taisei no Seiritsu*, vol. 1 (Tokyo,
1970), p. 705 and vol.2 (Tokyo, 1972), p. 496; E.H.Carr, *Socialism in one country 1924-
1926*, vol. 2 (London, 1959), pp. 282-292.

Table 4   The Number of Administrative-Territorial Units in the Ukrainian Soviet Socialist Republic

	1897	1922	1923	1935	1940	1965	1970	1979
area (1000 km²)	516.1	451.8	-	443.1	-	603.7	-	-
Guberniias	9	9	-	-	-	-	-	-
Aut. Republic	-	-	-	1	-	-	-	-
Oblasts	-	-	0	7	23	25	25	25
Uezds	99	102	?	-	-	-	-	-
Okrugs	-	-	40	8	-	-	-	-
Volosts	1811	1989	-	-	-	-	-	-
Raions	-	-	579	483	746	394	476	479
Sel'skie obshchestvos	18 514	-	-	-	-	-	-	-
Sel'skie sovets	-	?	10 990	11 136	16 289	8 486	8 598	8 522
population places (M)	29.5	?	?	?	?	?	?	29.7
volosts/a uezd*	18.3	-	-	-	-	-	-	-
sel. o-vos/a volost**	10.2	-	-	-	-	-	-	-
selsovets/a raion***	-	-	19.0	23.1	21.9	21.5	18.1	17.8
pop. places/a selsovet**** (or a sel.o-vo)	1.6	/	/	/	/	/	/	3.4

*   Average number of volosts in a uezd.
**   Average number of sel. obshchestvos in a volost.
***   Average number of selsovets in a raion (or a volost).
**** Average number of population places in a selsovet.

Sources: Tsentral'noe statisticheskoe upravlenie Ukrainskoi SSR, *Narodnoe khoziaistvo Ukrainskoi SSR (Statisticheskii ezhegodnik)*, 1982, p. 6; Tsentral'noe upravlenie narodno-khoziaistvennogo ucheta Gosplana SSSR, *Sotsialisticheskoe stroitel'stvo SSSR (statisticheskoe ezhegodnik)*, 1936, L-LI; Goskomstat Rossii, *Sbornik analiticheskikh dokladov po materialam perepisi naseleniia 1989 goda* (1992), p. 123; *Entsiklopedicheskii slovar' (Brokgauz i Efron)*, tom XXIX (1900), pp. 382-383; Y.Taniuchi, *Sutarin Seiji Taisei...*, vol. 1, p. 706.

Table 5   The Number of Administrative-Territorial Units in the Belorussian Soviet Socialist Republic

	1897	1923	1924	1935	1979	1989
area (1000 km²)	194.8	91.2?	126.8	126.8	207.6	207.6
Guberniias	4	-	-	-	-	-
Oblasts	-	-	0	0	6	6
Uezds	40	15	-	-	-	-
Okrugs	-	-	8	4	-	-
Volosts	729	238	-	-	-	-
Raions	-	-	101	88	117	117
Sel'skie obshchestvos	6 757	-	-	-	-	-
Sel'skie sovets	-	3 405	1 419	1 473	1 508	1 482
population places (M)	41.6	?	?	?	26.1	24.6
volosts/a uezd	18.2	15.9	-	-	-	-
sel.o-vos/a volost	9.3	-	-	-	-	-
selsovets/a raion	-	-	14.0	16.7	12.9	12.7
pop.places/a selsovet (or a sel.o-vo)	6.2	/	/	/	17.3	16.6

Sources: Tsentral'noe statisticheskoe upravlenie Belorusskoi SSR, *Narodnoe khoziaistvo Belorusskoi SSR (Statisticheskii ezhegodnik)*, 1979, p. 11; Goskomitet Belorusskoi SSR po statistike, *Narodnoe khoziaistvo Belorusskoi SSR (Statisticheskii ezhegodnik)*, 1988, p. 20; Goskomstat Rossii, *Sbornik analiticheskikh dokladov...1989 goda*, p.123; *Entsiklopedicheskii slovar' (Brokgauz i Efron)*, tom XXIX, pp. 382-383; E.H. Carr, op.cit., p. 282; Y.Taniuchi, *Sutarin Seiji Taisei...*, vol. 1,p. 706.

Table 6   The Number of Administrative-Territorial Units in the
Moldavian Soviet Socialist Republic

	1897	1971	1981	1987
area (1000 km^2)	44.4	33.7		
Uezds	8	-	-	-
Volosts	213	-	-	-
Raions	-	32	39	40
Sel'skie obshchestvos	1 241	-	-	-
Sel'skie sovets	-	700	771	827
population places (M)	1.5	?	1.6	1.6
			('79)	('89)
volosts/a uezd	26.6	-	-	-
sel.obshchestvos/a volost	5.8	-	-	-
selsovets/a raion	-	21.9	19.8	20.7
pop.places/a selsovet	1.2	/	2.1	1.9
(or a sel.o-vo)				

Sources: Gosudarstvennyi komitet Moldavskoi SSR po statistike, *Narodnoe khoziaistvo
Moldavskoi SSR v 1986 g.*, 1987, p. 17; Goskomstat Rossii, *Sbornik analiticheskikh
dokladov...1989 goda*, p.123; *Entsiklopedicheskii slovar' (Brokgauz i Efron)*, tom XXIX,
pp. 382-383; *Bol'shaia sovetskaia entsiklopediia (3-e izdanie)*, vol.16 (1974), p. 424.

Table 7   The Number of Rural Population Places and Their
Structure in Each Soviet Republic

	Population places (M)		1989 in % against 1979	proportion of population places according to their population in % (1989)		
	1979	1989		100 or fewer people	101-1000 people	1001 or more people
USSR	383.1	331.8	87	61	31	8
Russia	177.0	152.9	86	61	34	5
Ukraine	29.7	28.6	96	19	63	18
Byelorussia	26.1	24.6	94	66	32	2
Moldavia	1.6	1.6	99.7	7	43	50

Source: Goskomstat Rossii, *Sbornik analiticheskikh dokladov...1989 goda*, p. 123.

Table 8 Comparison of the Sizes of Volosts and Sel'skie Obshchestvos (Selsovets) Between in 1897 and 1929

Guberniias	1929			1897	
	Average number of selsovets in a volost (% to ⟨x⟩)	Average radius of a selsovet (km.)	Average radius of a volost (km.) (% to ⟨y⟩)	(x) Average number of sel.o-vos in a volost	(y) Average radius of a volost (km.)
Severo-zapadskii raion					
Vologodskaia	4 (57%)	10.0	12 (50%)	7	23.9
Tsentral'nyi raion					
Brianskaia	21	3.4	15	-	-
Ivanovo-Voznesenskaia	11	4.0	13	-	-
Kaluzhskaia	28 (200%)	2.5	13 (188%)	14	6.9
Kostromskaia	11 (138%)	4.8	13 (129%)	8	10.1
Moskovskaia	15 (68%)	2.5	9 (113%)	22	8.0
Riazanskaia	24 (120%)	3.0	14 (192%)	20	7.3
Tverskaia	8 (47%)	5.0	14 (152%)	17	9.2
Iaroslavskaia	6 (55%)	4.5	12 (145%)	11	8.3
Srednevolzhskii raion					
Votiag aut.obl.	10	5.3	17	-	-
Viatskaia	15 (167%)	5.0	20 (159%)	9	12.6
Nizhegorodskaia	9 (82%)	5.0	15 (188%)	11	8.0
Bashkirskaia ASSR	17 (155%)	5.0	20 (134%)	11	14.9
Povolzhskii raion					
Penzenskaia	24 (240%)	3.0	15 (208%)	10	7.2
Samarskaia	14 (200%)	4.4	17 (134%)	7	12.7
Saratovskaia	14 (175%)	4.5	16 (163%)	8	9.8
Stalingradskaia	12	6.0	19	-	-
Tatar ASSR	24 (141%)	3.0	14 (132%)	17	10.6
Ul'ianovskaia	15 (100%)	4.0	15 (149%)	15	10.1
Tsentral'no-Chernozemnyi raion					
Voronezhskaia	12 (133%)	4.5	15 (158%)	9	9.5
Kurskaia	11 (65%)	3.0	14 (169%)	17	8.3
Orlovskaia	16 (80%)	3.4	13 (149%)	20	8.7
Tambovskaia	8 (73%)	4.5	13 (163%)	11	8.0
Zapadnyi raion					
Smolenskaia	21 (131%)	3.5	17 (207%)	16	8.2

Source: Y. Taniuchi, *Sutarin Seiji Taisei...*, vol.2, p.497. The data for 1897 are procured from Table 1 of this chapter.

Table 9 Grouping of Guberniias in European Russia According to the Population Structure

	Population density (person/ sq.km)	Average number of selenies in a commune	Average population in a selenie (in male)	Average population in a commune (in male)	Guberniias
A	Very small (from 0.4 to 3.4)	Very large (from 7.8 to 11.9)	Small (from 37.5 to 49.4)	Large (from 359.0 to 485.5)	Arkhangel'skaia, Vologodskaia, and Olonetskaia
B	Small (from 17.0 to 34.2)	Very large (from 6.1 to 15.2)	Small (from 28.0 to 62.9)	Large (from 244.6 to 501.3)	Vitebskaia, Pskovskaia, Kostromskaia, and Viatskaia
C	Small/large (9.1, 11.8 and 47.1)	Medium (from 2.0 to 4.1)	Small (from 56.4 to 97.1)	Medium (from 111.0 to 394.5)	S.-Peterburgskaia, Novgorodskaia, and Permskaia
D	Small/ medium (from 23.6 to 41.9)	Large (from 2.7 to 6.5)	Small (from 45.4 to 71.3)	Medium (from 151.5 to 393.8)	Grodnenskaia, Minskaia, Mogilevskaia, Smolenskaia Tverskaia, and Iaroslavskaia
E	Medium/ large (from 32.2 to 73.1)	Small (from 0.9 to 1.5)	Medium (from 97.1 to 150.5)	Medium (from 142.8 to 186.4)	Moskovskaia, Kaluzhskaia, Tul'skaia, and Vladimirskaia
F	Medium/ large (from 28.6 to 72.1)	Small (from 0.8 to 1.2)	Large (from 208.2 to 506.3)	Large (from 172.7 to 601.2)	Simbirskaia, Penzenskaia, Saratovskaia, Riazanskaia, Tambovskaia, Orlovskaia, Voronezhskaia, Kurskaia, Ekaterinoslavskaia Chernigovskaia, Kievskaia, Podol'skaia, and Bessarabskaia
G	Medium/ large (from 31.2 to 56.0)	Midium (from 1.3 to 2.3)	Large (from 172.0 to 298.6)	Large (from 223.1 to 587.8)	Kazanskaia, Nizhegorodskaia, Khar'kovskaia, Poltavskaia, Khersonskaia, and Volynskaia
H	Small (from 17.8 to 23.9)	Midium (from 1.4 to 2.8)	Large (from 244.2 to 367.0)	Large (from 443.7 to 724.6)	Ufimskaia, Samarskaia, and Tavricheskaia

Profiles of Contributors

ENGELSTEIN, Laura (born in 1947)

Professor, Princeton University (USA)
Publications: *Moscow, 1905: Working-Class Organization and Political Conflict*, Stanford, 1982; *The Keys to Happiness: Sex and the Search for Modernity in Fin-de-Siècle Russia*, Ithaca, 1992.

HASLAM, Jonathan (born in 1951)

Senior Research Fellow, King's College, Cambridge (UK)
Publications: *The Soviet Union and the Struggle for Collective Security in Europe, 1933-1939*, New York, 1984; *The Soviet Union and the Threat from the East, 1933-41: Moscow, Tokyo and the Prelude to the Pacific War*, Pittsburgh, 1992.

KOLONITSKII, Boris (born in 1955)

Senior Researcher, the St. Petersburg Branch of the Institute of Russian History, RAS (Russia)
Publications: "A.F. Kerenskii i Merezhkovskie v 1917 godu," *Literaturnoe obozrenie*, No. 3, 1991; "Antibourgeois Propaganda and Anti- 'Burzhui' Consciousness in 1917," *The Russian Review*, Vol. 53, No. 2, 1994.

KÖVÉR György (born in 1948)

Associate Professor, Budapest University of Economic Sciences (Hungary)
Publications: "The London Stock-Exchange and the Credit of Austria-Hungary," *Acta Historica*, No. 2-3, 1988; "The Austro-Hungarian Banking System," R. Cameron and V.I. Bovykin (eds.) *International Banking 1870-1914*, Oxford, 1991.

MATSUZATO, Kimitaka (born in 1960)

Associate Professor, SRC, Hokkaido University
Publications: "Sel'skaia khlebozapasnaia sistema v Rossii 1864-1917," *Otechestvennaia istoriia*, No. 3, 1995; "The Fate of Agronomists in Russia: Their Quantitative Dynamics from 1911 to 1916," *The Russian Review*, Vol. 55, No. 2, 1996.

SUBTELNY, Orest (born in 1943)

Professor, York University (Canada)
Publications: *The Mazepists: Ukrainian Separatism in the Early 18th Century*, New York, 1981; *Domination of Eastern Europe: Native Nobilities and Foreign Absolutism, 1500-1715*, Gloucester, 1986.

TAKENAKA, Yutaka (born in 1953)

Professor, Osaka University
Publications: "The Russian Local Nobility in the Era of the Great Reforms," *Suravu kenkyu [Slavic Studies]*, No. 39 (1992); "The Local Politics of Russia in the Great Reform Era: The Case of the Nizhegorod Province," *Handai hogaku*, Vol. 43, Nos. 2-3, 1993. [Both in Japanese]

TOMITA, Takeshi (born in 1945)

Professor, Seikei University
Publications: "Comintern Reconsidered under Perestroika," Teruyuki Hara and Wakio Fujimoto (eds.), *Crisis of <Socialist> Soviet Russia*, Tokyo, 1992; "The Soviet Union in the 1930s," *Slabu-no sekai*, Vol. 3, 1995. [Both in Japanese]

TSUCHIYA, Yoshifuru (born in 1958)

Associate Professor, Nihon University
Publications: "Political General Strike in October of 1905," *Gendai-shi Kenkyu*, No. 37, 1991; "Bloody Sunday and the St. Petersburg Workers," *Shiso*, No. 51, 1993. [Both in Japanese]

ZYRIANOV, Pavel (born in 1943)

Senior Researcher, Institute of Russian History, RAS (Russia); Visiting Professor, SRC, Hokkaido University (1994/95)
Publications: *Petr Stolypin: Politicheskii portret*, Moscow, 1992; *Krest'ianskaia obshchina Evropeiskoi Rossii. 1907-1914*, Moscow, 1992.